Matthew B. Schwartz, PhD
Kalman J. Kaplan, PhD

Biblical Stories
for Psychotherapy
and Counseling
A Sourcebook

Pre-publication
REVIEWS,
COMMENTARIES,
EVALUATIONS . . .

"This is a much-needed book. In a clear and accessible manner, the authors—both eminent psychologists—demonstrate how and why much of post-Freudian psychology, psychotherapy, and psychiatry are both conceptually and clinically flawed. Schwartz and Kaplan propose an alternative anchored in values embedded within the narratives of Hebrew Scriptures, such as: creative freedom, committed love, faith in God, affirming life, nurturing children, articulating individuality, acquiring wisdom, and embracing a life of meaning and joy rather than a life of suicidal fatalistic depression. Fifty-eight biblical narratives are examined in terms of the lessons they teach, how they contrast with the worldview represented by Greek mythology—the foundation of contemporary psychotherapy—and the clinical implications of these narratives for understanding a wide variety of common life situations. Clergy seeking themes for homilies and insights into pastoral counseling, psychotherapists and social workers desiring to improve their clinical effectiveness, individuals who take Scripture seriously and who want to see how past wisdom speaks to contemporary social and personal perplexities, and people who want to understand themselves and others better will find this compelling volume helpful, enlightening, and inspirational."

Rabbi Byron L. Sherwin, PhD
Distinguished Service Professor,
Spertus Institute of Jewish Studies,
Chicago, Illinois

More pre-publication
REVIEWS, COMMENTARIES, EVALUATIONS . . .

"The great anthropologist Claude Levi-Strauss discovered the ahistorical importance of myth as a link between nature and culture. Matthew Schwartz and Kalman Kaplan realize that myth is even more than that. It has a basis of historical veracity in the sense that it records new experiences. Further, myth is projection of the longing and normative undertaking of the group. The authors undertake the gigantic task of analyzing stories of the Hebrew Bible within the framework of personality formation, the acquisition of morality, interrelationship with parents, despair, and redemption. They also highlight the interrelationship of Freud with the Oedipal myth as well as the Hebrew Bible."

Shlomo Giora Shoham, PhD
Professor, Faculty of Law,
Tel Aviv University

"Matthew Schwartz and Kalman Kaplan have long been champions of the importance of the Bible for psychotherapy. This book puts it all together in a highly illuminating and readable manner. It is full of insight and is helpful for the full range of challenges we face in life, from love to suffering, from parenting to aging.

Anyone reading this book will be impressed with the depth of psychological wisdom that saturates the Bible, and will appreciate the Bible as the unending wellspring of advice to guide us through life."

Rabbi Reuven P. Bulka, PhD
Congregation Machzikei Hadas,
Ottawa, Ontario, Canada

The Haworth Pastoral Press®
An Imprint of The Haworth Press
New York • London • Oxford

Biblical Stories
for Psychotherapy
and Counseling
A Sourcebook

THE HAWORTH PASTORAL PRESS
Religion and Mental Health
Harold G. Koenig, MD
Senior Editor

Biblical Stories for Psychotherapy and Counseling
A Sourcebook

Matthew B. Schwartz, PhD
Kalman J. Kaplan, PhD

The Haworth Pastoral Press®
An Imprint of The Haworth Press, Inc.
New York • London • Oxford

Published by

The Haworth Pastoral Press®, an imprint of The Haworth Press, Inc., 10 Alice Street, Binghamton, NY 13904-1580.

Cover design by Lora Wiggins.

Library of Congress Cataloging-in-Publication Data

Schwartz, Matthew B.
  Biblical stories for psychotherapy and counseling : a sourcebook / Matthew B. Schwartz, Kalman J. Kaplan.
    p. cm.
Includes bibliographical references and index.
    ISBN 0-7890-2212-5 (hard : alk. paper)—ISBN 0-7890-2213-3 (soft : alk. paper)
    1. Bible—Psychology. 2. Psychology and religion. 3. Psychoanalysis and religion. I. Kaplan, Kalman J. II. Title.
BS645.S38 2004
296.3'71—dc21

2003009817

To my parents.

—Matthew

A belated wedding present to my son and daughter-in-law,
Daniel and Reva.
With deepest love and hope for all that is good in life.

—Kalman J. Kaplan

ABOUT THE AUTHORS

Matthew B. Schwartz, PhD, teaches ancient history and literature in the Departments of History and Near East Studies at Wayne State University. He is a Contributing Editor of *Menorah Review* and Associate Editor of the *Journal of Psychology and Judaism*. Dr. Schwartz has authored or co-authored six books and numerous articles that deal largely with Graeco-Roman and Jewish thought. The books include *Roman Letters: History from a Personal Point of View* and several works in partnership with Dr. Kaplan, including *A Psychology of Hope; Jewish Approaches to Suicide, Martyrdom, and Euthanasia;* and *The Family: Biblical and Psychological Foundations*.

Kalman J. Kaplan, PhD, is Professor of Psychology at Wayne State University and Clinical Professor of Psychology in the Department of Psychiatry at the University of Illinois at Chicago College of Medicine. Dr. Kaplan is Editor of the *Journal of Psychology and Judaism* and on the editorial board of *Omega* and also is a reviewer for *The International Journal of the Psychology of Religion*. Dr. Kaplan is a licensed clinical psychologist and has published widely in the area of interpersonal and international relations, in the emerging field of biblical psychology, in schizophrenia, and in suicide/suicide prevention. He was the co-recipient of the 1998 Alexander Gralnick Award for outstanding original research in suicide and schizophrenia. Dr. Kaplan was also consulting psychologist for the *Detroit Free Press* study of physician-assisted suicide. He has authored or co-authored over 60 refereed articles and given over 100 presentations internationally. He has also authored or co-authored a number of books, including *A Psychology of Hope; Jewish Approaches to Suicide, Martyrdom, and Euthanasia;* and *The Family: Biblical and Psychological Foundations* (in partnership with Dr. Schwartz) as well as *TILT: Teaching Individuals to Live Together; Right to Die versus Sacredness of Life;* and *Living with Schizophrenia* (published in English and Italian).

CONTENTS

Foreword

The continuity of human beings is evident when we realize that although the particulars of daily life, work, and opportunities for the good life differ in extreme ways from ancient times to the present, basic needs and core aspects of wisdom remain the same. Those gems of wisdom whose lessons endure through the centuries form the heart of this book. Wisdom is old, so the stories that are written down here come from the Bible and are old. However, coupled with each story are concrete ways in which psychotherapists and counselors might use this material to help people. This book is a storehouse of treasures. I recommend it not only for its stated purpose—as a sourcebook of biblical stories for therapists and counselors—but also for anyone who wishes to read narrative examples of life's dilemmas that come from one of the richest literary sources.

The underlying conceptual distinction of the book is the difference between Athens and Jerusalem. A contrast is drawn between the assumptions about human nature that come from classical Greece and those originating in biblical Israel. This is illustrated, for example, by the difference between a Greek tragic view of life in which characters are controlled by fate, the gods, and necessity, forces outside of them, versus a Hebraic view that views humans as created with the ability to act and effect change. One characteristic of the difference between the Greek and Hebraic views is illustrated by the notions of disunity versus unity of a person's mental and physical components. In the classical Greek view, the mind and body were separate entities and death meant liberation of the mind or spirit from its earthly vessel. In contrast, the Hebraic version views human beings as unities so that death, although a part of life, is not to be idealized as liberating the spirit from the body, for it tears the unified creature that God had created. Important implications of this distinction exist for suicide and euthanasia. Which assumptions psychotherapists adopt have implications for the practice and goals of therapy. One assumption leads to tragedy and the other leads to hope, is the message delivered here in a delicate but clear way.

This is not a psychology of religion book; instead, it is a book whose task is, in part, to integrate biblical foundational stories and legends with the practice of psychotherapy. The book gives the working therapist fifty-eight Bible stories that can be used for specific sorts of cases. It is a practical sourcebook that is written upon a clear conceptual foundation.

Problem areas for which biblical narratives are presented cut across the whole gamut of important human experience. For example, individuals must confront the question of whether life is meaningful even when terrible events have occurred (David after the death of his son); spouses must respect and trust each other (Jacob and Rachel); couples need to learn to grow together and express appropriate care for common concerns even though they may have begun a relationship with mutual misfortune (David and Bathsheba); individuals need to recover from weariness (Elijah); people need to face difficult tasks even when hampered by disabilities (Moses and Aaron); people must live with the consequences of succumbing to temptation (Adam and Eve) as well as learn the necessary skills to face temptations squarely (Joseph and Potiphar's wife); people must accept the reality of evil, sickness, and disease in the world and are nevertheless bound to carry on with some level of faith for goodness in the future (Abraham and Isaac).

Because suffering and human problems are ageless, wisdom coming to us from the ages applies to the life stories of people today. At the end, one comes back to the theoretical distinction that is the foundation of the book, Athens or Jerusalem? These authors have a compelling message to send.

Raymond F. Paloutzian, PhD
Professor of Psychology, Westmont College
Editor, The International Journal for the Psychology of Religion

Acknowledgments

The authors acknowledge the help and encouragement provided by Laval Brown, Reuven Bulka, Stan Jones, Arthur Kurzweil, Jean McLellan, Byron Sherwin, and Shlomo Shoham.

Introduction

If you ask most people to tell you their earliest memories, they will recount a story about their childhood that, if carefully studied, bears great symbolic meaning. The conscious memory may not be very accurate, but it is nevertheless of profound importance for understanding the teller's psyche. The story is remembered out of many events of childhood because it had and still holds some very deep meaning. For example, a person with a continuing fear of abandonment might remember being separated from parents in a department store. A compulsively clean person might remember an old summer cottage with a malodorous bathroom and buzzing flies. One who recalls the warmth and kindness of attentive and loving grandparents might later take great pleasure in being attentive to children.

Such memories are termed foundation or master stories. As individual persons have foundation stories, so do nations, cultures, and religions. A nation's story of its beginnings tells much about its self-concept. The pessimism of ancient Mesopotamian society is expressed in its creation myth, the Enuma Elish, which describes the chaos and bitterness of a war between gods and monsters and then, as an afterthought, mentions the creation of man as a puppet to wait upon the victorious gods. Likewise, patterns of gender hostility, family triangulation, and violence are reflected in the Olympian creation stories of ancient Greece. The greater optimism of the biblical religions is reflected in their own foundation story of a loving God who created the world and man as an act of love and in a mood of harmony, not foreboding and conflict. Yet modern psychology and psychiatry seem dominated by the ancient Greek rather than the biblical experience.

Fifty years ago, Eric Wellisch, medical director of Grayford Child Guidance Clinic in England, called for a biblical psychology, arguing:

> The very word "psyche" is Greek. The central psychoanalytic concept of the formation of character and neurosis is shaped af-

ter the Greek Oedipus myth. It is undoubtedly true that the Greek thinkers possessed an understanding of the human mind which, in some respects, is unsurpassed to the present day, and that the trilogy of Sophocles still presents us with the most challenging problems. But stirring as these problems are, they were not solved in the tragedy of Oedipus. In ancient Greek philosophy, only a heroic fight for the solution but no real solution is possible. Ancient Greek philosophy has not the vision of salvation.

No positive use has been made, so far, of the leading ideas of Biblical belief in the attempts of modern psychology to formulate basic findings and theories. But there is no reason why the Bible should not prove at least if not more fruitful than the concepts of Greek or Eastern religious experience. . . . Psychology and theology are at the crossroads. The atheistic and pantheistic aspects of modern psychology lead to dangerous conclusions. The non-biological aspect of theology is doomed to lead to frustration. . . .There is need for a Biblical psychology. (Wellisch, 1954, p. 115)

The unique contribution of our book is to present biblical stories that can be used by therapists, clergy, and patients/clients alike, and also people who simply want to help themselves psychologically in a manner that addresses their spiritual concerns. In traditional societies, religious leaders performed this integrative function, applying the psychological wisdom implicit in the biblical religious traditions to the particular life problems of members of their congregation. Rabbis, priests, and pastors used biblical wisdom to help people with their concrete, real life problems.

The situation in contemporary America and the West is dramatically different. The religious leader may present a biblical story in a sermon but is typically unwilling or unable to apply it to the life problems of a member of the congregation. If someone approaches a religious leader with a serious personal problem, the leader is likely to refer to a card in the upper right-hand drawer of his desk with the phone number of a local psychotherapist. The therapist, however, is largely ignorant of, if not antagonistic to, religion, often in a manner incongruent with the patient's own orientation.

For example, in a 1990 sample of 409 clinical psychologists, only 40 percent believed in a personal transcendent God, compared to 90 percent of the general public (Shafranske and Maloney, 1990). There may be many reasons for the resistance toward religion on the part of psychologists. For one, the fields of religion and psychology have historically been in conflict with each other, with psychology allying itself to science. Second, psychology often has approached issues of spirituality at a highly superficial level, treating spiritual development as something extrinsic to the development of individual personality. Third, issues regarding life meaning are often relegated to the theological realm. Finally, much of traditional psychotherapy has been based on classical Greek foundation legends (for example, Oedipus, Electra, and Narcissus). For all these reasons, many potential patients eschew traditionally trained mental health practitioners in search of spiritual salvation from a variety of new age practitioners. However, many of these practitioners actually espouse pagan forms of spirituality, quite antagonistic to biblical beliefs. This volume will present biblical foundation stories as a basis for integrating spirituality into psychotherapy.

THE GREEK BIAS IN MEDICINE

Throughout their history, Jews have been greatly involved in medical science. In his article "Medicine in Ancient Israel," Sussman Muntner, professor of the history of medicine at Hebrew University, sees the Hebrew Bible as showing knowledge in areas such as etiology of disease, anatomy, communicable and infectious diseases, visiting the sick, and doctor-patient relations (Muntner, 1977). Another observation of Muntner's is very disturbing:

> It is surprising to note that talmudic pathology seems to have had no impact on medieval medicine, not even on the great Jewish physicians of the Middle Ages, such as Moses Maimonides and Isaac ben Solomon Israeli, (I. Judaeus) who were thoroughly familiar with the Talmud. Medieval medicine was so completely under the spell of (the Greek physician) Galen that anything he ever said about medicine was accepted as infallible, while the health rules of the Talmud were ignored. . . . *The Talmud was regarded as a purely religious code and not as a medical treatise of any kind. . . .*(emphasis ours) (Muntner, 1977, p. 20)

It was not until 1911 that Julius Preuss, the renowned physician and Judaic scholar, published his *Biblisch-Talmudische Medizin* as an alternative view of medicine to that emerging from Greek civilization. Preuss's work presents the great amount of medical knowledge in biblical and rabbinic literature with regard to anatomy, epidemiology, surgery, dentistry, and otology, neurological disorders, mental disease, obstetrics, and more (Preuss, 1978; Rosner, 1977).

Perhaps the single most important distinction between a Greek and a biblical approach to medicine lies in their different views on treating a disease versus treating a whole person. This difference is dramatically illustrated in the contrast between the Hippocratic oath (see *Hippocratic Writings,* 1984, p. XIII) and the physician's prayer attributed to Maimonides (see Golden, 1990, pp. 414-415). Hippocrates' view can be summarized as follows:

1. The physician is the servant of the "art" or "nature."
2. The "art" consists of three parties: the disease, the patient, and the physician.
3. The disease is the enemy, something to be combated by the patient along with the physician.
4. With regard to the disease, the physician is exhorted to do good or to do no harm.
5. In the Hippocratic oath, the physician swears to "give no deadly medicine to any one, if asked, nor suggest any such counsel."

The physician's prayer attributed to Maimonides is fundamentally different:

1. The physician has been chosen by God, in his mercy, to watch over the life, health, and death of his creatures.
2. The physician prays for inspiration from God for love for his art and for God's creatures. There are three involved parties: God, the physician, and God's creature (the patient).
3. The disease is a beneficent messenger sent by God to foretell approaching danger and to urge the patient to avert it.
4. The physician specifically prays to remove from the patients "all charlatans and the whole host of officious relatives and know-all nurses, cruel people who arrogantly frustrate the wisest purposes of our art and often lead Thy creatures to their death."

Perhaps the most important distinction for our purposes is the contrasting view of disease. In the Hippocratic oath, the disease is the enemy and the fight of the physician is to eradicate the disease or to cure the symptom. The patient seems secondary to this. In the prayer attributed to Maimonides, in contrast, the physician must treat the person (God's creature), and the symptom can be seen as an ally warning the physician of danger to the patient and as a signal to avert it. This latter view resonates quite well with more modern views of disease, especially with regard to disorders of the immune system. Nevertheless, biblical and rabbinic views of healing have received little attention in general medical literature.

THE GREEK BIAS IN PSYCHOLOGY AND PSYCHIATRY

A Greek bias also exists today in the field of mental health. The Hebrew Bible is filled with rich, psychological stories involving relations between parents and children, husbands and wives, and the individual and God. Nevertheless, modern psychology and psychiatry have made very little use of these materials, basing therapies instead only on a classical view of mental life. Bennett Simon (1978) points out this dependence in *Mind and Madness in Ancient Greece: The Classical Roots of Modern Psychiatry*. Despite the prominence and number of Jews in the fields of psychology and psychiatry, they too seemed to be under the spell of Hellas. Yosef Yerushalmi (1991) argues that Freud himself carried the Greek cyclical view of history and sense of hopelessness into psychoanalysis. Most psychologists, psychoanalysts, social workers, and even pastoral counselors learn a psychology based on the Freudian system—psychosexual stages, Oedipus complex, narcissism, and the like.

However, as brilliant and as penetrating as Freud's insights are, they are limited in the sense that Freud relied heavily on Greek myth and literature for his models and ideas. His view of man was in many ways that of the Greeks—a view that concentrated on the pathological underside of man and on the bedrock of his developmental problems. The Greeks could never really shake the sense of doom, the foreboding, and the fatalism that led so many great figures in Greek literature and in actual Greek history to depression and in a surprising number of cases to suicide. The long list of Greek and Roman suicides includes generals, philosophers, statesmen, and warriors—Lycurgus of Sparta, Zeno the Stoic, Marc Antony, Nero. To delve deeply into the Greek themes means, in a sense, to accept the premises of uncertainty and pessimism that they preach.

In contrast, in the Hebrew Bible, depression can be successfully managed, and suicide is a sad error that should be and usually can be avoided. The focus of the Bible is far more optimistic. It encourages people to hope (an important word) and teaches that day-to-day human effort has a purpose and meaning and that heroism is not a fair or useful aim for people to set themselves. There is no doom or fatalism. The Bible teaches that God created the world in a spirit of harmony and kindness, and this spirit has not changed. Also far more than in most Greek and in Freudian thought, the Hebrew Bible recognizes the human yearning for true greatness of character and for closeness to a caring God. The Bible offers the hope (again that word) of filling every moment of human life with greater meaning and feeling. People can work with their problems (all people have them) and can make their own lives and world better.

Recently, several books have attempted to delineate a specific Hebrew vision of psychology and psychotherapy. The Norwegian clergyman Thorlief Boman (1960) has attempted to differentiate Hebrew and Greek ways of thinking. While Greek thinking emphasizes "seeing," the static, the logical, and the nomothetic, Hebrew thought stresses "hearing," the dynamic, the psychological, and the ideographic. Kaplan, Schwartz, and Markus-Kaplan (1984) and Kaplan and Schwartz (1993) compare Greek and Hebrew approaches to families, stressing the dysfunctional oscillation between isolation and enmeshment in Greek family life and the healthy Hebrew integration of self and other. Yet modern psychology and psychotherapy largely continue to ignore Hebrew ideas. Psychiatric medicine too has "been under the spell of Galen." The treatment of the "psyche," the fetishization of "freedom," the fixation on the Oedipus complex, and the lack of emphasis on sibling rivalry and its resolution are four profound examples of the Hellenistic bias in contemporary psychology and psychotherapy.

Body and Soul

The earliest mention of the psyche in Greek literature is Homer's morbid picture of the unhappy shadowy existence of the Trojan War heroes in Hades. Homeric souls disappear like smoke, in the manner of ghosts, if someone attempts to touch them (*Odyssey*, 11.206). They dwell in Hades and can only regain their vitality and memory by drinking blood (*Odyssey*, 11.25).

Centuries later, Plato wrote of the soul as lofty and sacred with the body being merely its earthly prison. The soul was "elevated" from a materialistic double to a dematerialized divine being, of a nature totally different from the body *(soma)*. Plato, following the Orphics teachings, called the body a prison of the soul, and others with comparable ideas called it a tomb (*The Oxford Classical Dictionary,* 1970, p. 895). In Plato's thinking, the relationship between body and soul is conflictual and unfortunate. The soul is a helpless prisoner chained hand and foot in the body, compelled to view reality not directly but only through its prison bars, and wallowing in their ignorance (*Phaedo, 82d*).

In Hebrew thought, the human body and soul are both sacred, both created by God. They can and must function in harmony to fulfill God's purposes in the world. Emotion, intellect, and body are all integral components of a human being and there is no opposition between body and soul or flesh and spirit (Urbach, 1979).

The contrasts between Greek and biblical views regarding the body–soul relationship are exemplified in the following talmudic passage, which contains a discussion between the Roman Emperor Antoninus (perhaps Marcus Aurelius) and Rabbi Judah the Prince, the author of the Mishnah.

> Antoninus said to the Rabbi: "The body and the soul can both free themselves from judgment. Thus, the body can plead: The soul has sinned, [the proof being] that from the day it left me I lie like a dumb stone in the grave [powerless to do aught]. Whilst the soul can say: The body has sinned, [the proof being] that from the day I departed from it I fly about in the air like a bird [and commit no sin]." He replied, "I will tell thee a parable. To what may this be compared? To a human king who owned a beautiful orchard which contained splendid figs. Now, he appointed two watchmen therein, one lame and the other blind. [One day] the lame man said to the blind, 'I see beautiful figs in the orchard. Come and take me upon thy shoulder, that we may procure and eat them.' So the lame bestrode the blind, procured and ate them. Some time after, the owner of the orchard came and inquired of them, 'Where are those beautiful figs?' The

lame man replied, 'Have I then feet to walk with?' The blind man replied, 'Have I eyes to see with?' What did he do? He placed the lame upon the blind and judged them together. So will the Holy One, blessed be He, bring the soul, [re]place it in the body, and judge them together, as it is written, *He shall call to the heavens from above, and to the earth, that he may judge his people: He shall call to the heavens from above*—this refers to the soul; *and to the earth, that he may judge his people*—to the body." (*Babylonian Talmud,* 1975, 91a-b)

The difference between the Greek and biblical views has direct implications for issues of psychological freedom and attitudes toward life, death, and suicide. This inevitably will produce different orientations in the process of psychotherapy.

Freedom and Suicide

Freedom is a central and fundamental idea in the literature and thought of both the ancient Greeks and Hebrews, but the way in which the two cultures understand freedom is very different. To the Greeks, freedom is a struggle against the control of others and an effort to establish some sense of control over one's own life. The highest form of control over one's self is the freedom to decide whether to continue to live or to die, i.e., suicide. Jews, in contrast, see freedom as a central feature of their foundation stories, and the issue of control is resolved in a direct manner. Freedom can be achieved only in the acceptance of the realities of man's relationship with God. This sets the stage for a striking psychological contrast. For Greeks and Romans, suicide represents a very high form of creativity. In Judaism, life itself is the essence of creativity, and suicide only destroys this opportunity.

For Plato (*Phaedo,* 83a), the evil acts of the body pollute the soul and prevent it from achieving a complete and clean separation and returning to the world of Ideal Forms. Only the soul can perceive Ideal Truth but it cannot do so as long as it must perceive Reality by use of the five bodily senses. Thus, the real attainment of truth can come only in the higher world when souls can perceive directly without interference of the body. This idealizing of a state of existence after life is not necessarily a direct call to suicide, yet the philosopher is encouraged to believe that separation from earthly life is the only road to the ideal human existence.

Plato calls philosophy "preparation for death," and indeed argues that death frees the soul. While awaiting his execution, Socrates maintains in an argument to Simmias and Cebes:

> Other people are likely not to be aware that those who pursue philosophy aright study nothing but dying and being dead. Now if this is true, it would be absurd to be eager for nothing but this all their lives, and then to be troubled when that came for which they had all along been eagerly practicing. (*Phaedo,* 64a)

In a subsequent passage, Socrates again emphasizes that philosophers desire death, though he leaves the reasons vague. "And they would be speaking the truth Simmias, except in the matter of knowing very well. For they do not know in what way the real philosophers desire death, nor in what way they deserve death" (*Phaedo,* 64b). Later in this dialogue, Socrates further explains the linkage between philosophy and death—death frees the soul!

> For, if pure knowledge is impossible while the body is with us, one of two things must follow, either it cannot be acquired at all or only when we are dead; for then the soul will be by itself apart from the body, but not before. (*Phaedo,* 66e)

Socrates goes on to argue, "The true philosophers practice dying, and death is less terrible to them than to any other men" (*Phaedo,* 68a). His argument continues along the line that unlike the ordinary man, only the philosopher understands death is not a great evil. "You know, do you not that all other men count death among the great evils?" (*Phaedo,* 68d).

Given the preference for death over life, it seems only a short step for Socrates to be asked "then why not suicide?" Socrates responds with his famous guard-post allegory as an argument against suicide. Life is a sorry business but we must not leave our guard-post unless we are relieved.

> The allegory which the mystics tell us—that we men are put in a sort of guard-post, from which one must not release one's self or run away—seems to me to be a high doctrine with difficult im-

plications. "All the same, Cebes, I believe that this is true; that the gods are our keepers, and we men are one of their possessions. . . . If one of your possessions were to destroy itself without intimation from you that you wanted it to die, wouldn't you be angry with it and punish it, if you had any means of doing so? . . . so if you look at it this way I suppose it is not unreasonable to say that we must not put an end to ourselves until God sends some compulsion like the one which we are facing now. (*Phaedo,* 62b-c)

The equation of freedom with suicide is given more precise expression in the writings of the Greek and Roman Stoics. The Stoics attempt to conquer death by choosing it on their own terms. Zeno, the founder of the Stoic school, defined the goal of life as living in accordance with nature (Diogenes Laertius, 7:87). If this does not occur, suicide becomes the wise choice. Zeno was said to have committed suicide over sheer irritation when he wrenched his toe upon stumbling on his way home from school. According to Diogenes Laertius, Zeno held his breath until he died (7:20). His successor, Cleanthes, fasted initially to cure a gumboil but ultimately "as he had advanced so far on his journey toward death, he would not retreat," and he starved himself to death (Diogenes Laertius, 7:176).

Cicero argues in *De Finibus* that suicide is no great evil.

When a man's circumstances contain a preponderance of things in accordance with nature, it is appropriate for him to remain alive; when he possesses or sees in prospect a majority of the contrary things, it is appropriate for the wise man to quit life, although he is happy, and also of the foolish man to remain in life although he is miserable. (Cicero, 1914)

In the *Tusculan Disputations,* Cicero depicts death as freeing man from chains. The gods in their benevolence prepare for man a haven and refuge after he departs from worldly life (1:18). Some philosophers, he notes, disagree with this and some Stoics even feel that the soul is not immortal. Indeed, earthly life is not wholly evil; however, the afterlife holds far more joy (1:84).

Suicide also was a major topic in the letters of Lucius Anneaus Seneca, the brilliant Roman writer and statesman. The events of earthly existence are insignificant, not worth any emotional involvement. Who wins the Battle of Pharsalus or who wins an election is insignificant (Epistle 71). People may leave the world if they feel that they have overstayed their welcome (Epistle 120). The human body is an unpleasantness to be endured only as long as one wishes, and when one thinks fit, let one dissolve the partnership with this puny clay (Epistle 65:22).

The Stoic feels bound by necessity and seeks a sense of freedom and release. One should escape from this life whenever one chooses; to die when one wishes is in one's hand. "Choose any part of nature and tell it to let you out" (Epistle 117:23-24). One should pick the means by which to quit life. The option of suicide leaves open the road to freedom. To grumble at life is pointless for it holds no one fast. "Do you like life, then live on. Do you dislike it? Then you're free to return to the place you came from" (Epistle 70:15). The philosopher may choose a mode of death just as one chooses a ship or a house. Leave life as one would a banquet—when it is time (Epistle 70:11; Plotinus, 1918, *On Suicide*, 1, 9). Seneca (and his wife Paulina) put these thoughts into action, calmly cutting their wrists at the order of Seneca's former pupil, the emperor Nero.

Hebrew thought provides quite a different view of the relationship between freedom and life. From the rabbinical point of view, body and soul should function together harmoniously in their joint service of God. There is none of the Platonic sense that the body must die to liberate the soul. Body and soul need not be in conflict. Man must keep his body both physically and morally clean. Hillel described the soul as a guest in the body; the body should keep itself fit in order to offer hospitality to so distinguished a guest. To Hillel, the body was neither an evil to be repressed nor a bastion of heroism to be glorified by Olympic victories. For him, both physical and spiritual activities were part of man's fulfillment of his obligation to God. Just as a king appoints someone to keep his statue clean, humans, created in the divine image, must certainly keep their bodies clean (*Avot*, 2.33).

In Rabbinic thought the choice between life and death is not one to mull over daily, as talk of suicide so fills the letters of Seneca and other writings of classical philosophers. Suicide is forbidden in the Hebrew scriptures. It was a choice made once: "See I have put before you today life and death, blessing and curse and you shall choose life so that you and your seed shall live" (Deuteronomy 30:19). The choice is not whether to destroy one's life but how to live it best. The Stoics saw fate as a powerful force controlling human destinies, typically in a capricious manner. Indeed necessity was so strong that they sought to escape it, and in particular they sought to escape from the inevitability of death in the illusion of gaining control over death through suicide. Knowing that he could bring death by slitting his wrist gave Seneca the "feeling of freedom in every vein" of his body (De Ira, 3.15, 3-4). The option of bringing death seems to give Seneca the sense of preventing death from striking by chance.

Biblical thought is not concerned with fate, and real freedom always exists in the human realm, i.e., the freedom to act righteously. However, there is no illusion of freedom or choice in matters beyond human control. In this way the rabbis are the polar opposites of the Stoics. Where the Stoics felt overwhelmed by necessity or fate in all things except in the time and manner of death, the rabbis argued that in such matters as death no choice exists. "Against your will you are born, against your will you live, against your will you die, against your will you shall in the future give account before the King of Kings" (*Avot,* 4:29).

The Stoics desperately seek a feeling of freedom that offers them at least a temporary illusion of control. The rabbis accepted that God controls these matters of life and death. Feeling no need to take these impossibly difficult decisions from the hands of the one omnipotent and benevolent deity, the human beings then gain the freedom to devote their attention wholly to those tasks which are peculiarly theirs, i.e., loving God and studying and fulfilling his commandments. The Mishnah goes on to offer its own statement on freedom. The Ten Commandments were carved *(harut)* on stone. "Read not *harut* but *herut* (freedom). One is not free unless he devotes himself to study of the Torah" (*Avot,* 6:2). Freedom here means freedom of the human spirit from fears and desires. When one's fears and desires run wanton then the person is dominated by them and there is no freedom. The Stoics seek freedom from the terror of death by choosing their own means of exit. The rabbinic Jews acknowledge God's total power over birth, life, and death. In so doing, they accept the responsibility of their freedom to make moral choices. Birth and death are events beyond human understanding that God alone will handle. The individual is given freedom in terms of following God's commandments.

The Stoic comparison of life to a banquet from which one may depart at will meets a striking antithesis in a second century Mishnaic statement: "This world is like a portico before the world to come. Prepare yourself in the portico so that you may enter into the banquet hall" (*Avot,* section 4). That is, prepare yourself in the world by living righteously so that you may merit the rewards of the next world. The two worlds are dissimilar in function. In this world, good deeds and repentance are appropriate ends more beautiful than all the rewards of the next world. At the same time, the peace of spirit attainable in the next world is preferable to all the joys of this world. Earthly life is thus not a banquet, which must inevitably end. It is a time for work and preparation. The contrast with Stoic views carries on to the second point. One must not assume that the next world is some sort of refuge from this one. There is still awareness, and one must come before the King of Kings for a final judgment that will be beyond anything earthly man can comprehend. Both earth and heaven are thus important—each in its own way.

The Oedipus Complex and the Akedah

The body–soul unity and harmony reflected in the biblical tradition expresses itself in concrete narratives, which may be employed in psychotherapy. This approach is specifically contrasted with the dualistic conception emerging in classical Greek narrative and in psychotherapies, which employ these narratives, either literally or metaphorically. We will focus here on Wellisch's previously mentioned contrast between Oedipus and Isaac.

Wellisch offered the story of the *akedah*—Abraham's binding of Isaac—as a biblical alternative to the Greek legend of Oedipus and as a "new approach to psychiatry" (1954, p. 79). The core of his argument is that the *akedah* narrative suggests an unambivalent resolution of the father-son relationship that is unavailable in the story of Oedipus. He suggests that the moral relationship of parents to their children can be conceptualized in three stages.

Intense aggression and possessiveness of the parents characterize the first and most primitive stage. The aggression is particularly severe in the father and directed mainly to his sons and in the first place to his first born son. In early societies it not infrequently culminated in infanticide.

The second stage is caused by a reaction of guilt about aggressive and possessive tendencies and, especially, about committed infanticide. It results in a compromise solution between the opposing tendencies of the wish to possess the child completely or even to kill him and the desire not to do so (i.e., Freud's Oedipus Complex). . . . These mental sufferings can only be overcome when the third stage of moral development of a parent–child relationship is reached. It consists in the entire or almost entire abandonment of possessive, aggressive and, especially, infanticidal tendencies and their replacement by a covenant of love and affection between parent and child. . . . (Wellisch, 1954, pp. 3-4)

The Story of Oedipus

To better examine Wellisch's arguments, let us examine the actual legend of Oedipus as it emerges in Greek writings. The most widely known sources of the Oedipus myth are the three Theban plays by Sophocles (*Oedipus Rex, Oedipus at Colonus,* and *Antigone*), although Aeschylus and Euripides treated the topic as well. The myth of Oedipus has been nicely summarized by Gayley (1893):

> King Laius of Thebes was warned by an oracle that there was danger to his throne and life if his son, new-born, should reach man's estate. He, therefore, committed the child to a herdsman with orders for its destruction. The herdsman, after piercing the infant's feet, gave him to a fellow-shepherd, who carried him to King Polybus of Corinth and his queen, by whom he was adopted and called Oedipus, or swollen-foot.
>
> Many years later, Oedipus, learning from an Oracle that he was destined to be the death of his father, left the realm of his reputed sire, Polybus. It happened, however, that Laius was then traveling to Delphi, accompanied only by one attendant. In a narrow road he met Oedipus. A quarrel broke out, and Oedipus slew both Laius and his attendant. Shortly after this event, Oedipus saved Thebes from the sphinx, a monster, part woman, part lion and part eagle, who had been devouring all who could not guess her riddle. . . . In gratitude for their deliverance, the Thebans made Oedipus their King, giving him the queen in mar-

riage. He had already become the slayer of his father; in marrying the queen, he became the husband of his mother. (pp. 261-264)

Several additional points about Laius' behavior are stressed by Wellisch (p. 32). Laius had earlier killed the father of his wife, Jocasta. Second, Laius may have been a pederast who refrained from sexual intercourse with his wife. Thus good grounds exist to believe Laius' marriage to Jocasta was not a happy one.

The Oedipus legend can be seen as fitting into a primary type of Greek worldview which subordinates God to nature. The Olympian theogony (story of the creation of the gods) provides examples of all three themes. First, Sky (the father) and Earth (the mother) precede the gods. Second, Mother Earth helps her son cut off the genitals of Father Sky.

> Grieved at the loss of the children who were thrown (by Sky) into Tartarus, Earth persuaded the Titans to attack their father and gave Cronus a steel sickle. . . . Cronus cut off his father's genitals and threw them into the sea. Having thus eliminated their father, the Titans brought back their brothers who had been hurled to Tartarus and gave the rule to Cronus. (Apollodorus, 1, 1, 4; Hesiod, 1914b, 116f)

The elements of this type of myth pattern are as follows:

1. The father is afraid that his son will attempt to displace him.
2. The son typically enlists the aid of his mother in attempting this displacement.
3. The mother is predisposed to provide this assistance because of her husband's ill treatment of her.
4. To retain his position, the father attempts to destroy his son and, sometimes, his own wife as well.

This pattern is reflected in the very first sentence in the Oedipus myth presented previously. "King Laius of Thebes was warned by an oracle that there was danger to his throne and life if his son, new-born, should reach man's estate."

The Story of Isaac

The narrative of the *akedah*—Abraham's binding of Isaac—can be found in the twenty-second chapter of Genesis. There are several significant elements to the story. First, God calls upon Abraham to offer his only son, Isaac, as a sacrifice: "And he (God) said: 'Take now thy son, thine only son Isaac, whom thou lovest, and get thee to the land of Moriah, and offer him there for a burnt offering upon one of the mountains which I will tell thee'" (Genesis 22:2). Second, Abraham prepared to go through with the sacrifice. Further, Isaac trusts his father:

> And Abraham took the wood of the burnt offering, and laid it upon Isaac his son; and he took the fire in his hand, and a knife; and they went both of them together. And Isaac spoke to Abraham his father, and said: "My father." And he said: "Here am I, my son." And he said: "Behold the fire and the wood; but where is the lamb for a burnt offering?" And Abraham said: "My son, God will provide himself a lamb for a burnt offering." So they went both of them together. (Genesis 22:6-8)

God sent an angel at the last moment to command Abraham not to sacrifice Isaac:

> And they came to the place whereof God had told him; and Abraham built an altar there, and laid the wood in order, and bound Isaac his son, and laid him on the altar upon the wood. And the angel of the Lord called unto him out of heaven, and said: "Abraham, Abraham." And he said: "Here am I." And he said: "Lay not thine hand upon the lad; neither do thou anything unto him; for now that thou fearest God, seeing thou has not withheld thy son, thine only son from me." (Genesis 22:9-12)

Wellisch argues that this *akedah* experience produced a modification of instincts. A fundamental effect of Abraham's change of outlook was the realization that God demanded life and not death.

> Abraham realized that the meaning of the commanded sacrifice was not to kill his son but to dedicate himself and his son to life-

long service to God. He completely rejected the former dominance of his death instinct and entirely abandoned his aggressive tendencies against Isaac. His life instinct was tremendously promoted and with it a new love emerged in him for Isaac which became the crowning experience of his religion. (1954, p. 89)

Nevertheless, Wellisch's analysis fails to explain the concrete mechanism by which the "instinct modification" may come about. Our own approach is to read slightly earlier in the biblical text:

And God said unto Abraham: "And as for thee, thou shalt keep my covenant, thou and thy seed after thee throughout their generations. This is my covenant, which ye shall keep, between me and you and thy seed after thee, every male among you shall be circumcised. And ye shall be circumcised in the flesh of your foreskin: and it shall be token of a covenant betwixt me and you." (Genesis 17:9-11)

The merging of the physical and spiritual domains provides the dynamic for the biblical transformation of the father-son relationship described in the story of the *akedah*. The father knows that the son is not motivated to displace him because the son knows he will inherit from him. The father's identity is not threatened by the son. Indeed, he wants to see his son develop and surpass him. Circumcision of the son's foreskin addresses directly the son's fear of castration by representing a sanctified, noninjurious substitute. Covenantal circumcision actually transforms the primordial fear on the part of the son into his assurance that the father's own interests lie in the son's being fit to carry on the covenant.

The father willingly passes down the covenant, making displacement by the son unnecessary. The son, in turn, becomes increasingly aware that the father could have castrated him but chose not to, and offered, instead, a sanctified noninjurious substitute as the symbol of his (the father's) love and assent to the son's right to succession. The two generations have a vested interest in each other's well-being. The son wants a teacher; the father wants an heir. It is a concrete physical act, circumcision, which internalizes this spiritual transformation.

Jacob's Blessing and the Curse of Oedipus

Another major difference between biblical and Greek writings follows from the differing views of sibling rivalry and its resolution. Both the Hebrew Bible and the literature of ancient Greece present stories of family conflict. However, several basic differences between these literatures can be quickly noted. First, the stories of Genesis abound with sibling conflict, beginning with Cain slaying Abel, and continuing with the rivalries of Isaac and Ishmael, Jacob and Esau, and Joseph's brothers. Many of these stories involve sons vying for their father's blessing or favor.

The earliest myths of ancient Greece are very different, portraying conflict between father and son rather than between brothers, with the brothers often banding together, joined by the mother (see Freud, 1912-1913) to kill or castrate the menacing father. Hesiod's *Theogony* begins significantly not with God but with nature polarized into Sky father (Uranus) and Earth mother (Gaea). They marry and produce children. Uranus, however, was angry over the birth of the offspring and he shoved them back into Gaea as they were born. Groaning with pains, Gaea instigated their son Cronus to castrate Uranus and overthrow his rule. Cronus repeats his father's pattern, imprisoning his brothers, the Titans, in Tartarus. He then marries his sister, Rhea, and, fearful of the prophecy of Earth and Sky (his parents) that he would lose the rule to his own son, he devours his offspring as they are born.

The second basic difference between the literatures is even more striking. The Hebrew Bible offers a plan to resolve family conflict by employing the father's blessing. Originally the source of the sibling conflict, the blessing may work to achieve some level of reconciliation between the sons. As the father becomes more involved with his family, his blessing becomes more potent. This blessing from the father, in turn, reduces the degree of sibling rivalry.

Greek literature offers no such balm. The father represents an obstacle and a threat, not a blessing or a teacher, and the sons remain united against him for survival. As the power of the father diminishes, he curses the sons, leaving them to turn their enmity on one another.

The Biblical Pattern

In the Genesis story of the biblical patriarchs, the succession of generations is accompanied by blessings of the father to the sons, and by some level of reconciliation, or at least cooperation, among the sons.

The practice of the father blessing his children is introduced in the Hebrew Bible with the patriarchs. The blessing formally registers the father's recognition of the son and his confidence and hope that the son will find fulfillment in his natural gifts. It is not a magical formula designed to bring good fortune. Although the father formally administered the blessing, the mother also played an important part in deciding what blessing would be given to each son.

The Scriptures make no mention of fathers blessing sons before Abraham. However, the blessing became increasingly important with each generation of the patriarchs, until Jacob was able with his blessing both to affirm the unity of his twelve sons as the basis of the twelve tribes of the nation of Israel and to recognize and encourage the unique individual qualities of each.

Consider the stories of (1) Adam, (2) Abraham, (3) Isaac, and (4) Jacob. They indicate an increase in the father's involvement across these four generations, a greater degree of blessing, and ultimately a resolution of sibling rivalry.

Adam and his sons. God alone gave blessings to all mankind at creation, "And God blessed them and God said to them 'be fruitful and multiply and fill the earth and dominate and rule over the fish of the sea, and over the birds of the heavens and over every beast that walks on the land'" (Genesis 1:28). God also gives blessings directly to Adam and Eve (Genesis 1:28) and to Noah and his family (Genesis 9:1), but there is no indication that God blesses Cain and Abel directly or that Adam gave either son a blessing.

Notably absent in this account is any mention of direct communication between Adam (and Eve) and the two sons. Could Adam and Eve have been so unaware of the rivalry developing between Cain and Abel and of Cain's jealousy toward Abel? A direct blessing by Adam to his sons, showing each his place in the larger divine purpose, may have helped prevent the murder of one sibling by the other. However, it was lacking and God's intervention alone without the underlying blessing did not prevent the killing. In other words, Cain may not have felt sufficiently loved to withstand his sense of rejection.

Abraham and his sons. God told Abraham that he himself would be a living blessing and that through him all the peoples of the world would be blessed (Genesis 12:2-3). The ability to bless people was given to Abraham and passed on to his descendants (cf *Midrash Rabbah,* Genesis 39:11; Tanhuma Buber Lekh Lekha 5; *Numbers Rabbah* 11:2; Babylonian Talmud Sota 14).

Abraham circumcised both Ishmael (Genesis 17:26) and Isaac (Genesis 21:4). According to some interpretations (Rabbi Nehamiah) Abraham gave his blessing only to Isaac, though others (Rabbi Hama) interpret Abraham as giving only gifts to Isaac (Genesis Rabbah 61:6, Rashi on Genesis 25:9). Subsequently, Abraham trains Isaac as his successor and the receiver of God's special covenant. He gives his other sons gifts and sends them away to the east (Genesis 25:6). Abraham apparently had become closer again to Ishmael after a period of estrangement (Genesis 25:9), and both sons join together in burying Abraham.

Nevertheless, there is no indication of any real meeting of minds between the two sons. Isaac and Ishmael do seem to be able to cooperate when necessary, and one does not kill the other. Moreover, they seem to pursue largely separate paths without any real common purpose, although later Isaac's son Esau does marry a daughter of Ishmael (Genesis 28:9).

Isaac and his sons. Esau, the son of Isaac and Rebecca, had angrily threatened to kill Jacob, his twin brother. He accuses Jacob of stealing his birthright and his father's blessing. However, years later the brothers were reconciled and coexisted at least in peace if not in harmony of purpose. These peaceful outcomes of potentially explosive sibling clashes could result only because the parents, Isaac and Rebecca, did not saddle their sons with insurmountable emotional burdens and tried instead to be supportive of their sons.

God first told Rebecca when she was still pregnant that Jacob and Esau would be two great nations and that the older would serve the younger (Genesis 25:23-24). This is more a prediction than a blessing per se. God subsequently did bless Jacob (Genesis 25:23, 28:14, 32:30), but does not specifically bless Esau.

Isaac, however, did bless both Jacob and Esau, repeating God's prediction that the older (Esau) shall serve the younger (Jacob). Significantly, however, he gave each son a blessing that seemed suitable for him. First Isaac blessed Jacob, who had disguised himself as Esau, with the dew of the heaven and the leadership of other nations (Genesis 27:27-30). Esau, distraught over Jacob's trickery, also received a blessing of the dew of the heaven and to live by the sword and serve his brother (Genesis 27:39-40).

Esau naturally hated Jacob because he felt his blessing was stolen from him and so threatened to kill him (Genesis 27:41), but with the intervention of the mother, Rebecca, peace between the brothers was restored and ultimately Esau indicated satisfaction with his portion. "I have plenty, my brother" (Genesis 33:9). The fact that Esau too had been blessed by his father gave him the resiliency to gain great success. Significantly, both founded successful families and lines of kings.

Jacob and his sons. In the succeeding generations each father blessed his own children, joining them closer to the covenant with God and helping each son define and affirm his own sense of identity. The father permitted and encouraged them to enjoy the good things of life, both spiritual and material.

Jacob had the joy of seeing his sons reconciled despite their many problems with him and with one another. Even the selling of Joseph had a happy ending when Joseph, as viceroy of Egypt, saved the family from famine in so wise a manner that the old wounds were appreciably healed.

There is no mention of a direct blessing given by God to Jacob's sons. Moreover, in his last moments, Jacob conscientiously and lovingly blessed his sons each according to his own personality and his own needs (Genesis 49). Going a step farther, Jacob also blessed his grandsons Ephraim and Manasseh and added that they would be the highest examples of blessing: "In you will Israel give blessing saying, 'May God make you like Ephraim and Manasseh'" (Genesis 48:21).

Jacob used the blessing to prepare each son for the unique problems and challenges of his own personal situation. This recognition of the importance of each son did much to deflate the potential dangers of sibling rivalries and of parent-child conflicts. For example, when Jacob blesses his sons, he criticizes Simeon and Levi for their violent ways. "Simeon and Levi are brethren, weapons of violence their kinship . . ." (Genesis 49:5). Brotherhood must have a positive purpose and consist of more than simply being violent together. Nevertheless, Jacob does not disown Simeon and Levi but spreads them in Israel rather than giving them their own territory (Genesis 49:6-7).

The Greek Pattern

The Greek myths, in contrast, never develop the idea that a father should bless his children. The result is that conflict in the families grew more angry and nasty in each succeeding generation until the families self-destructed, as the family of Oedipus did. Not only do successive generations of parents not bless their offspring, they actively reject them. Oedipus indeed cursed his sons to kill each other. It was common enough both in myth and in historical reality for Greek parents to expose newborn children.

Many children were born out of wedlock or by incest. Not surprisingly, these children later find it difficult to relate to other people. Narcissus, for example, was born of a rape. His father abandoned him and his mother showed little affection for him. When the baby was born his mother went to the seer Tiresias and asked him if Narcissus would live a long life. A loving parent might express a joyous wish for a newborn child to be a dedicated physician, a great athlete, or a heroic soldier, but Narcissus' mother asked only how long he would live, as though she hoped it would not indeed be long. Narcissus grew to be a very handsome young man but one who could not relate to people and could not deal with himself. He died terribly, by stabbing himself (Conon, 24), or by simply pining away in his misery (Ovid, 3, ll. 497-502), according to different versions of the story.

Consider the following four Greek families: (1) Uranus and Cronus, (2) Cronus and Zeus, (3) Zeus and Heracles, and (4) Oedipus and his sons. There seems to be a decrease in the threatening aspects of the father over the generations, culminating with a blinded, scorned, and helpless Oedipus. The decline of the father allows the emergence of the previously latent sibling rivalry culminating in the mutual killing of the two sons of Oedipus, Polynices and Eteocles, at the Gate of Thebes.

Uranus and his sons. In Hesiod's horrifying stories, Uranus is portrayed as a menacing figure, hating his sons from the first. As soon as each was born, Uranus shoved him back into Gaea for fear of being usurped. Groaning with pain, Gaea banded her sons together and urged them to take vengeance against their father and gave Cronus a saw-toothed scimitar. Cronus cut off his father's genitals and threw them into the sea while he lay stretched out fully against Earth, longing for love. Uranus reproached his sons and called them Titans, for he says, "They strained in insolence and did a deed for which they would be punished afterwards" (Hesiod, *Theogony*, ll. 155-210).

This is clearly the model employed by Freud in "Totem and Taboo" (1913) in his description of primitive families. According to Freud's historical reconstruction, men in primeval times lived in small hordes, each under the domination of a strong male. All females were his property. If the sons excited the father's jealousy, they were driven out. Freud argued that this kind of social organization was altered by a banding together of the driven-out sons, who collectively overcame and murdered their father and ate of his body in an attempt to identify with him through displacing him and incorporating a part of him in themselves.

The sons have a common purpose but it is based on fear of the father rather than on any anticipation of blessing. Indeed, Uranus warned his sons that they would be punished for their misdeeds. The banding together of the sons is defensive against a hated father who threatens to destroy them. Identification is accomplished through incorporation and the father's curse is lurking in the background, threatening to punish them for their misdeed. After the threat of Uranus recedes, the previously repressed sibling rivalry has a chance to emerge, as Cronus himself, according to some interpretations, imprisons his brothers, the Titans (Hesiod, *Theogony*, ll. 504-505).

Cronus and his sons. This same pattern of a paternal threat to the sons emerges in the next generation described in Hesiod's *Theogony*. Cronus (Hesiod, *Theogony*, l. 453f) begat many children by force whom he proceeded to swallow because he had learned from Earth and Heaven that his destiny was to be overcome by one of his sons (*Theogony*, l. 453f). Rhea, Cronus' sister and wife, appealed to her parents Gaea and Uranus (Earth and Sky), who sent her to bear her youngest son Zeus in Crete. She tricked Cronus into swallowing a huge stone in swaddling clothes, thinking it was Zeus.

Zeus meanwhile grew up and led his siblings, the Olympian gods, to overthrow Cronus and his allies, the Titans (Hesiod, *Theogony*, l. 629f). Zeus and his siblings hunted their father Cronus and their uncles down to Tartarus (Hesiod, *Theogony*, ll. 720-725). Afterward, Zeus and his siblings need not cooperate in any meaningful way.

Once again, we have a case in which the sons (Zeus and the other Olympian gods) are banded together not out of any positive sense of purpose but as a defensive necessity against their threatening father, Cronus. When he is removed as a threat (hurled down to Tartarus) the Olympian gods no longer need unity.

Zeus and Heracles. Our third example of the relationship between paternal threat and sibling rivalry can be seen in Ovid's narrative of Heracles and Iphicles. Although the two boys are twins born from the same mother, they have different fathers. Heracles is the son of Zeus while Iphicles, his twin, is the son of Alcmene's husband, Amphitryon. This occurred as a result of Zeus's impersonation of Amphitryon during the latter's absence.

Despite this trickery, neither father seems a threat in the sense of Uranus or Cronus. However, they seem largely absent or powerless. Zeus boasts that he has fathered a son whom he provocatively names Heracles (which means "the glory of Hera") who will rule the noble house of Perseus. However, Zeus is tricked by an enraged Hera who delays Heracles' birth long enough so that Zeus's promise goes instead to a relative, Eurystheus, who had been born just before Heracles (Hesiod, *Shield of Heracles,* ll. 35, 56, and 80). Again note here the similarity to the biblical theme of birth order as discussed in the Jacob and Esau story—but with such a different purpose. Hera acts out of personal pique; Rebecca, and even Sarah, act out of a sense of suitability of inheritance.

In any case, this story seems to support our basic theme. As the power of Zeus wanes, rivalry between the young males emerges in earnest, encouraged by Zeus's wife Hera. Eurystheus is able to force Heracles into twelve labors which involve great danger. Later, after Heracles' death, Eurystheus expels Heracles' children from Greece.

Oedipus and his sons. The final Greek family we examine is that of Oedipus—in relation to his sons rather than to his father. Four children are born out of his incestuous union with his mother, Jocasta: two sons, Eteocles and Polynices, and two daughters, Antigone and Ismene.

When the horrible truth becomes known, Jocasta kills herself and Oedipus takes out his eyes. His sons, who were to share the power of Thebes, mistreat their now powerless father. They allow him to be exiled from Thebes and he wanders, cared for by his daughters. Before his death, Oedipus announces a curse that his sons should die by each other's hands.

According to the legend, Eteocles, now king of Thebes, exiles his brother Polynices, who in turn leads a vast army from Argos against Thebes in order to seize the throne for himself. In the ensuing battle, the brothers slay each other in individual combat, fulfilling their father's curse.

This episode is so striking that it has been covered from slightly different angles by a number of Greek plays. In Sophocles' *Oedipus at Colonus,* Oedipus disowns his two sons and curses them to kill each other. He says to Polynices,

> And thou, begone, abhorred of me and unfathered!—begone, thou vilest of the vile, and with thee take my curse which I call down on thee—never to vanquish the land of thy race . . . but by a kindred hand to die, and slay him by whom thou hast been driven out. . . . I call the Destroying God who both set that dreadful hatred in you twain. Go with these words in thine ears . . . that Oedipus has divided such honours to his sons. (ll. 1386-1394)

Oedipus' conduct is diametrically opposite to that of Jacob with regard to his blessing of Simeon and Levi. Jacob criticizes Simeon and Levi for their violent acts but does not disown them. Oedipus disowns Polynices and Eteocles and causes them to be violent together! In Aeschylus' *The Seven Against Thebes,* the curse is described as follows:

> And both alike, even now and here have closed their suit, with steel for arbiter. And lo, the fury-fiend of Oedipus, their sire, hath brought his curse to consummation dire. Each in the left side smitten, see them laid—the children of one womb, slain by a mutual doom! (ll. 879-924)

Again note the striking difference between this curse and the prophecy given by God to the pregnant Rebecca regarding Jacob and Esau (Genesis 25:23-24). Polynices and Eteocles are cursed to a mutuality of doom, within one womb. Jacob and Esau are described as two separate nations, albeit of the same womb!

In both of these plays, the mother, Jocasta, is described as already dead. Euripides' *The Phoenissae* presents a revised version. Here

Oedipus and Jocasta are still alive and Jocasta engages in a futile attempt to bring about reconciliation between the two brothers. She describes Oedipus' curse as the product of his mental illness,

> He [Oedipus] is still living in the palace, but his misfortunes have so unhinged him that he imprecates the most unholy curse on his sons, praying that they may have to draw the sword before they share the house between them. (ll: 1-91)

Unlike Rebecca, Jocasta fails to bring about a peaceful reconciliation between her sons. Even when the Greek mother tries to resolve sibling rivalry, she is unsuccessful.

A Comparison of Greek and Biblical Family Narratives

In summary, then, we argue that the greater incidence of sibling rivalry in narratives in Genesis than in Greek mythology is misleading. It is a function of the underlying purpose of the biblical family—the sons compete to inherit the covenant of the father. The father's blessing can resolve this rivalry as culminated in Jacob's blessing of all his sons.

The Greek family, in contrast, is purposeless. The father is not a source of inheritance but an impediment. Sibling rivalry is initially masked by the threat of the father to the sons who must band together to protect themselves. However, this bonding is shallow and fear based and will disappear as the paternal threat recedes. This pattern is consummated in the curse of Oedipus to his two sons to slay each other.

A purposive family therapy would benefit from taking seriously the biblical idea of parental blessing as a means of overcoming potentially disastrous sibling conflict. Each child may require a unique blessing suited for his or her particular talent, leaving a feeling of unconditional love. This is the biblical message to family dynamics.

BIBLICAL STORIES

New solutions to mental health problems are always welcome. Ours is a new approach, yet a very old one. We present in these pages a series of stories that can be read on the level of simple narratives but that also offer a vast treasure of knowledge and wisdom about the way people think and act and why they do so. The stories are drawn from the Hebrew Bible, a compendium whose latest books are already 2,400 or so years old. Through all those centuries, the basic story of man's searching and yearning has changed little. We shall concentrate on the psychological meaning of these narratives and what they tell us about how their characters met the challenges of family, handicap, depression, and much more.

We also present information from actual clinical research of our own day that parallels the biblical narratives. The wisdom gained from the ancient stories is applied to help the people of today gain self-understanding and handle their own situations. The story of Moses, who overcame a speech problem, can be applied to the problems of a Midwestern college student, and the account of David and Goliath can help a businessman overcome his fears of lack of macho.

The field of mental health has not really taken these issues to heart, maintaining a severe separation from the biblical tradition(s). The reluctance to mix religion and psychology can be understood in a liberal democratic society such as America with an insistence on the separation of religion and state. However, the baby has been thrown out with the bath water. Contemporary psychology and psychotherapy have gone to the other extreme, implicitly reflecting much of the Greek value structure discussed previously, and even transmitting the pathology in Greek stories in an attempt to cure people. This is a little bit like giving medicine to cure influenza in a glass infected by the virus. This book presents a collection of biblical foundation stories with psychologically oriented commentary.

A point should be emphasized in closing: The biblical stories are presented in order to provide the therapist with tools to help in a particular case. The decision to use the biblical story itself in treatment must remain a case-by-case decision. It may be extremely helpful with an overtly religious individual. With less religious people, the biblical metaphor may be used profitably without going into detail. Finally, with people hostile toward religion the underlying message may be transmitted using secular metaphors. Our reliance on the stories of the Hebrew Bible should make these stories of value to Jew and Christian alike. The Jew sees these stories as Torah, the Christian as Old Testament, but the underlying message of help transcends formal theological differences.

Would it not be wonderful if we could have a personality such as Cain or Jonah on the psychotherapist's couch in front of us? Failing this, however, we must instead rely on our understanding of the Bible and its characters, on the text, and on a 3,000-year-old uninterrupted tradition of interpretation. The earliest of these interpreters passed down their ideas largely by oral teaching. Later, scholarly interpretations began to be preserved in written form beginning with the Talmud and the various works of Midrash.

Over the centuries, a serious body of biblical interpretation has been produced that has been honest and insightful in the highest manner. We have sought to work closely within these sources, being careful to take account of this wisdom of the ages rather than venturing into untried speculations.

Chapter 1

Self-Esteem: Strengths, Sources, Disabilities, and Healing

INTRODUCTION

The issue of self-esteem is central to mental health. Without a healthy self-esteem, an individual typically is unable to succeed either in love or work. In love, individuals may be afraid to express unique, even idiosyncratic, aspects of their own personalities for fear of being rejected by others. Instead they will disguise more personal expressions of self under the mask of social convention. For example, an individual with low self-esteem often may appear stilted and pompous.

The situation in work is analogous and equally constricting. Individuals may be afraid to express their own ideas and, thus, their own creativity because of their fear of criticism and their need for approval. They will be afraid to be different and thus inhibit what might be their most valuable contributions. They may be totally unable to utilize their special gifts and may be paralyzed by any imperfections or disabilities.

Many people never develop a healthy self-esteem. Indeed, it demands hard work and understanding of some concepts that people find difficult to accept. In biblical terms, one must begin by accepting the very fundamental premise that people are created by God and that God does not make mistakes. It would be a foolish and false modesty for a person to feel that God had blundered or mixed the wrong ingredients in making him or her. All human beings are created unique and important and with the opportunity and the obligations of doing their best. Indeed, man was created in the image of God. To derogate man, including and especially oneself, is to degrade God.

The rabbis have stated that a person must believe that the entire world was created solely for his or her benefit (Sanhedrin 37a). A person's role in the world is unique and everything he or she does is very important and meaningful. People's actions may have effects on themselves and on others years and even generations later in ways they never imagined. People should not feel guilty about talents or gifts with which God has blessed them. Instead, they should thank God for the gifts and use them as best they can. For people to act as though they do not have a gift or talent that they do have is highly counterproductive and shows a low self-esteem.

Low self-esteem resembles modesty only in a superficial and distorted way. True modesty demands realistic insight into one's self and a proper respect for God and for people. It involves recognizing the limitations of mortal man's power and control while using the abilities that one does have. A man should not think of himself as slow-witted when he is, in fact, very bright, or consider himself homely when he is, in fact, of pleasing appearance. If a woman is a great scholar, she should acknowledge that fact and use her learning well. She should not insist on seeing heself as unlearned nor should she use her talents to arrogate herself above other people. To think one is less than one is, is to demean God's creation and belittle the divine image in whose form man was created.

People often seek to build themselves up by gaining honors or by accomplishments—by piling up wealth, publishing their writings, or winning ball games. In fact, no accomplishment, no matter how great or heroic, can produce self-esteem. It may produce short-term satisfaction or pride. However, true self-esteem must be based on the belief that one is created by a loving God.

Man's work in this world, whether in studying or in fulfilling what he learns, is never complete. Nor does it need to be complete. It is the work itself that is important, not the accomplishment or result. The results of the work are in God's hands. Man's job is to work—not to complete the task or achieve some self-appointed goal. To stray from this belief is to embrace deep self-disappointment. The ancient Greeks devoted themselves to victory and achievement in every area of endeavor but could never shake a deep sense of fatalism that drove many famous people to suicide. No achievement was or is ever sufficient to overcome a basic lack of self-esteem. The failure to esteem one's self, as God wants man to do, leaves man hurt and vulnerable to tragic depression and suicide.

The present chapter will focus on six biblical stories related to self-esteem, and will draw implications for clinical treatment. The first, Adam and Narcissus, deals with the basis of self-image. The second, David and Goliath, discusses the issue of recognizing the basis for one's strength, whether physical or psychological. The third, Samson and Delilah, highlights the problems of dealing effectively with special gifts one may have. The fourth, Elisha and Naaman, deals with the basis of health and the healing of disease. The fifth, Saul, describes the basis of self-esteem and how to face life's challenges. The sixth, Abraham, deals with maintaining and strengthening one's identity while immigrating to a new land.

THE BASIS OF SELF-IMAGE: ADAM AND NARCISSUS

Biblical Narrative

A realistic sense of self helps one to deal with all situations more positively and effectively. Let us consider two classic views of self-image. One is presented in the Greek myth of Narcissus and the second in the Genesis account of the creation of the first man.

Narcissus' inability to deal with his self-image led him to a life of alienation and fleeing from reality, culminating in a wretched suicide. In contrast, Adam's self-image was based on his knowing that he was created by God and in the image of God. Biblical man, too, will deal with alienation and unrealistic ideas, but the solid base of the positive self-image helps to save him from destruction and certainly from self-destruction.

The most complete version of the myth of Narcissus comes from Ovid's *Metamorphoses,* a first-century Latin poem, although the original story is far more ancient. The nymph, Liriope, was raped by Cephisus, a river god, and gave birth to a son, Narcissus. She sought out the seer Tiresias to ask if the boy would live to old age. Tiresias prophesied that Narcissus would be just fine as long as he would never know himself. This sort of prediction was typical of Tiresias who is known in other myths as a deceptive man who would taunt people by telling the truth in so obtuse a manner that they would invariably misunderstand. Tiresias' prediction about Narcissus set him up for a life pattern of alienation from others and from self-knowledge as well.

Narcissus was very handsome and was sought after eagerly by admirers and lovers of both sexes, particularly the nymph Echo. However, he scorned them all, preferring a solitary life in the forest. One day he came upon a clear pool, and looking into it, fell in love with the image that gazed back up at him, not realizing at first that it was his own image. This realization finally grew upon him as he sat obsessed with the image in the pool. Feeling that he could never possess the image, he pined away until death overcame him or, in another version of the story, stabbed himself to death (Conon, 1978).

Narcissus could deal with the world, at least in a limited way, only as long as he did not need to face himself. Dealing with himself truthfully and with proper self-love should have been the beginning and the foundation of his human development. However, this had been denied him by the prophecy. He apparently had never looked into a mirror and certainly had never touched his own psyche. Emotionally underdeveloped and with no means of growing, unable to deal with others or with himself, Narcissus suffered an intense and debilitating shock when forced to confront himself.

The Genesis account of the creation of Adam is very different. God himself created the first man and expressed his love by sharing with him his divine image, i.e., something of his own creative ability. God also blessed man to "be fruitful and multiply . . ." Man is thus a unique being, the highest form of creation and especially beloved by God. Adam's beginnings were glorious and bright compared to Narcissus who began life as the child of a rape and then had to live with the obtuse and hostile predictions of the seer instead of the idea of himself as a divine image who benefited from God's blessing.

After placing Adam in the beautiful garden, God stated that "it is not good for man to be alone" (Genesis 2:18). Adam will have a wonderful companion and will not have to suffer lifelong alienation as Narcissus did. Even when man erred, God still intervened lovingly and truthfully to save him. Although Adam must leave the garden and will find earning a livelihood a far tougher challenge and burden than before, man's capacity to grow and develop remained great. He could still create and think. Despite the threat to their marriage, the man and woman emerged with their relationship strengthened by God's therapeutic intervention (Genesis 3:17-21).

Clinical Implications

Unlike Narcissus who destroyed himself at his first challenge, Adam and Eve recovered from mistakes to produce the human race. They were still human beings created by God in his own image. If they would look into a pond, they would see the images of God and understand that the world continues to have meaning. What they do and how well they fare is important to God, whose images they are. People must remember, although it is sometimes hard to do, that they are special to God and that God did not commit a foolish mistake in creating them. Narcissus looked into the pool and saw nothing of this, only an alienated self who could not interact with anyone, who could not dream of pursuing wisdom or goodness, and who could not handle even day-to-day realities. He certainly had no inner resources nor did he have a God to help him recover from his mistakes.

Adam and Eve and their successors can go on, can pursue the highest goals, and can have wonderful lives despite setbacks, precisely because they never can forget the fact that they are images of God, that they are important, and that they have God's unconditional blessing and love. Several striking points emerge from the Greek story of Narcissus. First, Narcissus is the child of a rape. Second, he is promised a long life as long as he does not come to know himself. Third, he never seems to have any authentic relations with himself or anyone else. Fourth, he is looking to outside images for a confirmation that should come from within. The narrative of Adam provides a key for a clinical approach to the treatment of individuals so cut off from meaningful relationships with themselves or others. First, Adam is created by God and infused by him with the breath of life. The idea that a person is worth something no matter what the sad history of the family background cannot be emphasized enough and is stressed in Psalms 27:10, "Even though my father and mother abandon me the Lord will take me in." Second, Adam is taught about the world by God himself (Genesis 2:19-20). Third, God gives Adam a mate because he knows it is not good for man to be alone. Finally, Adam is forbidden to enmesh himself in illusory knowledge (Genesis 2:17) because it obscures his fundamental relationship with God and his search after real understanding and acceptance of self and others. While the Greek Narcissus is forbidden to know himself, Adam is commanded to know himself. This emphasis on authentic self-knowledge is central to psychological health.

DEFINITIONS OF STRENGTH: DAVID AND GOLIATH

Biblical Narrative

The famous duel between David and Goliath is more than the tale of the victory of a plucky young lad against a giant warrior. It is also a confrontation between two views of strength—those of the Hebrew Bible and of the Greek epic. The giant Goliath was a Philistine, the people who conquered the Gaza area about 1200 B.C.E. They were one of a group called the Sea Peoples of which different branches had overrun the Hittite Empire and much of Phoenicia and had almost destroyed Egypt at about the same time. These Sea Peoples, including the Philistines, seem to have been recipient to the Aegean tradition of Homeric style warriors. Goliath is a spiritual descendant of the *Iliad*'s Achilles and Ajax (Homer). He is a fighter who devotes himself to the search for military glory. Fighting and winning is his life.

The Philistines and Hebrews were constantly at war. On one occasion, the Philistines invaded Israel, and King Saul gathered his army to meet them. As the two armies faced each other, the giant Goliath stepped forth from his own ranks to challenge an Israelite champion to single combat. He was huge and his armament was impressive.

In the true form of an Iliadic hero, Goliath heaped verbal abuse on the Israelites. They are "slaves" (1 Samuel 17:8). "I scorn the ranks of Israel." The Israelites are cowards. If no one comes voluntarily, let them pick one man to face the giant (17:10). It was part of the warrior's plan to frighten his opponent and to build his own reputation, similar to heavyweight boxers today before a big fight. Saul and his army were overwhelmed with fear. No one felt ready to fight Goliath in single combat, nor could they seem to develop any other strategy. They allowed themselves to be trapped in Goliath's game plan and to be demoralized.

At this point, David came to the Israelite camp, bringing food and other provisions for his brothers in King Saul's army. Goliath had been coming forth daily, morning and evening, for forty days to hurl his challenges and abuse at the Israelite army, whose morale steadily declined. David saw how terrified the Israelites were. They told David about Goliath and how he "scorns Israel," and that the king had promised to enrich the man who could defeat Goliath. The winner would marry the king's daughter, and his family would be free of taxes (17:25).

David, however, was a more original thinker, and his answer showed that he understood a certain reality that his countrymen did not. The promised rewards were not the issue to David. The question was "who will smash the Philistine and remove the humiliation from Israel, for who is this uncircumcised Philistine that scorns the ranks of the living God?" (17:26). David saw this not as a challenge match between gladiators but as a battle between the Philistine lifestyle, which failed to recognize God, and the Israelites, whose entire world was God-centered and for whom circumcision was a sacred mark of a life of special dedication. When David said this, the people could only repeat their earlier assurances of material rewards. His own brothers expressed their irritation with him (17:28). David nevertheless continued to voice his opinion and finally he was called before Saul. David offered to fight the giant. Saul did not understand: "You cannot go to fight against this Philistine. For you are an inexperienced lad and he is a warrior trained from youth" (17:33).

David replied with a story of how he slew a bear and a lion that had attacked his sheep . . . "and this uncircumcised Philistine is like one of them, for he has scorned the ranks of the living God" (17:34-36). David thus expressed his belief that God rules the world, and nothing happens by chance. His fights with the animals attacking his sheep had helped prepare him for his encounter with Goliath. He convinced Saul that God was with him, and Saul reluctantly consented to allow David to fight Goliath. "And Saul said to David, 'Go and God be with you'" (17:37).

What made David think he could actually defeat this fearsome warrior? Was he delusional? Was he relying on a miracle? As a devout Hebrew, David certainly believed in miracles, yet here, David did not seem to have felt a need to change the course of nature in order to win. David understood something that the other Israelites had forgotten—the importance of the mental and spiritual element in warfare. He seemed to have correctly sized up the braggadocio of Goliath whose spirit could not match his muscles. David knew, too, the value of a slingshot in a battle, even against a heavily armed professional warrior. Did either David or Goliath know the story of the archer Paris standing in safety on the ramparts of Troy and slaying the mighty Achilles?

David picked up five stones and approached the Philistine. Goliath seemed a bit nonplussed by his challenger. While David moved directly toward him, the giant walked more hesitantly with his armor bearer in front of him. He heaped derision on David's youth and good looks. He was surprised and befuddled, indeed almost insulted. "Am I a dog that you come to me with sticks?"(17:43). Why did Goliath refer to himself as a dog? David must have sensed Goliath's inner weakness. Like many macho bullies and like the typical Homeric hero, Goliath had, in fact, a very poor self-image.

"Come to me and I will give your flesh to the birds of the sky and the cattle of the field" (17:44), Goliath continued. David understood that Goliath was concerned about his lack of mobility under the heavy armor. He heard, too, that Goliath was befuddled, as "cattle" do not eat meat.

David replied very directly. "You come to me with sword, spear and shield, and I come to you in the name of the Lord of hosts, the God of the ranks of Israel whom you have scorned" (17:45). This was not to be a battle between warrior champions but between two lifestyles. David assured Goliath that he would cut off his head and would leave his corpse "for the birds of the heaven and the beasts of the earth" (beasts, this time, not cattle) (17:46). Victory is in the hands of God, and does not depend on military panoply. With that, David charged at a run straight toward Goliath and the Philistine army. While moving, he slung a stone at Goliath and hit him in the head, killing him.

Slingers were an important arm of ancient armies. It would not have been unusual for David to have been expert in the use of the sling. Had he missed the first shot, he probably would have had time for several more. David was not relying on miracles. He was acting on a very intelligent plan and knew exactly what he was doing.

However, this was not only a matter of the young shepherd outwitting the warrior, like the crafty Odysseus in the *Iliad* and the *Odyssey*. David's entire concept of the world was different. He understood and took seriously a higher concept of humanity. Compared to this, Goliath was a brute, who floundered in situations where he could not overwhelm his opposition with macho. His self-concept collapsed when he was challenged. David, on the other hand, did not depend on macho brutality like Goliath and Ajax. He had a deep feeling for God and his own people, and his self-concept was in good shape.

This important distinction appears too in their differing concepts of war. To Goliath, war was a means of achieving glory and expressing control and power. However, no victory could ever bring him more than a momentary thrill. His deeper fears and confusions remained as painful as before. For David, war was a practical means of preventing enemies from disrupting the purposes in life for which man was created—creativity and good works in both intellectual and practical matters. His self-concept stemmed from his awareness that God loved him unconditionally. He did not need to seek grandiose and destructive ways to express himself.

Clinical Implications

Sometimes patients will come to treatment feeling that they have no significant strengths in their personalities. They feel unworthy of being loved and incapable of serious work. It is especially surprising that these people often have a great deal going for them. They may be sensitive, kind, intelligent, resourceful, and likable. Why do they discount all their attributes, instead focusing on their limitations? They mistakenly see sensitivity as weakness, kindness as foolishness, intelligence as useless, and resourcefulness as trickiness. They may admit that they are likable but for no good reason. This orientation may be a consequence of nonconstructive parental criticism of any imperfection on the part of the patient as a child. Our approach with these people is to provide a therapy that will help them to accurately assess both their strengths and weaknesses. Such an approach is necessary to make them feel good about attributes they previously discounted. The therapist can find in the biblical story of David and Goliath a guide to help the patients resolve their problems. David cannot beat Goliath at his own game. He must go with his own strength to succeed. Such an awareness of one's strengths and weaknesses is essential for an individual to cope with the opportunities and setbacks of life and to convert potential disasters into triumphs.

DEALING WITH SPECIAL GIFTS:
SAMSON AND DELILAH

Biblical Narrative

Jose Carreras, the great operatic tenor, loves playing the role of Samson in Saint-Saen's opera, *Samson and Delilah*, despite his wiry build. This, he says, is because he believes that Samson was not a hulking athlete. Rather, his strength had a spiritual base in the special mission that God had given him. Several biblical stories tell of people who overcame personal handicaps. The career of Samson, in contrast, depicts a man who possessed a gift and had to face the unique problems and challenges that came with it.

The Philistines had subjugated the Israelites by virtue of superior arms. God sent to save the Israelites a man who did not use weapons but was himself the weapon. However, Samson's great physical strength also brought the danger that his physical desires could master him and eventually lead to his destruction. "Once Samson failed in the battle for his own soul, he could no longer fight the battles of the Lord" (Leibowitz, 1981, p. 80). It was to prevent this that the angel ordered Samson's parents to consecrate him as a Nazarite even from the womb.

Samson was to drink no wine, avoid ritual uncleanliness, and never cut his hair. It is important to stress that Samson's long hair was not a pagan symbol of macho virility and unbridled sensuality but a brake on his great physical prowess. Samson was to remain sober and pure and to keep a physical sign on his head of the purpose that God had set for him—to be God's sacred instrument for overthrowing the Philistines.

Samson apparently kept his vows throughout his life, until the day Delilah cut his hair. However, he fell to another weakness. He followed his eyes; i.e., he was very susceptible to feminine charms. "And Samson went to Timnah and saw a woman . . . and he said, 'I have seen a woman in Timnah. . . . She is pleasing in my eyes'" (Judges 14:1f).

At first Samson seemed to use his connections with women to strike at the Philistines. When he told his parents that he wanted to marry a Philistine girl he had seen in Timnah, they did not realize that he was merely "seeking a pretext against the Philistines" (Judges 14:4). Samson used his marriage to the girl to kill thirty Philistines and to establish himself as a champion of the Israelite people. Whatever beneficial intent may have motivated him, however, Samson's interest in Philistine women continued. The Bible mentions a harlot in Gaza and the affair with Delilah, and the Midrash adds more names to the list.

Samson did use his strength for several momentous one-man destructions of Philistines, and he brought peace to his people for some years. However, in the end, his weakness undercut his strength. The Philistine leaders bribed Delilah to learn the secret of Samson's prowess. Using the feminine wiles to which Samson was so susceptible, she induced him to reveal that cutting his hair would make him like any other man. Delilah had his hair cut while he slept. He awoke greatly weakened; the Philistines seized him, put out his eyes, and sent him to hard labor in prison. "Samson followed his eyes; therefore the Philistines gouged them out," notes the Talmud (Sota 9b).

Samson's weakness in following his eyes led him to yield to Delilah and finally to lose both his eyes and his special strength as well. There was no magic in Samson's hair, no elixir of superhuman strength. Rather, God was displeased that Samson was so careless about the main sign of his special mission. However, Samson's mission had not failed. For over twenty years, he had protected the Israelites from the oppression of the Philistines. Even in his blindness, he struck one more smashing blow that would cow the Philistines for years, when he pulled on the pillars of the temple of Dagon in Gaza and destroyed thousands of enemies in a moment.

Even here, while saving his people, Samson did not entirely elevate and purify his own motivation. He prays to God to strengthen him so that "I may be avenged of the Philistines for my two eyes" (Judges 16:28). In one sense, he was praying for satisfaction for his eyes, a personal victory and a fulfillment of the weaker part of his life. Although his destruction of the Philistine temple did bring peace to the Israelites, he prayed not only for their welfare but for his own personal revenge as well.

Clinical Implications

Unlike Greek tragedy, man is brought to destruction not through an arbitrary decree of the gods but through his own willfulness. Samson brought about his own downfall. He had a special gift and the free will to make good use of it. He succeeded greatly for he accomplished the protection of his people, but he also "went after his eyes" and diminished the sanctity of his life and work. It is not enough for a person merely to be gifted. One must learn to use these gifts in a healthy way for himself or herself and others and must work against being stultified by them.

Part of the therapeutic process is to help people accept their talents as God given and to constructively utilize them. This means to neither seek self-aggrandizement through them nor to ignore them, but to use them positively and modestly as part of a purpose and context larger than one's self. The therapist must help individuals to accept their strengths and to use them well.

THE SOURCE OF HEALTH: ELISHA AND NAAMAN

Biblical Narrative

The meeting of Elisha, the Israelite prophet, and Naaman, the powerful Syrian general, portrayed a confrontation between two wholly different approaches on how to live. Naaman had lived in a pattern that made it seem both difficult and unnecessary for him to try to find anything better. He was the glorious and highly honored commander of the armies of the warlike King Ben Hadad of Aram (Syria). However, he was afflicted by *tsora'at,* a very uncomfortable disease.

The transformation of Naaman's life proceeded from empty power, pomp, and ceremony to a deeper simplicity that is the beginning of truth. This process sheds the false burdens and misconceptions that block the individual from fulfillment.

The first hint of hope for Naaman and the first sense, as well, of an area of life not subject to his own sort of power came in a piece of advice from a little Israelite girl who had been captured in a Syrian raid into Israel. "Let my master entreat of the prophet in Samaria. He will recover him from his *tsora'at*" (2 Kings 5:2-3).

The king heard this idea from Naaman. Pleased to help his general, Ben Hadad sent Naaman to King Jehoram of Israel, demanding that he cure Naaman of his disease. Naaman traveled in state to Samaria, the capital of Israel, with great stores of silver, gold, and garments. The Syrian king had, however, missed the point, for he assumed that

King Jehoram had prophets and soothsayers who would obey his desires just as those King Ben Hadad himself had employed in Syria. He merely sought a new sorcerer, with some more potent magical incantations. Jehoram also missed the point. Upon receiving Ben Hadad's demands, he fell into a mood of despair, feeling that Ben Hadad knew that Israel had no better magic than Syria and that this was all a pretext to start another war with Israel (5:7).

While King Jehoram was pointlessly tearing his clothes in frustration and fear, help arrived from an unexpected quarter. The prophet Elisha sent a message to the king to send Naaman to him for he wished to teach Naaman that a prophet is in Israel (5:8). This was an obvious truth, although it seemed that no one but Elisha and the slave girl had yet grasped it. Kings did not cure anyone from illness, physical or psychological, by their politics and power any more in antiquity than they do today. Ben Hadad was foolish to think Jehoram could cure Naaman, and Jehoram in his reaction showed his lack of faith and understanding of his role as king of a country such as Israel with its rich spiritual and cultural heritage. Elisha now intervened as God or his representatives often did in a way that both taught and strengthened the ailing patient.

Elisha understood the nature of Naaman's deeper problem. He knew what Naaman must learn in order to improve his life, and he taught the lesson in a supportive nonpunitive manner. Naaman came out both wiser and stronger. His misconceptions were removed gently, and hope of a more meaningful life awaited him.

Naaman now proceeded with his large retinue of horses and riders and his great display of wealth and power, and he alighted before the door of Elisha's humble home. The contrast between the two worlds was immense: the general with all his pomp and glory and the prophet whose gift was of the mind and spirit. Elisha would not even step out of his home to talk to Naaman. In doing so, Elisha showed that he rejected the superficiality and emptiness of Naaman's world. He would not meet Naaman on Naaman's terms but only on his own. Instead the prophet sent a message whose deeper meaning did not become clear until later. "Go and wash seven times in the Jordan, and your skin will be restored and healed" (5:10). Elisha did not address the general by his accustomed titles. He merely issued a seemingly frivolous command.

Naaman was miffed. He had expected the prophet to come out to him, pronounce some incantations to his God, and wave his hands over the diseased body. Elisha, however, had done none of these things. He was not playing the game by Naaman's rules, was not assuming his expected role, nor allowing Naaman his accustomed status. Certainly, too, the rivers of Syria are far better than the Jordan, thought Naaman, and he had already bathed in them often and not been healed. His servants then said to him that if the prophet had sent him to some great and difficult task, he would have carried it out. Surely, he should try something so simple as bathing in the Jordan (5:12-14). How much more fruitful this is than the oppressive labors given to Heracles in Greek legend!

This was exactly the point that Naaman needed to learn. The best way of living is not with pomp and arrogance. It is not any magical power of the river that heals and elevates man, but his learning the importance of realism and humility. Naaman was cured both of his illness and of his illusions. A changed man, he returned to the prophet, who now came out to greet him. Naaman explained to Elisha that he must return to the Syrian court and must conform to its practices. However, at heart he will remain faithful to his newfound ideals (5:15-19).

Naaman departed a new man. Gehazi, Elisha's assistant, however, was tempted by the very pomp and display above which Naaman had risen. He followed Naaman and told him that the prophet would like some of the gifts Naaman had unsuccessfully urged on him. Gehazi took them and hid them away for himself. His greed and materialism had now removed him from the spirit of Elisha's world and into the neurotic, defensive, and materialistic unreality of what had been Naaman's old world. Gehazi's greed was not hidden from the prophet, who informed him that he would be stricken with Naaman's old disease. "And he went out from his presence with *tsora'at*, as white as snow" (5:20-27).

Clinical Implications

Many psychological problems manifest themselves in physical ailments. A child from an overbearing family finds it difficult to breathe and develops an asthmatic condition. Another patient is referred to a therapist by a rheumatologist because of back problems resulting from poor posture. It becomes clear in the process of therapy that the patient finds it difficult to stand up for himself in a healthy way. He either walks bent over or thrusts his body forward aggressively. As the patient learns to be properly assertive rather than submissive or domineering, his body posture improves and his back pains subside. The biblical story of Elisha and Naaman offers the therapist a model for working with such patients. A psychological view of disease is contained in this story. An individual must learn the emptiness of external display. A simple approach can offer an access to wisdom obscured by overly complicated solutions, which themselves are products of a defensive posture toward life.

THE FOUNDATION OF SELF-ESTEEM: SAUL

Biblical Narrative

Sometimes individuals can use an exceptional gift or talent in such a way as to ruin their happiness rather than to bring good to themselves and others. Saul, the first king of Israel, displayed admirable qualities of strength, majesty, quickness of action, and modesty. He was also very tall and handsome, of imposing physical appearance (1 Samuel 9:2). Unfortunately, he seemed to rely on his imposing physical appearance rather than on other abilities in dealing with people. He never developed a more mature sense of responsibility that was so necessary for a king of Israel. This weakness of character began to show itself from the very start of the story of Saul in 1 Samuel 9. First, Saul was not arrogant or grasping. He is introduced as on an expedition with a companion to find his father's donkeys that had strayed. After several days without success, they turned, at the worker's suggestion, to consult the prophet Samuel.

When Saul approached the town to find Samuel, he paused to ask directions from a group of young girls. The choice was well made. Obviously taken with the tall, handsome stranger, the girls babbled on with a prolonged description of where the prophet was and what he was doing (9:11-13).

Saul went on to meet Samuel and to learn that God had chosen him to be king over Israel. Samuel also described to Saul several events that would occur while he was on his way home including that Saul himself would be visited with the spirit of prophecy. Scripture notes that "Saul turned his shoulder to go from Samuel and God gave him a new heart" (10:9). Once again, it seems that Saul felt easiest in expressing himself with his height.

Samuel now invited the entire nation to a public assembly at which he would announce God's selection of the new king they had demanded. He used lots to demonstrate that God had chosen Saul. However, when the choice was proclaimed, Saul was nowhere to be seen. Shy of the crowds of people and lacking confidence in his ability to rule, Saul was hiding among the piles of vessels (10:22). The people found Saul and brought him to the platform, "And he stood among the people, and he was tallest among the people from his shoulder and up" (10:23). As Saul finally stood before the multitude of his new subjects, it was his height that gave him confidence before them and made him able to accept his position over them.

A short time afterward, the new king reacted quickly and surely, raising an army and smashing an Ammonite invasion. Yet, when facing a major battle with the Philistines, he showed an unwarranted timidity by not waiting for Samuel to come and offer sacrifice before the battle; "Saul said, 'Because I saw that the people scattered away from with me, and you did not come by the appointed time . . .'" (13:11). It was again a fear of the people's disapproval, albeit not a fear of the Philistine army. Fear would prod Saul once more in a crucial moment and would cost him his throne. He disobeyed God's order by allowing his soldiers to keep the cattle and sheep they had taken in their war against the Amalekites. His excuse to Samuel was that he feared the people (15:24).

Any sincere man might have fears about accepting a royal throne, but Saul could have expressed his doubts to God himself or at least to Samuel as God's prophet. Instead Saul simply fled. His modesty was real and becoming to him, but it was mixed too with fears that were not suitable and which led later to tragically wrong decisions and the loss of his kingship and his life.

Clinical Implications

Many individuals will be somewhat apprehensive when confronted with a new task. A problem emerges when they are so intimidated by the task that they become overly sensitive to rejection by others and make decisions solely aimed at pleasing others rather than following an inner voice. They may go to the opposite extreme, imposing their will in a ruthless fashion, totally disrespecting the opinions of others. Saul shows this vacillation in his life. First, he disobeys God in sparing Agag, the king of Amalek, and his cattle because he is too worried about what other people think. Then, he is too severe, with the priests of Nob, killing them for their alleged disloyalty in shielding David. One who pities the wicked will eventually be cruel when one should be merciful (Babylonian Talmud Yoma 22b; Rosenberg, 1996).

The therapist must help the patient strike the proper balance between listening to one's inner voice and being sensitive to the opinions of others. An individual can do as much damage by being overly forgiving as by being totally unforgiving. The therapist must help patients modulate their responses in proportion to the precipitating action.

THE COURAGE TO EMIGRATE: ABRAHAM

Biblical Narrative

America is today a very mobile society. It is not unusual for a person to move from one city to another a number of times, first to new schools and later to new jobs. Each move requires readjustment and an altering of relationships and lifestyles. The biblical Abraham also went through several changes. At the hoary age of seventy-five, he was told by God to go from Haran to Canaan, where he would prosper and become father of a new religion and a great nation. This was not an easy move physically, and it meant separating from his extended family. However, the anticipation of the realization of God's promise must have been uplifting to Abraham even at his advanced age.

Abraham was not long in Canaan before the land was stricken with famine. With a large household to support, Abraham was forced to wander once again, this time to Egypt, where food was plentiful. Abraham could have felt deeply disappointed. All his dreams associated with the promised land of Canaan now must be put aside for a while. Egypt was a land of great culture and wealth. Abraham was a godly man who practiced kindness and hospitality, while ancient Egypt was noted for its xenophobia and animal worship. Abraham dealt with the challenges of his move to Egypt, including the temporary abduction of his wife Sarah. As with each of the many trials in his life, he endured and grew stronger because of his faith and his sense of God's purpose working through him. One can best deal with the disruption of a move by maintaining focus on values and ideals that are truly important.

Clinical Implications

The story has great practical value for today's mobile society. How shall one maintain a loyalty to his or her own values and central life-mission while going through a series of disruptions and temporary situations? Therapists can help patients focus on their main goals in life, while helping them maintain a practical sense of survival. Deep in the Jewish tradition is the notion that "without food there is no Torah, and without Torah there is no food" (*Avot*, 3:21). One must balance the immediate with the long range.

A very good example of this problem emerges from the rules of American football. A team must advance ten yards in four downs to keep possession of the ball, though the overarching goal of a team is to score points (either through a touchdown or a field goal). The ability to pursue the larger goal may be undermined if the short-term necessities are not met.

When a man moves to a new location, he must take his identity with him. The individual's core must remain solid and transportable, an essential requirement in today's mobile world.

Chapter 2

Obligations and Loyalty
to Self and Others

INTRODUCTION

"On three things does the world stand: on Torah, service and kindness" (*Avot,* 1, 2). One has obligations to (1) self, (2) God, and (3) other people. By means of all three, one reaches toward holiness and closeness to God.

Study

The basis for all these, in the view of the Mishnah, is the study of Torah. This obligation is continuous—without respite, both religious and intellectual. It sharpens the mind and teaches right from wrong at every level from the simplest behavioral to the most esoteric spiritual. It helps avoid errors and misconceptions in understanding and wrong decisions in moral and practical matters.

Even when a person is alone and has no immediate duties to others, study must continue. Part of the aim of study is to gain knowledge and sharpen the mind, but study is also an elevating spiritual activity similar to prayer. It should intensify one's feelings of joy and of love for all that God has created.

The study of Torah also constitutes an important part of the relationship between parents and children. "And you shall teach your sons diligently" (Deuteronomy 11:19) is a means of imparting knowledge, but it is also much more. It serves as a means of bonding between parents and children based on growing together and striving together toward mutual ideals. Beyond even that, the bonding helps to affirm and strengthen the children's identities by connecting them not only with the spiritual riches of Torah and with their parents but with the many generations back to the biblical patriarchs. The parents also feel the strengthening of their own identities by taking their place in the linking of generations both past and into the future.

Service

Along with the obligation to study and understand God's commandments, man must follow them through. Divine service demands specific acts of ritual, which are designed to express and strengthen emotional commitment. In the biblical worldview, both ritual act and emotional commitment are necessary, and neither can be neglected without loss. Indeed an important part of service is the linking of man's spiritual and physical parts in a total relationship with God. Both body and soul are necessary, and both are blessings from God. Neither is a useless burden. Neither is inherently evil or sinful. Man must recognize God's infinite goodness and benevolence toward people and his constant concern with every individual. God created man in his own image, i.e., with a creativity so great that man himself, like God, can bring new people into being. God blessed men by sharing with them this unique ability of his own. God wants man to do well, and he sets up for him a system, i.e., Torah, in which he can work and thrive.

Kindness

Man must learn and practice kindness to others. People were not permitted to live in glorious isolation or in alienation from one another. God himself gave Adam a companion, stating that "it is not good for a man to be alone" (Genesis 2:18). People learn much from associating with others, and they have special obligations to close relatives, honoring and respecting parents and spouses and teaching their children. People are also deeply obligated to sustain the poor and downtrodden and to provide emotional support to those who need it.

The problem of balancing loyalty to oneself and to others is central to mental health and for social adjustment. Veering too much in either direction can create a distortion in one's ability to function successfully. Long ago the Jewish teacher Hillel taught the simple but profound rule: "If I am not for myself, who will be for me? If I am for myself only, what am I? If not now, when?" (*Avot*, 1:14).

Individuals totally immersed in looking out for themselves may appear self-absorbed and indifferent to others. However, total involvement in others at the expense of the self leaves individuals unable to develop their capacities.

This chapter will focus on six psychological issues related to this balance, again illustrating each with a biblical story. The first, Jonah, deals with the problem of overcoming disengagement tendencies and assuming responsibility to others. The second, Lot's wife, deals with the complementary problems of overcoming enmeshment tendencies and assuming responsibility to oneself. The third story, Miriam, stresses the importance of expressing one's own voice in a larger group product. The story of Joshua and Moses involves the issue of completing another vision, but in one's own way. David and Jonathan's story highlights the great love that can emerge between friends. Finally, the story of Esther involves the issue of placing one's resources in the service of a larger goal, saving one's people.

ASSUMING RESPONSIBILITY FOR OTHERS: JONAH

Biblical Narrative

To act responsibly includes doing what is right even in opposition to one's own views or perceived interests. In biblical terms, right is defined as fulfilling God's commands and wishes. Whether based on selfish greed or altruism, one's own views must give way before God's. For the prophet Jonah, learning the true nature of responsibility was a perilous adventure, but God stayed with him through a series of mistaken judgments until He was able to drive home to Jonah that God, not man, decides where man's responsibility lies.

Jonah was commanded by God to travel to Nineveh, capital of the mighty Assyrian Empire, and to urge the people to repent of their wicked way of life. Fearful, however, that his own people of Israel might look bad by comparison if the Ninevites repented, Jonah disobeyed God and instead fled by ship in the other direction. Jonah's concern for his own people and his lack of interest in the lot of the Ninevites was well-intentioned but inappropriate. He should have obeyed God. Certainly, he could have discussed with God any matters of doubt or disagreement as had Abraham, Moses, and other prophets before him. He should have even expressed his anger at God.

Although Jonah had disobeyed him, God still wanted to help Jonah both to fulfill his mission to Nineveh and to fulfill himself. God watched over him closely. He sent a storm, and Jonah responded by telling the sailors to throw him into the sea, almost an act of suicide. However, God still did not abandon Jonah, and He sent a large fish to swallow him and save him from drowning. From the fish's belly, Jonah prayed, and God had the fish spout him up onto dry land.

God sent Jonah again to Nineveh, where he was successful in persuading the people to mend their ways. Jonah, however, was still disgruntled and almost suicidal, and he sat outside Nineveh unsure what to do next. God had still not given up on Jonah. He caused a plant to grow overnight to give Jonah shade from the blazing Asian sun. Jonah felt much better. God then caused the plant to wither, again leaving Jonah without shade and feeling miserable. God already knew that it was important for Jonah to recognize and deal with the anger that he felt against God. Disturbed about the loss of the gourd, Jonah finally turned the direction of his anger from himself to God, "I am greatly angry even unto death" (Jonah 4:9). God as therapist could begin to deal with Jonah directly.

> You have had pity on the gourd for which you did not labor, nor did you make it grow; which came in a night and perished in a night. Shall I not have mercy on Nineveh that great city in which there are 120,000 people. . . . (4:10-11)

God used the incident of the gourd to drive home to Jonah the immensity of God's care for mankind. Jonah had the right and indeed the obligation to understand both his own duties and God's intentions. Jonah was responsible to do what was right, i.e., what God required of him. He was so despondent at the failure of his own plans that on several occasions he expressed a wish to die. God wanted to salvage not only Nineveh but Jonah as well. Jonah had to learn that clarity of understanding and joy in life would come only by fulfilling the responsibilities that God placed on him and not by merely following his own plans.

Clinical Implications

The clinical message here is clear. Jonah is refusing to go to the people of Nineveh because he is disengaged from them. Perhaps he is afraid of being corrupted by them or that they will surpass him. In either case, Jonah's approach shows a lack of perspective and an inability to communicate with God. He is to be contrasted to Abraham who argued with God to save the city of Sodom. Individuals must learn that they can interact with people who are having problems in life without being overwhelmed by them. People in the helping professions need not be weighed down by their patients' problems. Therapists have a right, and indeed an obligation, to live their own lives.

Often, an individual's inability to help another emerges from a lack of mature perspective. One does not have to lose if the other one wins. One's success is not always measured against another's failure. Understanding this involves communication. Individuals locked into this underdeveloped perspective must be encouraged to communicate if they are able. If they are not able to communicate at a particular time they must be protected until they are able to. God does not give up on Jonah but shields him from self-destructive tendencies. Finally the message of compassion is transmitted not just intellectually, but experientially. Jonah only understands God's attachment to Nineveh when he experiences his attachment to the gourd.

ASSUMING RESPONSIBILITY
FOR SELF: LOT'S WIFE

Biblical Narrative

A person faced with a new set of circumstances may well find it necessary to give up long-established patterns of behavior in order to survive and even to grow and improve. The name of Lot's wife is never mentioned in the Scripture, yet she figures in one of the Scripture's strangest and most remarkable episodes (Genesis 19). Two angels had come to Lot's home to warn him to take his family and escape that wicked city because God would destroy it with fire and brimstone that very night. Lot's wife was apparently reluctant to separate from Sodom and the family and friends that were not going with her. Even if she was not as evil as her fellow townspeople, she was too involved, too deeply enmeshed with them. Perhaps she was enamored of the lifestyle of Sodom. Alternatively, it may have been difficult for her to separate from something familiar.

Whatever her motivation, Lot's wife was ambivalent about leaving. Fiery destruction was already striking Sodom as Lot and his family fled the city. Lot's wife, however, was still unable to separate, for her heart was still in Sodom whether because she actively loved it or simply tolerated it. Impelled by misplaced loyalties, she turned for one more look at her beloved city, and she was caught in its destruction and turned into a pillar of salt. Lot's wife's self-definition seemed totally determined by her experiences with the people of Sodom. Therefore she was unable to see herself in any way other than as a Sodomite. Lot, however, with his experience of the family of Abraham and a self-definition independent of Sodom was able to break away.

Clinical Implications

Lot's wife preferred to continue familiar, if unsatisfactory, patterns of acting rather than change for the better, and she was trapped in the unfortunate results of that way of life. People may find themselves in situations where they are being abused or hurt, yet they seem unable to extricate themselves from this abuse as if they are receiving an unconscious sense of nurturance from it. Separating oneself from a familiar environment is not a simple task psychologically. It requires identifying with a transcendent force that provides a basis for self-esteem that is independent of the destructive environment. Consider a young boy from a highly abusive family. He is continually taunted by siblings and humiliated by parents. He unconsciously seeks the same punishment in adult relationships. He seems to feel that he deserves to be punished, and he cannot extricate himself from the destructive pattern. How can he? The very humiliation he receives so diminishes his sense of self that he thinks he deserves no better. Even if he summons the courage to leave, he will be confronted with severe criticism as he tries to leave. The job of the therapist is to provide a basis for self-definition that transcends his situation and enables him to withstand the criticism he will encounter when he leaves.

SINGING ONE'S OWN SONG: MIRIAM

Biblical Narrative

The entire Israelite nation had just lived through the tremendous experience of the crossing of the Red Sea. They could feel intensely both the power of God and his caring intimacy, and they had seen the Egyptians, their former oppressors, powerless and dead, hurled in the waves of the sea returning to its place. Moses then led the Israelites in singing a great song of praise to God, commemorating his great love and their deliverance. Indeed, they sang, and all the nations of the world trembled and stood in awe of this immense event (Exodus 15:14-15). Moses was the man of the hour. His devotion and hard work through many trials had led his beloved people to this moment. It was certainly fitting that the spirit of prophecy should now rest on him and that he should lead the singing of the great song of praise, "Then did Moses and the Children of Israel sing this song to God, and they said . . ." (15:1). In this great moment, however, something was lacking. Miriam, who was a prophetess, realized it. "And Miriam, the prophetess, the sister of Aaron, took the timbrel in her hand and brought the women out after her with timbrels and dancing, and Miriam responded, 'Sing to the Lord for He is exalted'" (15:20). Miriam saw that the women too must participate in the great song of praise, for they needed to understand and never forget their own integral role in making all this come to be. Also, Moses' song of praise was lofty and grand, but it lacked music. The Hebrew Bible on several occasions associates music with the spirit of prophecy. Miriam, as a prophetess, knew that the women with their singing and playing would add whole new dimensions to the greatness of the moment. For Miriam herself, this song marked not only a day of miraculous national salvation but a culmination of a lifelong personal quest, for it was she who, as a little girl, had stood near the river to watch over the small reed basket in which lay her infant brother Moses, hiding from the Egyptian persecutors. The sense of faith and confidence that she expressed even in her actions as a child had now reached a point of high fulfillment. Although Moses was perhaps more visible on this momentous day, the song of Miriam and the women needed no less to be sung.

Clinical Implications

The story goes to the heart of the relationship of men and women in society. Miriam's song brought a new dimension to Moses' song of praise. Each person has the uniqueness of his own expression, much like the musical instruments of an orchestra. Even to as great a leader as Moses, Miriam's song makes a distinctive contribution. In the midrashic interpretation, rather than silence themselves, Miriam and the women brought musical instruments from Egypt in anticipation of this moment.

Individuals involved in a major event may think they have little to contribute. A therapist must help these people learn to express their own voices even when they feel overwhelmed. This story with its indications of gender differences may be especially helpful in marriage therapy where many problems arise between a man and a woman who are trying to do the same things. Each can learn to bring his or her distinctive voice and skills to the same event. Moses may bring the great vision, while Miriam brings the more lyrical sound. In a successful marriage, each partner must see the importance of the other's contribution to the final product rather than see the other as a threat to oneself.

COMPLETING ANOTHER'S VISION:
JOSHUA AND MOSES

Biblical Narrative

The Israelites would never have another leader as great as Moses (Deuteronomy 34:10). Replacing him could have been a difficult process, which could have brought dissension and demoralization to the Israelite people. Instead, the succession of Joshua was carefully orchestrated so that Moses and Joshua could both perform well, and the people would feel minimal disruption. Possible friction between the two leaders was avoided and each was able to do what he could do best. Without careful planning this likely would not have happened. Several problems had to be handled. First, it was necessary both to satisfy the people and to keep them in line. Second, Moses must relinquish the leadership. Third, Joshua must be prepared to succeed him.

Although Moses would always be revered as the greatest of Israelite leaders, a new day was coming. Joshua would need to respond to the demands of his own time and not fixate the people in a stifling worship of Moses. Moses would find peace only when he knew he could safely relinquish the ongoing burden of his work and pass it to the next generation. Moses' concept of leadership could not work for Joshua. God informed Moses that he would not lead the people into the promised land of Canaan. There would be a new leader. Moses had felt a fatherly protectiveness toward the Israelites. These were, after all, the people whom he had led out of slavery and through many perils in the desert.

Moses, was now, however, rejected as leader because of his error in striking the rock to bring water out of it in the wilderness of Zin instead of speaking to it as God had commanded. Moses' primary concern at this point was not for his own glory but for his people's well-being. He asked God to appoint a leader who would understand the problems of individuals and who would work closely with them, not a distant and imperious figure.

Drawing an image perhaps from his own experience as a shepherd, Moses prays that the people will not be "as sheep which have no shepherd" (Numbers 27:15-17). Moses conceived of a leader as a gentle man who leads with moral persuasion and empathy, as Moses himself did, not with strictness and a heavy hand. God then told Moses that the new leader will be his own disciple, Joshua. Moses is to appoint Joshua in front of all the people, and the divine command would be publicly confirmed in a miraculous manner by the breastplate of the high priest. This was all performed publicly so that no one could later claim that Joshua was not worthy to lift up his head while Moses was still alive.

Moses seems to have been accustomed to treating Joshua paternally. Moses loved and respected him, and he seemed to feel a need occasionally to support or to correct him. Thus, Moses had prayed for Joshua and even changed his name for fear that Joshua might be caught up in the plotting of the twelve spies (Numbers 13:16). He later rebuked Joshua for urging him to silence two men from prophesying (Numbers 1:28). Now at God's command, Moses helped to set up Joshua as his successor.

Despite all this, Joshua must have been hesitant about assuming the leadership. Moses and God were continually reminding Joshua to "be strong and courageous" (Deuteronomy 31:7; Joshua 1:6). Joshua may have been concerned too because of what had befallen his master Moses, who, after over forty years of wonderful service to his people, was not allowed to lead them into Canaan. God reassures Joshua that he will, indeed, lead the Israelites into their promised land (Joshua 1:6).

What sort of leader must Joshua be? Moses would like him to be as gentle to the Israelites as Moses himself was. Joshua must be one of them, and he should consult closely with the elders, leading as a first among equals and not by force. Joshua, however, will not be Moses, and times have changed. God wants Joshua to enter the promised land not as one of the people but as a tough leader, forcing them to obey even by threat of punishment if necessary (Numbers 27:15-23; Numbers Rabbah 21:2; Sifre Netzavim, 305).

Human beings probably do not much differ as personalities from one generation to the next, but circumstances do change, and leaders must develop policies suitable to their own times. No leader can govern effectively under the shadow of another leader whether living or not. The Israelites knew that Joshua was a leading disciple of Moses. At first, they saw him only as a reflection of Moses, not as his own man. People would say that Moses was like the sun and Joshua the moon (Bava Batra 75a).

In order to establish Joshua as leader in his own right, several steps had to be taken. First, God ordered Moses to appoint Joshua publicly, and then God gave Joshua private instruction in the tabernacle without Moses present. This would commend Joshua to the people and show that he could lead even when removed from Moses' tutelage. Then Joshua himself must be prepared. Moses appointed him before all the people and God repeatedly instructed the new leader to rule strongly: "Be strong and courageous" (Numbers 27:22; Deuteronomy 3:28 and 31:7f; Joshua 1:6, 7, 18). Joshua heard the same at least once from Moses and again from the leaders of the tribes of Gad and Reuben.

A new leader should neither follow his predecessor in all things nor change merely for the sake of change. The task and success of every great leader is to help the nation fulfill itself. For the Hebrew people this always meant devotion to God and to one's fellow man, not only to someone else's dreams.

Clinical Implications

Individuals may feel impelled to carry on someone else's work and that they are blocked in life until they do. This may involve carrying on a parent's legacy or a teacher's. The individual needs to understand where this feeling comes from. Is it a self-imposed illusion or does it reflect an accurate appraisal that one is equipped to succeed another in fulfilling God's vision? Further, is one the best person to do this?

Even if this is the case, however, the individual should continue God's work in *his own* way. Joshua can successfully succeed Moses only by being Joshua, not by being Moses, which he cannot be, and not by ancestor worship.

The therapist must help patients find the balance between what they must do and what they need not do to fulfill their obligations to their parents. Jacob's experience with God was not exactly the same as Isaac's or Abraham's. Each generation must define its unique path to God within its own idiom.

FRIENDSHIP AND LOVE: DAVID AND JONATHAN

Biblical Narrative

Poets and songwriters in every language have long exalted the glories of what they call love. However, what they typically describe is, in fact, infatuation—the excitements and disappointments of a relationship that is essentially immature, selfish, and unhealthy. Their lyrical praises beautify but do not resolve the threat of how destructive an unbridled infatuation can be. Shakespeare's *Romeo and Juliet* is a masterful study of two young people whose immaturity leads to a tragic double suicide. It is remarkable that the world thinks of Romeo and Juliet as the epitome of star-crossed lovers and forgets their terrible end.

The biblical Book of Samuel tells of a very different sort of friendship in its account of David and Jonathan. Jonathan was the son of

Saul, Israel's first king. He was beloved by the people and a man of courage both in war and in his humanity. In the early days of Saul's reign, parts of the land of Israel were under the control of the warlike and aggressive Philistines. Jonathan sparked the Israelites' revolt by killing the Philistine governor. It was again Jonathan who sparked a great victory by wiping out a Philistine outpost at Michmash with the aid of only one other soldier.

Saul's army was, however, soon challenged by a new Philistine invasion led by the giant warrior Goliath. For forty days Goliath challenged the Israelites to send out a champion to meet him in single combat. The Israelites, including King Saul and Jonathan, were unable to react to the giant's bombast, and the humiliation went on day after day. Finally, David the shepherd came from guarding his sheep to kill the giant with his slingshot. When David returned to the camp after his victory, Jonathan greeted him in a most remarkable manner. The Scripture says that Jonathan's soul became bound (bonded) with David's, and he loved him. The two entered a pact of friendship, which Jonathan sealed by giving David fine gifts, including his jacket, bow, and sword.

What sort of love was this that arose so suddenly between the two men? It was a love that had no ulterior motive or profit. It did not depend on physical attraction, nor on the faulty empathy of mutual weakness. It emanated rather from the deep draw of goodness for goodness. Jonathan was deeply moved by David's selfless courage and his devotion to God and his people, as well as his intelligent handling of his combat with Goliath and his skill with the sling. Jonathan appreciated and loved the goodness in David even though David would now supplant him as hero among the people of Israel. Only a man of Jonathan's own courage and high-minded character could tolerate the coming of a rival and indeed rejoice in it. David's goodness called forth the goodness in Jonathan, and goodness was the greatest moving force in Jonathan's own life, the force behind his courage and his empathy for others.

Jonathan and David's devotion to each other went on even after Jonathan later realized that David, and not he, would become the next king of Israel. Their friendship deepened even during the times when Saul unjustly sought David's life. Jonathan would not disrespect his father, for he loved him too, but he knew that Saul was wrong, and he maintained his contact with David and helped him whenever he could.

David's lament over the deaths of Saul and Jonathan in battle against the Philistines on Mount Gilboa again expressed and helps to explain his feeling for Jonathan, "Your love was more wondrous to me than the love of women" (2 Samuel 1:26). David understood the greatness of Jonathan's power to love. Love of children or of a husband is often thought of as a special quality of women but, says David, Jonathan's love and loyalty to both his friend and his father remained steadfast and exemplary even in the turmoils and conflicts of the end of Saul's reign and in the time of Saul's emotional decline. "They (Saul and Jonathan) were never separated in life, nor in death were they apart" (2 Samuel 1:23).

Clinical Implications

This story can be of particular value in helping adolescents and young adults deal with issues of friendship and love. These need not be limited to a sexual relationship. Certainly, no sign indicates that David and Jonathan had any sort of homosexual connection.

Sometimes a friend will do better on an exam or will get a date with someone that your patient likes or will be wealthier or better looking, a better tennis player—or be more popular. This need not destroy a friendship, and actually can enhance it. The job of the therapist is to help the patient accept that a friend may be better at something and to love him or her because of it. This does not mean negating one's self, but rather seeing that life is not a zero sum game. Friendship can instill this lesson well.

SAVING ONE'S PEOPLE: ESTHER

Biblical Narrative

Rabbinic thought contains the concept that a very high quality of human character is the ability to act in a manner out of line with one's usual personality when a situation requires it. Can the leader become an effective follower, or vice versa? Can the flexible person show some stiffness and rigidity? One of the great stories of the Hebrew Scripture centers around Esther, a kind, gentle, and somewhat reticent woman who was brought against her will into a position of power and who found placed on her shoulders the task of saving her people from annihilation.

According to the biblical Book of Esther, the Emperor Ahasueros of Persia, besotted with wine, had executed his queen, Vashti, for snubbing him. Sorry and lonely when he sobered up, the king began to search for a new queen by rounding up beautiful women from all over the empire. One of those taken was Esther, a Jewess of the tribe of Benjamin whose family, related to the line of King Saul, had been among those exiled to Mesopotamia when Judah had been conquered. Esther's parents had died when she was very young, and she had been raised devotedly by her cousin Mordecai, a distinguished scholar who was known at the royal court.

Esther seems to have been a patient, loving young woman who reacted to events by flowing with them. Perhaps this was a suitable way of reacting to events that she could not control—the loss of her parents, the forced removal from Mordecai's home by the king's men, and the year spent in the harem waiting to be called before the king. She did not even ask for anything from Hagai, the harem keeper, as did the other women, who prepared themselves diligently for their night with the king. Esther "found favor in the eyes of all who met her" (Esther 2:15). She apparently had a genuine warmth and empathy for other people, which they found very attractive. Finally Esther was brought to the king although still much against her will, and Ahasueros, as impressed by her as was everyone else, fell in love with her and made her his new queen. Esther would have rather returned to her people and to her family, but this was no longer possible, and she again felt she had no choice but to accept her new situation.

Mordecai stayed as close to the palace as possible. He knew the king's instability and, remembering the fate of Queen Vashti, he feared for Esther's safety. In the meantime the king was very pleased with Esther, and he celebrated her accession to the throne with great splendor.

Then came trouble. Haman, the king's leading minister, wrote up a plan for the annihilation of all the Jews of the Persian Empire and obtained the king's consent. Esther, on Mordecai's advice, had never told the king that she was Jewish. Mordecai, with his connections in the palace, soon learned of the plot and sent word secretly to Esther, along with a copy of Haman's decree, to urge her to intercede with the king.

A gentle empathic woman long accustomed to being accepting and reticent, Esther was now faced with a threatening situation that demanded action. Esther's message sent back to Mordecai shows her hesitance.

> All the king's servants and all the people of the kingdom know that any man or woman who enters the inner court of the king without being summoned will be put to death unless the king raises his golden scepter so that he shall live. And I have not been called to the king in thirty days. (4:11)

Esther hesitated. She did not so much as mention the danger to her people, but dwelt instead on her own fear that she could not succeed in her mission. She preferred to delay and let matters take their course.

Mordecai realized that things must now be done to prepare Esther to approach the king. First, she must understand that the evil decree has already been enacted and that it would not go away by itself. She must take on an assertiveness that moved against the grain of her whole life's story. Second, she must understand the necessity and importance of what she now must do, and she must do it with confidence if she is to be successful.

Esther thought that a delay would help. The king had not called her in a month, and he was certain to call before much more time passed. Perhaps the king was angry at her, in which case again it was better to wait a few days.

Mordecai, however, was more politically attuned. The decree of annihilation had already been set in motion and there was not a moment to spare. Only Esther might be able to win the king over. Mordecai's message to Esther impressed upon her the need for immediate action.

> Do not think that you will be safe even in the king's palace if trouble comes for the Jewish people. If you are silent now, you will never be able to face yourself again. In any case, God will not let the Jewish people be destroyed. He will bring rescue from some other source, if not through you. (4:13-14)

Mordecai began bluntly but ended by holding up before Esther the wonderful opportunity she had to be God's instrument of the saving of her people "for who knows if for such a time you have been raised to the throne" (4:13-14). Esther knew that Mordecai was right, and she accepted his plan, agreeing to go to Ahasueros and asking only that all the Jews fast and pray for her success.

The last words of her message to Mordecai are very telling: "I and my ladies shall also fast and so I shall go in to the king, which is not according to the law, and if I perish, I perish" (4:16). The last phrase seems unduly pessimistic even in a moment of such tension and peril. Rashi, citing an opinion in the Midrash, explains it as expressing Esther's deeper sense of abandonment. She had felt abandoned by her parents and now she felt that Mordecai too had been taken from her, although in reality he had constantly done his best for her welfare even after she had been taken to the palace. Perhaps it was this sense of abandonment that had made Esther somewhat reticent.

Now, however, Esther must set aside her personal problems and show an assertiveness that was unfamiliar to her. She was aware of the importance of what she must do, and of her own role, and the rest of the Book of Esther recounts how she won the support of the king and brought about the fall of Haman and the neutralization of the decree of destruction. The story is important both for telling how the planned annihilation of the Jewish people was averted and also for showing how Esther could overcome her own weaknesses to save herself and her people.

Clinical Implications

This story illustrates a person being called upon to do things that he or she has not typically done. It could be a woman who finds herself suddenly alone and faced with caring for young children. It could be a person who is suddenly thrust into a position of leadership. Esther, despite her shyness, grasps the importance of what she must do, and thus is able to act with an assertiveness that must have been very difficult for her. Likewise, individuals must find their life purpose in order to meet a significant life challenge.

The therapist must decide whether patients are able to take on new challenges. If they can, then the therapist must guide them in this direction, but this must be done carefully because not every person can handle every task and a great deal of damage can result. It is destructive to block a person who is ready to move ahead, but it is equally destructive to push someone ahead who is not ready for it.

Chapter 3

Making Difficult Decisions

INTRODUCTION

Holiness

To strive toward completeness as a human being means, in biblical terms, to devote both body and spirit to the service of God so that every act and every hour of life can be made holy and meaningful. There is no sense, as in Greek philosophy, that the soul is imprisoned by the body and must seek separation. The body and soul are not by nature in conflict. Instead, obeying the commands of God means to sanctify every human act whether by body or soul. Holiness is not something of the heavens nor does it mean alienating or even separating oneself from day-to-day activities. Rather it means sanctifying even the most mundane activities by closeness to God. Indeed, every blade of grass and every drop of water are also holy parts of God's world.

Holiness involves intimacy with God whether one is engaged in physical or spiritual activities. It is actually beyond one's limited ability to achieve such intimacy with God all by oneself, and true holiness is attained only with God's help. What people must do is persevere in pursuing wisdom and understanding with the aim of sanctifying all their acts. "A person sanctifies himself a little, and God will help him to attain great holiness" (Luzatto, 1966, p. 326f). The person who lives in holiness is himself a holy tabernacle, a temple. The righteous are the divine chariot, says the Midrash. Everything that the righteous man does is elevated because he does it (Luzatto, 1966). To live in holiness comes as result of many years of hard work. It is a high goal that (1) offers the individual a new perspective of what is important in a life far beyond the mundane and (2) can arouse a desire to seek human greatness far beyond the baggage of one's past and one's present perceived limitations.

People face difficult decisions again and again. Often they are caught between conflicting loyalties. They may find it difficult to know what issues to focus on in a myriad of factors. Becoming aware of one's life purpose helps provide a framework enabling one to establish the priorities necessary to making difficult or even agonizing decisions. This section will present five biblical stories each focusing on an issue relating to this theme.

Rebecca, the first story, focuses on distinguishing between abilities for a specific task. The second story, Sarah and Hagar, discusses the importance of focusing on one's main aim. The story of Michal, David, and Saul involves distinguishing different motivations behind similar actions. The famous story of Solomon and the two mothers involves integrating implicit knowledge with explicit demonstration. The final story in this section, Cain and Abel, focuses on distinguishing whether a gift is given toward a particular end or is given freely.

WEIGHING ABILITIES:
REBECCA AND HER TWO SONS

Biblical Narrative

It is sometimes important to be able to weigh accurately and realistically the abilities of others. This is an important skill day by day and absolutely essential for an effective teacher or business manager. General Robert E. Lee was reportedly brilliant at analyzing the military abilities of opposing Union generals and predicting their strategies.

One of the foundation stories of the Hebrew Bible tells of the patriarch Isaac blessing his sons, Jacob and Esau. Blessings are taken seriously in the Hebrew Bible, not, however, because they have a magical effect, for they do not. The blessing usually constitutes the passing from father to son of a special purpose in life and explains and supports the receiver's ability to carry it out. Thus were Isaac's blessings to his sons and also Jacob's to his, many years later. In other cases it was God himself who blessed a human being—Adam, Noah, Abraham, and others.

Isaac's plan to bless Esau and Jacob might, however, have gone awry had it not been for the insightful and brilliantly planned intervention of Rebecca, Isaac's wife. Rebecca understood the two young men and what they needed better than Isaac did. She also understood Isaac, and she formed her plans knowing what each participant was able to do and what role she would have to play in helping them to do it. Rebecca's insight was crucial in preserving the continuation of the Abrahamic covenant with God.

Esau and Jacob were twins, and during her pregnancy Rebecca had been told by a prophet that both boys could be great and that great nations would come from them, but they would be very different. Indeed, even at birth, they were very different. Esau was born hairy (the attribute for which he is named) and ruddy. Jacob came out with his hand grasping Esau's heel, as though trying to hold him back (Genesis 25:25-26). The two boys received the same schooling, and in their early years seemed to be following the same path. As they grew older, however, differences between them grew more apparent. Esau became a cunning hunter, a man of the outdoors, while Jacob was a quiet man devoted to scholarship ("dwelling in tents") (25:27).

Each parent favored a different son. "Now Isaac loved Esau because he did eat of his venison; and Rebecca loved Jacob" (25:28). What were the characteristics in each son that seemed to draw the favor of the parents? S. R. Hirsch (1976) treats the question at length in his commentary. First, he says, the parents erred in not better recognizing the natural differences between their two sons. Esau was more athletic and not well suited for the usual classroom situation. Perhaps his physical cunning and ability, if properly directed and trained, could have helped him to a useful and productive life, dedicated to God. However, pushed into a lifestyle not suited to him, Esau learned to suppress his nature and to be crafty and tricky—useful skills for stalking and hunting. A hunter he became, a man of the wilds who gloried in the chase and the kill, not one who harnessed his physical prowess to the service of God and humanity.

Isaac was a deeply spiritual man who had risen from the altar of the akedah and devoted himself to a spiritual and somewhat withdrawn lifestyle. Esau's physical vigor appealed to him. Rebecca had grown up in a home that respected devotion neither to scholarship nor to honesty, both characteristics in which Jacob flourished, and Rebecca prized her younger son. The parents' own needs and feelings influenced their attitudes toward their children in ways that could be unhealthy. In any case, Rebecca was right in realizing that Jacob was far better suited than Esau to carry on the great work of Abraham's family.

When Rebecca learned that Isaac was planning to give his special blessing to Esau, she knew that Isaac was making a serious error that could have destructive consequences. She realized that she must arrange matters so that Isaac would give the main blessing to the more worthy Jacob and also that Isaac must be brought to agree with her. Rebecca worked out a brilliant plan that accomplished all her aims. Isaac had sent Esau out to hunt to bring him venison before receiving the blessing. Rebecca persuaded a reluctant Jacob to bring lambs from the flock to serve his blind father and, pretending to be Esau, to receive the blessing intended for the elder brother. Rebecca reassured Jacob by taking full responsibility should the plan fail. Jacob, thus disguised as Esau, succeeded in obtaining Isaac's blessing, and when Isaac learned what had happened he quickly grasped Rebecca's point. He was tricked so easily in this mummery by the quiet, honest Jacob. Had he been fooled all these years by the persuasiveness of Esau as well?

This moment of coming to his senses was a shock to Isaac "and he trembled exceedingly" (27:33) at the disastrous mistake he had almost made. However, he realized that Rebecca was right. He gave a different blessing to Esau and full-heartedly confirmed his blessing to Jacob (28:1). Understandably, Esau was fiercely angry with Jacob and threatened to kill him. However, Rebecca's decision had been correct. No human relations can thrive on falsehood. With the passage of time, Esau's anger calmed, and the two brothers reconciled and lived in peace, each in his own way (33:1-16).

Clinical Implications

It is interesting to consider how difficult it would have been for Esau to pretend to be Jacob. It would not have been a matter of Esau shaving his arms. Rather he would have needed to emulate some of Jacob's spiritual qualities as well. This points to an important principle in weighing others' abilities. The qualities that are important cannot be easily imitated.

A therapist can take from this story the message that patients must be in touch with those qualities that define them as unique. This can be done only if they separate the self from the image that they may reflect to the outside world. Our culture stresses image, which is easily reproduced at the expense of the underlying self.

FOCUSING ON ONE'S MAIN AIM: SARAH AND HAGAR

Biblical Narrative

God had promised Abraham that he and Sarah would have children, but Abraham had reached his mid-eighties and Sarah her mid-seventies with that promise unfulfilled. Sarah urged Abraham to take Hagar, her maidservant as a second wife, and "it may be that I shall be built up through her" (Genesis 16:2). In due course, Hagar did become pregnant, and she began to look down on her mistress, Sarah. This was more than Sarah could bear and she treated Hagar so harshly that she fled from Abraham's household.

An angel came to Hagar and told her to return to Abraham and that her son to be born would be a powerful man. Rabbinical commentators, especially R. Moshe ben Nachman and R. David Kimchi (see *Mikraot Gedolot,* 1978) have argued that Sarah's behavior did not fit her usual noble character. Although she had acted generously in encouraging Abraham to take a second wife, she treated Hagar too harshly when things went wrong. About thirteen years later, God fulfilled his assurances to Abraham and Sarah by giving them a son of their own, Isaac, when Abraham was 100 years old and Sarah was ninety. Isaac was to be the successor to Abraham as the carrier of his special covenant with God.

As Isaac grew, Ishmael, Hagar's son, became increasingly jealous, and he made fun of Isaac and played up his own claims as Abraham's successor. Sarah was very disturbed about Ishmael's behavior, and thought that she had to act to protect both the covenant and Isaac's special role in it. She demanded that Abraham send both Hagar and Ishmael away, for she realized that Hagar was encouraging Ishmael's jealous behavior. This time Sarah was right. The covenant was threatened, and God told Abraham to do as Sarah demanded.

Abraham knew that Hagar was behind most of the trouble, and he accepted the need of sending her away. He hoped that Ishmael could still be salvaged. God, however, told Abraham that although Ishmael would go on to greatness, Abraham's special relationship with God and the special blessing he would bring to the world would come only through Isaac. Ishmael would have something of Abraham in him but more of Hagar. Isaac would be known as Abraham's son. Sarah and Abraham devoted their lives to the fulfillment of the high purposes that God had set for them and their descendants. Although they were kind people and although God loves kindness, sometimes they would have to be tough and carry out tough decisions to protect their unique mission.

Clinical Implications

Sometimes we find ourselves in quandaries, beset by conflicting messages. Our sense of loyalty to another person keeps us from fulfilling our own purposes. Making decisions to fulfill one's purpose must not be confused with selfishness. Rather it must be rooted within a broad framework that gives one's life purpose. Then one becomes open to fulfill priorities.

A therapist must help a patient distinguish between selfish egocentrism and healthy self-definition. A selfish person disregards others because they seem unimportant. The healthy person follows his or her own path not in disregard of others, but to help others enjoy the fruits of his or her labor.

DISTINGUISHING MOTIVATIONS: MICHAL, DAVID, AND SAUL

Biblical Narrative

Michal, the daughter of King Saul and the wife of King David, was a princess, bred strong and independent, with her own ideas as to how royalty should behave. King Saul was becoming frightened at the success and popularity of David, who was then his young lieutenant. Learning that Michal had fallen in love with David, Saul offered her to David in marriage on condition that David should slay 100 of his Philistine enemies. Saul hoped that either David would himself be killed in battle or that Michal would serve as a spy in David's household. However, Michal proved anything but docile. On one occasion, when Saul sent soldiers to seize David in his house, she helped David escape, delayed his pursuers for a long time on various pretexts, and later lied to Saul about the entire matter.

Some years later David became king. The holy ark of the tabernacle had been captured by the Philistines but now, after various mishaps, it was being brought to Jerusalem. The event was celebrated with a magnificent procession and great rejoicing. David, clad in a priest's tunic, led the procession dancing joyously with all his might, filled with the love of God. Michal watched from the royal residence and despised what seemed to her David's lack of royal dignity (2 Samuel 6:16). David completed the ceremonies, blessed the people in God's name, distributed gifts among them, and sent them on their way. He then turned to his own home, but before he entered the door, Michal came out and assailed him with a torrent of sarcasm: "How honored today was the king of Israel, who uncovered himself before the maidservants of his servants, just as the low class people are seen" (6:20).

The Midrash offers two different insights into what Michal was saying. In one view, she was saying to David that her father had ruled with royal dignity, always dressing and behaving every inch a king. How could David lower himself to dance in public in so undignified a manner? In this view, Michal, princess of a royal line, was embarrassed at David's behavior. (Did she perhaps feel some guilt for having supported David in his problems with her father years before?)

The second view notes that Michal is once referred to in the Book of Samuel by the name Eglah, meaning young heifer. This indicates Michal's fierce need for independence. She had often disagreed with Saul and rebelled against restriction just as the young heifer struggles against the yoke. In this view, Michal may well have been disturbed by the several instances when her father had given in to the desires of his subjects rather than forcefully carrying out his own will. In these matters, Saul insisted too little on his royal dignity, and it had hurt his kingship beyond repair. Michal loved David very much, and now she saw him leaping and dancing like a common man, and it disgusted her precisely because it seemed to be the same mistake her father had made. The two instances when her father had entered into a prophetic trance and had gone naked in public may have been particularly galling. If David had no sense of royal dignity, his rule likewise would crumble, so Michal battled her husband as she had battled her father. In fact, the two views are not necessarily in contradiction. Michal may well have felt a certain ambivalance toward both men.

Saul had acted toward Michal out of motives that set his interest above hers. David's answer did not directly respond to Michal's attack, yet David's actions were certainly moved by a higher purpose. He said to Michal,

> I rejoiced before the Lord, Who chose me over your father and all his house to be ruler over the people of God, over Israel. And I will humble myself indeed more than this, and I will be lowly in my own eyes, and with the maidservants of whom you speak I shall be honored. (6:21-22)

David told Michal that he had been raised to the throne at God's command, not by popular election, and the purpose of his rule was to dedicate himself totally to serving God. He did not have to demonstrate his royal status to the masses. He intended instead to lead them in serving God.

Clinical Implications

This story illustrates quite well the difference between attachment and deindividuation. Saul behaved in a way that diminished him as a king and weakened his self-definition. However, David's behavior was different. He decided to show his love of God and his attachment to his people, not as a diminishment of his own being but as a fulfillment of his being. Michal's failure to distinguish these two motivations leads her to put Saul's face on David. She interprets his openness as a weakness, or in more technical terms, attachment as deindividuation. This is a very common misinterpretation in our society, which often equates kindness with weakness, and strength with indifference. A wise therapist can help a patient make this distinction.

TWO VIEWS OF WISDOM: SOLOMON AND THE TWO MOTHERS

Biblical Narrative

World (Greek) literature from its beginnings displays a curious ambivalence toward wisdom and self-knowledge. On the one hand the oracle at Delphi issues the dictum "Know thyself" in the sense of knowing one's place; on the other hand, Narcissus is promised a long life providing "he does not come to know himself." This ambivalence may emerge from the impossible dilemmas, or Hobson's choices, facing many of the heroic figures. Wisdom is not really an ally when all of the several possible solutions are self-destructive. The myth of Oedipus provides a useful example of this problem. Oedipus may continue to seek the murderer of King Laius in order to save Thebes from divine punishment, but his learning that he himself is the murderer leads inexorably to the ruination of his own life and that of his family. No wonder his mother-wife Jocasta attempts to stop Oedipus' search.

The Hebrew Bible has a very different view of wisdom. Hobson's choices are not the norm. Problems have solutions and should be dealt with. Bad situations should be made better. The best way to solve problems is with hope and wisdom. The story of King Solomon and the two women illustrates this point well.

God appeared to the young Solomon in a dream, shortly after his accession to the throne of Israel, and asked him, "What shall I give you?" (1 Kings 3:5). Solomon's answer was significant. He was succeeding his father King David as ruler of a great nation but he was young and inexperienced. He realized he did not know "how to go out or come in" (3:7). Solomon tells God, give your servant "a heart that hears" so that he can lead the people and decide between what is good and what is bad (3:9).

God approves of Solomon's request and grants to Solomon more wisdom than to any other man (3:12). He also gives him immense wealth and power (3:13). This is God's way of telling Solomon that human wisdom is wonderful, but that wealth and power too are gifts of God and not the products of human activity no matter how wise. Solomon's work will be to use his gifts to follow God's will (3:14).

The first test of Solomon's wisdom comes soon in his encounter with two harlots, who lived in the same house. They had each given birth to a son within three days of each other. The first woman claimed that the child of the second had died during the night and that the second woman had switched babies, taking the living one for herself. The second woman replied, "No, for my son is the living and your son is the dead." The first woman said, "No, for yours is the dead and mine is the living" (3:16-22). There were no witnesses to the event nor other proofs, and to Solomon's courtiers the case must have seemed impossible to resolve.

Solomon, in fact, by his mental acuity and spiritual openness had already figured out which child belonged to which mother. First, Solomon very carefully repeated the statements of the two women. The king said, "This one says, 'This is my son that liveth, and your son is the dead.' And the other says, 'No, but your son is the dead, and mine is the living'" (3:23).

Listening carefully to the words of the women, (with "a heart that hears"), Solomon had caught that one woman consistently mentioned the living child first and the other consistently mentioned the dead child first, where she should have answered, "No, mine is the living and yours is the dead." Solomon understood that each mother was unconsciously expressing her attachment to her own child through her ordering of her words. That is, the mother mentioning the living child first was the mother of the living child and the mother mentioning the dead child first was the mother of the dead child.

However, Solomon grasped that an even greater problem of demonstrating this to everyone's satisfaction still remained so that later there could be no doubt as to the mother. Solomon called for a sword to cut the living child in half, counting on the women's reactions to reveal before everyone who the real mother was (3:24-25). The true mother, of course, could not bear to see the child killed and begged that instead he be allowed to live as the other woman's son. The false claimant advanced a very legitimate argument in favor of his death. "He won't be mine and he won't be yours" (3:26), i.e., this child will have a very unhappy life never knowing who his true mother is and always being uncertain of his identity. Since the women were prostitutes, it seems likely that the father was also not known.

Nevertheless, the false claimant's response made clear that always mentioning "your dead child" before "my living child" was no coincidence, and that in her grief over her own loss, she wanted the real mother to suffer the loss of her child too. Solomon had now demonstrated that his deduction (in 3:23) was absolutely correct, and he handed the child to the true mother. Not only had Solomon's wisdom solved a seemingly insolvable problem, but it had sliced right through the potential Hobson's dilemma by demonstrating to all, and perhaps to himself as well, that his judgment had been correct. The judgment helped to establish Solomon's reputation for wisdom and perceptiveness.

The fame of Solomon's wisdom and greatness spread far and wide. However, the Bible is always truthful about the failings of its heroes. After many years of great accomplishment, Solomon, perhaps overconfident in his ability to handle all challenges, did not prevent his wives from worshiping idols. His grip on the kingdom weakened, so that Rehoboam, his son and successor, could keep the loyalty of only two of the Israelite tribes, Judah and Benjamin. The other ten tribes seceded and formed a new nation under other rulers (1 Kings 11, 12). The breach was never healed and two separate Jewish kingdoms existed until they were conquered by the Assyrians and the Babylonians several centuries later.

Clinical Implications

This story illustrates how people often know unconsciously the answer to vexing problems, yet they must find some conscious way of demonstrating the truth of their inner instincts. The demonstration may be to oneself or to others. However, in either case, a public event may often demonstrate rather than determine the correctness of a decision. Implicit knowledge must be integrated with explicit demonstration to complete many difficult decisions. A therapist must teach a patient that it is often not enough merely to be right. A clear demonstration to others that the judgment is correct may be necessary. The act of working and the basis by which the person may know the truth can serve as a demonstration for others.

TWO TYPES OF GIVING: CAIN AND ABEL

Biblical Narrative

A healthy human relationship requires being able to give as well as to take, and the need to give is essential to human nature. The story of Cain and Abel depicts one brother who found it natural and easy to give and a second who would give only grudgingly and whose own acquisitiveness would have destroyed him had God not intervened to help him.

Adam and Eve gave birth to two sons, Cain and Abel. Eve gave Cain his name, saying, "I have acquired *(caniti)* a man from God" (Genesis 4:1). Eve emphasized her role as acquirer and owner of the child, and perhaps it was from this beginning that Cain became a farmer, devoted to acquiring and owning land, not only because he had bought it but because of the toil and sweat he had expended on it. God would seek, in the Ten Commandments, to modify the oppression of heavy work by commanding the Sabbath as a weekly day of both physical rest and spiritual rejuvenation.

The name Abel means ephemeral. Perhaps by the time Abel had arrived the parents were more impressed by the transitoriness and impermanence of human life. In any case, Abel fulfilled his name by becoming a shepherd with no attachment to the land. His was a lifestyle given more to contemplation than to acquisition and sweaty labor, and he learned to care for and to be responsible for living creatures. The difference in the lifestyles of the brothers must have become more marked as time went on.

Cain decided to bring an offering to God, "And after a period of time, Cain brought of the fruit of the ground an offering to God" (4:3). Abel too brought an offering—the best of the firstborn of his sheep. God accepted Abel's offering and rejected Cain's.

Sometimes two people do the same task, and yet the two acts differ profoundly in spirit and intent. Abel brought from the best of his flock, showing that he placed his relationship with God above his need for possession. Cain, however, while realizing that it was appropriate to offer God some show of thanks, could not bring himself to part with his best. His need to acquire and possess was primary. Interestingly, the brothers did not bring their offerings together. Perhaps Cain wanted to exclude Abel, feeling threatened by him or wanting God all to himself. Even Cain's giving was a form of acquiring and withholding from others.

Cain's worldview had no room for anyone else whether divine or human. The land that he owned and tilled and the crops that he harvested were his. He owed God a general thank you, but God was distant and did not concern himself with the mundane details of daily life. What Cain had produced by his own hard work was his own. Abel's view of the world was very different. The earth belonged to God, not to Abel, and his offering acknowledged that fact. Abel saw his role as doing something for God's world, and the sacrifice would symbolize that he had done his work well.

Cain could not accept Abel or his view of the world, and he rejected God's initial efforts to help him. Like many rulers of later history, he could deal with opposition only by dominating or eliminating it. So Cain murdered his brother only to find out that ideas are much more difficult to kill than people, "And the voice of Abel's blood cries out from the ground" (4:10). Cain did not see himself as beholden to or responsible to anyone beside himself—"Am I my brother's keeper?" he asks (4:9).

Clinical Implications

People who cannot give can never be as creative or productive as God had meant them to be, nor can they ever find deep satisfaction within themselves. God did not give up on Cain even after he murdered Abel. However, God knew that great changes were necessary in Cain's life. God removed Cain from the soil, to which he had bound himself, so that now he could begin to deal with reality. Only in this way could he build a new and better life. He founded a city and produced descendants who were very creative, inventing new tools and musical instruments. Some even took up Abel's profession of breeding cattle.

People must not give gifts unless they have put their personal stamps on them. Cain erred in giving God what he thought was his own. This reflected his sense of entitlement. Abel thought that what he gave God was God's and that Abel was the steward of it. This led to Abel approaching God with a sense of modesty. Cain's view can lead only to conformity and destruction. Abel's will lead to transformation and creativity.

Chapter 4

Commandments, Oaths, Parables, and Temptations

INTRODUCTION

Individuals may sometimes feel burdened with an unfathomable commandment they have received from a parental figure. They may not understand the commandment, yet not feel free to ignore it. Alternatively, people may take oaths in an attempt to gain some outcome: "If this happens, then I will do this." Often, no one asked the individuals to make the oaths. They elicited them on their own.

At other times, individuals may be engaged in destructive behavior and become quite defensive when confronted. Sometimes a parable may be raised to introduce that content without incurring resistance. Finally, individuals may be faced with the temptation of a magical solution to a vexing problem: "If you enact this ceremony, you will achieve your desired outcome magically."

Freudian man can seek mental health without God. In the view of the Torah, however, a world without God is unimaginable and pointless. God created the world and watches it always. He is not remote from man. In one biblical story after another, God intervened to help people even after they had sinned—Adam, Cain, Abraham, and so on. Freud defined a person's psychological balance by the capacity to love and to work. To this, Jewish thought adds the need to function in the area of the spiritual and the striving toward God. A highly important element of this striving is the concept of trust or faith. Both Hebrew Bible and rabbinic literature contain much on this topic.

One of the most venerated discussions of trust in God is the fourth chapter of Bahya Ibn Paquda's (1963) classic *Duties of the Heart* (eleventh century). R. Bahya argues that only by means of trust in God can man rise above the worries of this world and achieve inner tranquility and diminishing of anxiety. One can rely in complete trust only on God, not on one's own wisdom, not on other people, and not on wealth or power. R. Bahya (p. 292f) defines trust as "the peace of mind of the one who trusts and his heart is sure that the one he trusts will do good out of complete kindness and compassion."

The one who trusts God differs from the one who does not trust in seven respects.

1. One who trusts God accepts God's judgment in all matters and thanks him for what seems good and also for what seems evil. One who does not trust God boasts of his good fortune and is exasperated at his bad fortune, and he is more subject to the vacillations of life.

2. One who trusts God knows that God will always do only what is good, and his own mind can therefore be at rest. The other is always troubled and anxious even when he is prosperous, because he constantly drives himself to increase his possessions. He handles adversity poorly because it is so much against his desires and his nature.

3. The man who trusts relies on God and not on his own work. It is man's duty to work, but any success or accomplishment comes only from God. One who does not trust God occupies himself with means that he does trust (though wrongly) and grows angry and despondent if his means do not succeed.

4. One who loves God gives freely of the goodness of his heart. One who does not trust God regards the world as insufficient for his needs. He is more careful in earning and saving money than in fulfilling his duties to God and man.

5. One who trusts God occupies himself with his daily affairs as part of his spiritual life and his preparation for the world to come. One who does not trust God puts his trust in his own livelihood and may not refrain from using even dubious means to attain it.

6. One who trusts God will earn the trust of all sorts of people because they are sure he means them no harm and that he demands no benefits from them. One who does not trust God can have no true friend because he always covets what his neighbor has. He blames others when his desires are not fulfilled or when evils come on him, and he grows to hate other people.

7. One who trusts in God neither rejoices nor grieves about the future. He is concerned only with fulfilling his duties to God. He accepts the Mishnah's precept, "Repent one day before your death," and tries to improve himself steadily through his life. One who does not trust God worries about the future. He stores wealth as if it could give him security. He feels that his life will never end, yet he puts off his spiritual obligations and needs, thinking that it is more important to assure security for himself and his family by storing up wealth just in case death should strike him unexpectedly.

The basis of trust, in R. Bahya's view, centers on the idea that man must work because God commands it. All results and outcomes are totally in God's hands, and man must trust Him. Wise people realize that they hold worldly goods only on deposit from God, and that they must return them on demand. All things from God are a benefit so that if people even have losses or pains, they must thank God for them. Although people are unable to see the good in what God has done, it was certainly good. People of trust know that God will always do good for them—indeed better than they could do for themselves. They rejoice in whatever are their situations in life. Trust enables people to avoid being overwhelmed by day-to-day troubles and becoming depressed or embittered. Trust in God offers them a different perspective. They understand that events can happen only as God wants them to and that God's wisdom is always greater than man's.

This section illustrates these themes with five biblical stories. The first, Abraham and Isaac, deals with Abraham's reaction to an unfathomable commandment—to kill his beloved son Isaac. The second deals with an Israelite general, Jephthah, and the oath he has foolishly made to sacrifice his daughter. The third story in this section focuses on the parable David receives from Nathan regarding David's behavior. The fourth story concerns the first biblical couple, Adam and Eve, who in their quest for a quick solution to their problems, succumb to the temptation of an illusory freedom and violate God's commandment. The fifth, Joseph and Potiphar, addresses temptations that involve disloyalty to another.

DEALING WITH COMMANDMENTS:
ABRAHAM AND ISAAC

Biblical Narrative

One of the fundamental concepts of the Hebrew Bible is that God loves mankind and commands certain laws to guide them. No other philosophy or belief, whether liberal or conservative, laissez-faire or restrictive, can ever take precedence over God's command. What God asks man to do is always in man's own best interest, however unlikely this may seem to man's limited wisdom. To understand this, and more so to fulfill it, is difficult but deeply important for man.

In the Hebrew Bible, the story of the binding *(akedah)* of Isaac stands as a major peak experience. The *akedah* imprinted indelibly the concept of total trust in God's will and benevolence on the historical and emotional consciousness of the Hebrew people.

Abraham met a series of challenges beginning with leaving his home in Haran and traveling at God's behest to a new land that God would show him. These challenges culminated with the *akedah*. God commanded Abraham to take his son Isaac and to offer him as a sacrifice (Genesis 22:2). Abraham and Sarah had lived through the disappointment of many years of childlessness until God blessed them miraculously with Isaac when Abraham was 100 years old and Sarah was ninety. This son was to be the bearer and continuation of the special relationship between God and Abraham. Now Isaac was to be sacrificed. Abraham was a deeply kind and compassionate man who had devoted his life to helping others. Born into a family and society of polytheists, Abraham had searched for God and a more meaningful life, and he had been entrusted by God with a special mission and a special blessing to benefit all the inhabitants of the earth (Genesis 12:1-2). The command to sacrifice Isaac went counter to all that Abraham believed and all he had striven for through the years.

Yet, God planned the *akedah* to be the peak experience for Abraham. It would remove his lingering hesitations and fears regarding his own ability to carry out his work in this world. Pagans of Abraham's day regularly proved the fullness of their loyalty to their gods by sacrificing their sons. Was their religious fervor, even if misplaced, superior to Abraham's? In the *akedah*, God would teach Abraham two important lessons. First, people must accept that God's will is superior to their own. Second, they would learn that giving one's all to God need not be disgusting or sadomasochistic as is so much of idol worship. Man's relationship with God does not consist of placating a capricious and hostile deity but in obeying God's command in trust and love whether in great events or "at the level of every day's most quiet need" (Elizabeth Barrett Browning).

In Abraham's mind there must have long lurked the frightening question as to whether he could bear such a terrible stress. Now he would experience a test that would show him that his loyalty to God would indeed meet any danger, and that his world mission would be successful. Abraham accepted, although with some pain, that God must have a good reason for commanding the sacrifice of Isaac. He had argued with God over his intention to destroy the cities of Sodom and Gommorah because of their wickedness. However, he did not protest the order to sacrifice his own son.

Abraham brought Isaac to the site on Mount Moriah, prepared the altar and the firewood, and raised his knife to slaughter his son. At that point, a heavenly voice called to him, "Lay not your hand on the lad and do nothing to him, for now I know that you are a God-fearing man and you have not withheld your only son from Me" (22:12). Abraham learned from this experience that he could do whatever he needed to do to fulfill his mission and that he had an important purpose in life. God had also made clear to all the world that he did not demand human sacrifice. God did want man to obey his commandments and know that this would always be the best course for man to follow.

Clinical Implications

This story illustrates vividly the ways in which life tests us. Often we may know something intellectually but still have to play it out experientially. This hands-on experiencing, often involving actions that seem unfathomable at the time, allows a kind of wisdom that cannot be transmitted through the mind alone. We must allow ourselves to enter situations that we do not fully comprehend in advance and must trust that there is a higher meaning to what we do. Many people are blocked from growing because they lack the faith to enter into an undefined situation and lack also the confidence that they will emerge in strength after taking on the temporary position of an apprentice.

DEALING WITH OATHS:
JEPHTHAH AND HIS DAUGHTER

Biblical Narrative

Jewish thought does not encourage the making of vows. Often one makes a vow that is unrealistic or punishing to one's self or to others. It expresses a momentary intensity of emotion that may be rooted in flighty motivation and foolish goals. Vows of abstinence too are sinful, for a person must enjoy God's world. Jephthah was a leader who made an impetuous and ill-considered vow and brought tragedy on himself and others.

As so often happened in the period of the Judges, the Israelites fell under the dominion of a foreign power, in this case the Ammonites. In desperation, the Israelites called upon Jephthah, the head of an outlaw band, to lead them in battle against their oppressors. Jephthah accepted the call and began to organize an army and to negotiate with Ammon. When efforts at peace failed, Jephthah marched off to war. Before leaving, he

> vowed a vow to God and he said, "If you will give the sons of Ammon into my hand, then it shall be that whatever will go forth from the doors of my house to meet me when I return in peace from the Ammonites will be to God or I will bring it up as a burnt offering." (Judges 11:30-31)

(This translation and the following interpretation are based on Rabbi David Kimchi, twelfth century, and Rabbi Levi ben Gerson, thirteenth century).

The Torah does not wholly oppose a vow made in an hour of peril (cf Jacob's vow in Genesis), nor does it discourage a promise to donate to charity (Babylonian Talmud, Nedarim 8a). However, Jephthah's vow was foolish. Instead he should have promised a specific number of animal sacrifices or a specific donation to the tabernacle or to charity. Instead, Jephthah promised that if an animal came out of his property it would be designated as a burnt offering, or if a person, then he would devote his entire life to religious works. What if a donkey or a dog, which were not suitable as offerings, had come out?

As it happened, Jephthah's only daughter came out to welcome him with music and dancing to acclaim his victory. Upon seeing her,

Jephthah tore his garments and bemoaned his vow from which he felt he could not back down. Rabbinic writers are highly critical of Jephthah. Of course, he should have gone to the religious court and had his vow annulled, a perfectly acceptable procedure in this instance. Jephthah, however, would not go to the court, say the commentators, because he feared public embarrassment.

What happened to the unfortunate daughter is not specified in the text. Some commentators believe that Jephthah actually offered her up as a sacrifice. Most argue that she lived out her life as a sort of hermit, never marrying, and instead devoting herself to religious works. All opinions agree that Jephthah was one of the most unfit of Israelite leaders and that he was deeply culpable in the misfortunes of his daughter.

Clinical Implications

This situation must be distinguished from one in which an individual believes he or she is fulfilling a higher purpose. Jephthah is seduced by his own ego to make and keep an ill-considered and unnecessary vow. There was no reason for Jephthah to make a vow to begin with, and still less of a reason to keep it when he saw what was entailed.

A person under severe frustration may be tempted to bribe God by giving him something he does not really want. It is a person's desperation rather than any request from God that will prompt an ill-considered vow. If the person gains success, it may be despite the vow rather than because of it. The therapist must convince patients to concentrate on the intrinsic excellence of their actions rather than to seek approval through trying to ingratiate themselves with God or other people.

COMMUNICATING THROUGH PARABLES: NATHAN AND DAVID

Biblical Narrative

Any good teacher knows that ideas and information are often transmitted better by the use of example and parable than by pounding with facts. Parables are frequent both in the Hebrew Bible and in the rabbinic literature. They help to simplify difficult matters, they serve as memory devices, and they help overcome psychological barriers that impede learning. Remarkably, in the literature of the ancient Greeks, information was often given in a manner that could not be accepted or understood correctly, and the receiver would be hurt by it. When Oedipus sought the murderer of the old King Laius of Thebes, the prophet Tiresias gave Oedipus the information in a way so taunting and ambiguous that Oedipus was left confused and outraged. In another famous myth, a seer declared to the mother of the newborn Narcissus that the boy would be all right as long as he never knew himself. Clear knowledge was hardly a premium for Greek heroes.

Hebrew Scripture, on the other hand, emphasizes the importance of learning and knowing—"And you shall occupy yourself with it [Torah study] day and night" (Joshua 1:8; Deuteronomy 6:7). There are many memorable parables in Scripture, but perhaps few are more telling than Nathan's lesson to King David. The story displays a method of transmitting information that is important not only for a prophet or teacher but also for a psychotherapist whose client seems resistant and unaware of the need to bring change.

King David was attracted to Bathsheba, a beautiful woman whose home adjoined the royal palace in Jerusalem, and he slept with her. However, Bathsheba was already married to Uriah, a soldier off with the Israelite army fighting the Ammonites. David ordered his generals to place Uriah where the fighting was most dangerous and then to order a quick pullback abandoning Uriah on the field. This was done, Uriah was killed by the Ammonites, and David married Bathsheba. David reckoned himself clear of wrongdoing, say the commentators (Babylonian Talmud, Shabbat, 56a). Uriah was guilty of death anyway for having once spoken sassily to the king, and it was not David but the Ammonites who had killed him. However, although in a technical sense David may not have violated the law (because Uriah had given Bathsheba a conditional divorce before going to war), he had acted very badly. How could this point be impressed on a man who had closed his eyes to it?

God now sent Nathan the prophet to David with a parable that would drive its point home poignantly without arousing David's resistance (2 Samuel 12:1f).

Two men lived in a town, one rich and one poor. The wealthy man had very many sheep and cattle, and the poor man had nothing but one little lamb which he had nurtured and raised with himself and his own children. It ate of his food and drank from his cup and slept on his cot and was like his own daughter. Now a guest came to the rich man, and he had spared to take from his own sheep or cattle to prepare for the guest who had come and he took the poor man's lamb to make a meal for his guest.

The rich man's heartlessness infuriated David, and he angrily declared the rich man worthy of death. Certainly, at least the rich man should give the poor man four lambs in place of the one. Nathan then said simply to David, "Thou art the man." With David's resistance broken, Nathan went on to explain David's sin in detail.

Why have you despised the word of God to do evil in His eyes. You have smitten Uriah the Hittite with the sword, and his wife you have taken as your wife. Him you have slain by the sword of the Ammonites. . . . (12:9)

Nathan went on to describe the punishment that God had set for David. Great troubles would rise up against him out of his own family, and even his wives would be taken from him.

The problem was made entirely clear to David, and he made no effort to deny his miscreance either to Nathan or to himself. Having acknowledged that he was guilty, David could now begin to work on restoring his relationship with God. His repentance was sincere and real, and ultimately God blessed the marriage of David and Bathsheba with a brilliant son, Solomon. The prophet Nathan came again to David, this time to bring the message that God still loved David. God signaled this by giving Solomon an additional name, Jedediah, meaning beloved of God, and by assuring David of the continuity of rule over Israel by his descendants through Solomon.

Clinical Implications

Patients may need to address some misbehaviors on their part. The therapeutic problem becomes how to do this. If the patients are confronted directly, they may feel attacked and erect defensive walls. In such cases, the patients are blocking the content of the message in order to protect themselves. The trick is to present the content to the individuals in a manner that does not make them feel personally affected and thus allows them to accept it. A parable can be very useful in this respect.

David accepts the validity of Nathan's parable because he does not personalize it. By internalizing the content, David, with Nathan's help, is able to apply it to himself.

DEALING WITH TEMPTATIONS: ADAM AND EVE

Biblical Narrative

Socialization usually begins with familial relationships, which strongly affect how we deal with people and circumstances all through life. The family is the school in which one can learn love and compassion. All family relationships require work and care, and when an important relationship malfunctions, something must be done to resolve the problems.

In the Genesis account of Creation, God creates the first couple and then intervenes, almost in the role of a benevolent and competent therapist, to salvage their relationship when it runs into trouble (Genesis 2-3). God has created the first man without a companion, wanting Adam to see for himself how much better it is to have a companion than to be alone. Adam studies nature extensively and while learning much, he still finds in his work no satisfaction and no salve to his loneliness. None of the animals can afford him meaningful companionship or certainly intellectual, spiritual, or sexual fulfillment. God then forms a woman to be his companion. For her, man will loosen other relationships and will cling to her so that they may be united as one (2:24). Disagreements will occur between them upon occasion, but they shall help and support each other. Healthy disagreement need not lead to dysfunction. When God introduced the newly formed woman to the newly formed man, according to the Midrash (*Midrash Rabbah,* Genesis 18:1), God dressed her in beautiful clothes and gems suitable to so important an occasion. God's very active role in making this match demonstrates his belief in its importance. He had already called upon mankind to produce and create and had blessed them (Genesis 1:28). Now God formed the first human organization to help foster this creativity, i.e., the married couple.

God settled the couple in a beautiful garden, which required some care but they did not need to work too hard (2:15). They remained close to God and could enjoy the benefits of intellectual creativity and human relations amid the beauties of the garden. In this beautiful garden in all the wondrous harmony of Creation, however, was trouble—a cynical and deceitful snake. One may debate what the snake may symbolize, but it detracts nothing from the main point of the story to allow simply that this snake walked, talked, and thought in a very humanoid way.

The trouble that came shook the harmony of the garden and of the new couple. That the couple was not wholly destroyed by their own compounded mistakes was due to a kindly and effective intervention by God in a manner that set a model for marital therapy throughout history. The snake approached Eve and tried to convince her to turn against God. He sought to make her dissatisfied with what she had. He was clever enough to sense some vague dissatisfaction in her already and he stirred her interest in several areas. First, he lured her into conversation by challenging her authority and independence in the garden, sensing perhaps her need for control (3:1f). Then he convinced her that she need fear no retribution from God if she would eat the fruit of the forbidden tree. In fact, God was merely trying to prevent her from attaining the wonderful knowledge and independence of thought she would gain by eating the fruit. Eating would open her eyes and mind to many new wonders, and she would become like God. She ate of the fruit and gave it to her husband to eat, perhaps feeling that he might abandon her and find another woman. He eats, perhaps preferring to join Eve in her difficulty than to be left alone without her. However, Adam and Eve found that the snake's promises were lies. Not only were none of his promises fulfilled, but everything became worse than before. They gained no great wisdom or liberty or control.

Notice how different this story is from the parallel Greek story of Prometheus and Pandora. Pandora is described as a curse to man and Zeus' punishment for Prometheus stealing fire, which was necessary for man's survival. Thus woman and genuine autonomy for man are placed at odds. Eve, however, is a helpmate and blessing. She does not recognize the true freedom in Eden, and pushes Adam in a search for an illusory freedom. Woman and freedom are not at odds, but there is the danger that woman and man will be tempted by false freedoms, which lead to an overwhelming awareness of their own vulnerability.

Adam and Eve had no idea how to rectify their error, and they began a series of behaviors, refusing to recognize their real problem. They sought first to cover their vulnerability with simple garments that they made of fig leaves. At this point God as a therapist intervened to help them. This was not a jealous, punitive deity coming at them in an awesome theophany, hurling thunderbolts at the pitiful sinners who dared disobey him. God appeared gently, in the soft moments at the end of an afternoon (3:8). His aim was to rejuvenate his people, not to destroy them. The man and woman hid, denying that they had a problem. Adam clearly was not ready to take a first step on his own, so God opened a dialogue with him—"Where are you?"(3:9). The question is existential rather than spatial. Adam's answer betrayed his fear and confusion and inability to face his problem. "I feared because I was naked and I hid" (3:10). In fact, Adam was not naked by this point. He had his fig leaves on, but neither Adam's new outfit nor his hiding behind the trees was the issue. Adam was confused, and God now confronted him more bluntly though still not threateningly, asking Adam directly if he ate of the forbidden tree.

Adam's response was to blame both the woman and God himself—"the woman which You gave me" (3:12). He should have tried to protect his wife as best he could, to face up to his mistake and to make his peace with God, but he did none of these. Nor could Eve take responsibility for her mistake, pointing to the snake instead. Adam and Eve were angry and resentful toward each other too. God knew that he must assume the responsibilities that the two people could not handle. He must decide how to restore them to productive, meaningful lives and to a good relationship with each other as well.

His answer was to engage the people more fully in the divine plan for the world. This involved more work not for the purpose of mere busyness and drudgery, but as a part of their human development. Childbearing for Eve and work for Adam will be more difficult. However, God's love for them did not diminish. They can still have wonderful lives, creative and productive and in good relationship with God. He curses the ground so that it will not bear produce readily.

However, man himself is not cursed (3:17). The woman is named Eve, (Chava) mother of life, only when she leaves Eden.

God has preserved life and joy and creativity for mankind. He has also resolved the central problems of Adam and Eve by not allowing them to prolong the pattern of mutual recrimination and entrapment typical of Prometheus and Pandora. He reassures them of his support so that they need not fear abandonment by each other or by him. The renewed trust between husband and wife is evidenced in Adam's choosing the new title for Eve.

Also God provided Adam and Eve with new garments. In this way, he recognized their need for protection, both emotional and physical. The garments provided a mark of status and position as garments do all through history and often in the Bible, as with the priestly garments in Exodus or Joseph's coat in Genesis 37. This is a legitimate need of mortal man.

The new people had another important lesson to learn here. The species of the tree of knowledge is not stated. It does not seem to have produced any unusual fruit. Rabbinic commentaries theorize that the fruit may have been grapes, figs, citrons, or wheat. In any case, the fruit does not seem to have given Adam and Eve any great knowledge or benefit as did fire for Prometheus and Greek man.

Here lies the lesson. Knowledge and maturity of spirit and intellect are not attained by eating magical fruits or living in an idyllic garden. These require hard work and determination. Man can live well enough without the garden and the tree of knowledge. Perhaps sending the people out of the garden was a way of showing them that it is by obedience to God and by working to fulfill his aims that people live useful and healthy lives and not by eating magical fruits in a magic garden.

Clinical Implications

Sometimes a person is tempted by a seemingly magical solution to an ongoing problem. "If only you eat this," states the tempter, "you will magically achieve that outcome." Often we are obsessed with using seemingly magical pills to cure depression and anxiety rather than viewing depression and anxiety as signs of a deeper malaise, which must be worked through therapeutically. A magical solution is offered to provide an illusory relief, which comprehends the original problem and alienates the individual from himself or herself. So it was with Adam and Eve, who are offered a magical fruit that will enable them suddenly to know good and evil. When they eat this fruit, they are expelled from Eden, and they must work to overcome their dependency on what they perceived as magical fruit in order to reach their original God-given mandate to grow and develop.

REJECTING TEMPTATIONS: JOSEPH AND POTIPHAR'S WIFE

Biblical Narrative

Genesis' account of the confrontation of Joseph and Potiphar's wife involves encounter between not only personalities but between widely variant cultures. The focus is on the difference between a life devoted to meaningful obligations and commitments and one that seeks gratification and freedom without commitment or giving of oneself. The story also brings out contrasting views of sexuality.

Joseph, seventeen-year-old son of Jacob and Rachel, was sold to caravan traders by his brothers, who resented their father's favoritism of him. The traders carried him down to Egypt and sold him there as a slave to Potiphar, a government official of importance. Very bright and capable, Joseph did well in his new environment. Successful in his work, he maintained the moral and religious standards that his parents had inculcated in him. This was a difficult task, since Egyptian life was very different from Israelite life. The Egyptians worshiped a multitude of gods and fetishes with oppressive ritual and elaborate ceremony, and they built magnificent temples and pyramids, which stand to this day as monuments to Egypt's glory. Egyptian moral standards were far looser than in Joseph's family.

Joseph had the strength to resist the temptations of his new land, and Potiphar soon recognized both the excellence of Joseph's work and the depth of his commitment to God, "And his master saw that God was with him and that in all that he did God prospered him" (Genesis 39:3). Joseph was soon appointed as head over all of Potiphar's house, and again Joseph performed magnificently, so that Potiphar trusted him unquestioningly.

Potiphar's wife now stepped onto the stage. Scripture never mentions her name, but Midrash calls her Zulieka. She noticed Joseph's ability and striking good looks, and she tried to seduce him. Joseph was faced with a great dilemma. If he refused her, she could make terrible trouble for him. However, adultery was clearly against the Hebrew view of sex.

The Hebrew Bible praises sex as a wonderful activity that expresses many important facets of human creativity. It helps in the bonding of husband and wife, it gives great pleasure, and it makes the couple partners to God in the producing and raising of children. However, sexual activity was limited to the commitment of the marriage pact. In Egypt, the view of sex was very different. Promiscuity and sexual aberration were common enough to be socially acceptable. Masters slept with slaves and eunuchs were prominent. To Zulieka, Joseph was an attraction. An affair with him offered some excitement with no bonding or commitment and certainly no sanctification. Joseph could be sold or dispatched when she tired of him. Even if she was attracted by his intellect or his spirit as well as by his good looks, she was still seeking a relationship that offered quick physical gratification but neither bonding, commitment, nor security.

Joseph turned her down, trying to explain that he could never feel right betraying Potiphar. When that made no impression on her, Joseph tried to explain that adultery was forbidden by his God. Zulieka was not interested in excuses, and she continued to press Joseph day by day only to be rebuffed each time.

One day Joseph went into the main house when no one was there but Zulieka. Joseph may have known that all the men were away, and for a moment he was ready to yield to temptation. Finding Joseph alone, Zulieka again tried to seduce him. A midrash says that Joseph was ready to give in when the image of his father flashed through his mind and he remembered God's purpose in building a new faith on Jacob and his family. Joseph's life had too much meaning to be cast away for a meaningless flirtation with his master's wife. She seized hold of Joseph's jacket, but Joseph broke away and left the house, leaving the jacket in her hand. Angry and fearful that Joseph might report her to her husband, Zulieka planned to smear Joseph. She called in the servants, and showing them Joseph's garment, she accused him of trying to rape her, degrading him as a Hebrew foreigner in order to win them over. She told the same story to Potiphar when he came in, emphasizing not only Joseph's lowly foreign origin but also his slave status, which she had, of course, omitted to mention when talking to her slaves.

Potiphar probably knew both Joseph and his wife well enough to have guessed the truth of the matter, and he did not put Joseph to death. Instead he placed him in a jail for political prisoners, where Joseph with his great ability and high moral stature soon became the trusted aide of the chief officer. In prison, too, God was with Joseph, and he was still "a successful man" (39:2 and 23). Joseph became the viceroy of Egypt and, more important, was reunited and reconciled with his family and fulfilled his role as a major figure in the founding of a great faith.

Clinical Implications

This story illustrates the importance of people knowing who they are. As a therapist centers a person on what is essential to self-definition, many conflicts and temptations will disappear naturally. As patients realize who they are, they also realize who they are not. This in itself provides a more solid basis for avoiding destructive detours than lecturing a person on behaviors. Many temptations lose their power because they take a person away from his or her real purpose. Recollections of his father, Jacob, reminded Joseph of the depth of his commitment to the covenant and of the higher purposes of his life. Succumbing to the seduction of Potiphar's wife involves not only betrayal of Potiphar but ultimately betrayal of Joseph himself and God. From this point of view temptation can be seen as a failure to know oneself. Joseph must choose whether to know himself and be Joseph or to surrender himself to the oblivion of Narcissus.

Chapter 5

Good and Bad Anger

INTRODUCTION

"Sing, goddess, the anger of Peleus' son Achilles and its devastation, which put pains one thousand fold upon the Achaeans, hurled in their multitudes to the house of Hades strong souls of heroes . . ." So reads Richmond Lattimore's translation of the magnificent opening lines of Homer's *Iliad*. The bitter wrath of Achilles caused horrifying division and destruction. Achilles was moved by personal pique, operating within the social code of the Homeric aristocratic hero. However, he had little in him of the visionary statesman, who understands the unique potential of his people or his times. Other greater statesmen would express such feelings later, e.g., Pericles' paean of the greatness of Athens in his oration of 429 B.C.E. or Abraham Lincoln's sense of the meaning of American democracy as expressed in his debates with Stephen Douglas and in his Gettysburg Address. Achilles' passions were egocentric and destructive to others and to himself.

In Western thought, the strength and power of the athlete or warrior is glorified. People such as Achilles are admired as heroic because of their macho and their warlike deeds, with no regard to whether they behaved decently and morally. The Hebrew Bible praised physical strength and heroism (e.g., David and Samson), and Israelite armies often displayed their prowess on the field of battle. The Hebrew Scripture insists, however, that the race is not to the swift, nor the battle to the strong. It is not the warrior's powers that bring victory. The winning or losing of the war is God's decision.

The truest hero is the person who overcomes oppositions not by proving his macho nor by winning athletic or military contests, but by doing what is right and rejecting what is wrong. The opposition may come from the outside or it may come from barriers or weaknesses within one's own character. "To conquer one's own inclinations is greater than conquering a city" (Proverbs 16:32). The Hebrew Bible, unlike Achilles, prizes virtues such as kindness, honesty, and peace. Still, sometimes one must be rough or deceptive or militant in order to uphold those very virtues. Sometimes we must perform angry and violent deeds in defense of greater ideals, and at such times quiet and passivity may be inappropriate.

This chapter presents five biblical figures who found that the most appropriate response to their particular situations was to be strong and assertive, even perhaps violent. Only thus could they support the higher aims of virtue, peace, and harmony. These people would not go through life like Achilles, as machines of angry destruction. They could remain wholly loyal to their nobler purposes and their better selves. The stories discuss the zeal of Phinehas in confronting immorality; the excess of anger displayed by Simeon and Levi, who become obsessed with revenge for revenge's sake; King Saul, who first is too merciful, and then too violent; the healthy anger of Moses in protecting an innocent Israelite; and last, the story of Hezekiah and Rabshakeh, which highlights the role of anger in escaping cynicism.

CONFRONTING IMMORALITY: PHINEHAS

Biblical Narrative

Zealous vengeance is an act that modern man finds very disturbing and uncivilized. So does Scripture, enjoining its readers, "Thou shalt not take revenge." God rebuked Elijah, the great prophet, for being overly zealous. Sometimes, however, zeal and vengeance are the only effective means to handle a serious problem. Let us view two stories in which a person needed to act with zealous vengeance. In a biblical story the protagonist acted—with success. In a famous English play, the protagonist did not act—with tragic results.

The biblical Hebrew word, *kanai,* is often translated into English as zealot, and it is used thus in Numbers 25 to describe Phinehas. However, the word "zealot" connotes an angry fanaticism while *kanai* implies more an unflinching dedication to do what is right even with great personal risk or hardship. This can be a very positive force. Phinehas was a grandson of Aaron, the kindly high priest who loved peace. However, in the moment of need, Phinehas's vigorous action saved perhaps thousands of lives, and indeed brought peace.

Near the end of their forty years in the Sinai, the Israelites were encamped at Shittim. The Moabites, having failed to destroy them with Balaam's curses (see Chapter 9) and fearing to take arms against them, determined upon another means to destroy them. They sent their daughters to seduce Israelite men and lead them into the disgusting rites of their deity, Baal Peor. The plan seemed to be working. Many Israelite men were entrapped, and God sent a plague to punish them.

Moses set up special courts to deal with the crisis, but with little apparent effect for the orgies went on and so did the plague. Then Zimri ben Salu, a prince of the tribe of Simeon, brought a Midianite woman through the Israelite camp, flaunting her in full view of Moses and his advisers. The two proceeded to Zimri's tent. Moses and the judges wept, perhaps from sheer frustration, but they seemed unable to stop Zimri. National disaster threatened. Then Phinehas arose. No record indicates that prior to this moment he had ever done anything noteworthy or had ever held any public position. Now, however, he saw that the plague was spreading, and that the leaders could not act. He took upon himself the great responsibility required of that moment, working completely on his own with no authorization from the leaders, although in consonance with law. Although he was not an experienced warrior, he took a spear in his hand. At great personal risk, he followed Zimri and the Midianite woman into the tent where, finding them in flagrante delicto, he thrust the spear through them both, transfixing them in a way that showed exactly what they were doing: "And he came after the Israelite man into the tent, and he speared both the Israelite man and the woman through her belly" (25:8). The result of Phinehas's "zealous" act was that the plague finally ceased after having killed 24,000 people.

Phinehas was compelled by the need to honor God's name, to save lives, and to prevent a potential moral breakdown of the entire nation, not by a thirst for blood or attention. This was an act of personal growth for Phinehas as well as a great public service. Phinehas acted quickly and effectively. God confirmed Phinehas's act by establishing two covenants with him: (1) a "treaty of peace" (25:12) and (2) a treaty of "everlasting priesthood" (25:13). Phinehas now joined the rest of the family of Aaron as a full-fledged priest, serving in the tabernacle, a privilege he had not held before. This was the suitable reward for one who had brought atonement for the Israelites, which is one of the priest's main responsibilities. By acting as decisively as he did, Phinehas saved many lives and quieted God's anger at his people.

Compare the story of Phinehas to Shakespeare's Hamlet, surely one of the towering presences of Western literature. Hamlet is given the imperative of killing his uncle, King Claudius, to avenge the murder of Hamlet's father. A man of intellect and refinement, Hamlet fails to carry out this violent duty, procrastinating and thinking too much as opportunities pass him by. "Whether 'tis nobler in the mind to suffer the slings and arrows of outrageous fortune, or to take arms against a sea of troubles, and by opposing end them?" (Act III, scene I). Hamlet is a noble human being, but he lacks zeal. By not killing the king quickly, Hamlet makes the situation far worse, allowing the king to set up the final scene in which Hamlet, Laertes, the queen, and, too late, the king all meet violent deaths. Polonius and Ophelia have already died. By slaying the guilty Claudius earlier, Hamlet could have averted this tragic ending. Hamlet was a refined soul and a better swordsman than Phinehas, but his hesitation to strike when it was necessary brought all his goodness to naught and destroyed many innocent lives. Phinehas, by doing what the law required of him even though violence was not his usual way, struck the blow that stopped the plague and ultimately saved many lives and perhaps the essential character of a great world religion.

Clinical Implications

Modern sensibilities recoil from a story of vengeance, but this is an important story for therapists. The essence here is that Phinehas reacted and Hamlet did not. It is sometimes right and healthy to become angry. Not to become angry in the face of great wrong or danger can breed an insidious passivity that will "cast a blind eye" at all sorts of wrongs. Moreover, such inaction tends to diminish one's sense of self. It is an evasion of responsibility.

This story must not be interpreted as glorifying violence or macho per se, but at times action simply must be taken, and zeal and conviction need not be a mindless fanaticism but instead represent the deepest spiritual love of God, of goodness, and of right. Patients will grow if they develop the strength and stamina to take action when it must be taken. Often, like Phinehas, patients may find themselves acting alone—but so be it. The alternative is the endless inaction and self-recriminations of a Hamlet.

TAKING REVENGE: SIMEON AND LEVI

Biblical Narrative

When a man is attacked, should he react violently or absorb the attack more placidly and not risk escalating the tensions? Genesis 34 provides a case. The patriarch Jacob returned with his household to Canaan after many years in Haran working for Laban, his father-in-law. Dinah, Jacob's beautiful young daughter, wandered away from the safety of the family's camp and was abducted and raped by Shechem, the son of the local King Hamor. Shechem became very enamored of Dinah, refusing to let her go. He negotiated with Jacob for Dinah's hand in marriage as part of a general alliance between Jacob's people and the citizens of the town of Shechem.

Deeply saddened and angry, Jacob kept silent until his sons came home. The sons were enraged and Simeon and Levi devised a plan to take Dinah back. They pretended to be interested in Shechem's offer, but insisted that Dinah and other women of Jacob's clan could marry only circumcised men. Pressured by their king and anxious for the alliance, the Shechemites agreed to circumcise themselves. On the third day, when all the men were weak and in pain, Simeon and Levi entered the town and slew them all. They and their brothers then looted the town.

Can such an act of revenge be justified? The brothers believed it was necessary to rescue Dinah and that to uphold their family's honor and take a just revenge would discourage others from starting up with them. Jacob was much older than his adolescent sons and had gone through many trials. Although he felt the wrong probably even more deeply than they did, he was hesitant to use violence lest it draw upon him the anger of nearby nations and put his whole household in danger. He always abhorred violence and sought peace in his own life. Years later, he warned his sons about controlling their anger, expressed both in the story of Dinah and in the selling of Joseph. "Cursed be their anger for it is hard . . ." (Genesis 49:7). Jacob did not reject Simeon and Levi or disapprove generally of using appropriate force when one's well-being or one's cherished principles are threatened. He blessed Simeon and Levi among his twelve sons before his death, although warning them in strong terms that anger must be used only for good purpose.

Clinical Implications

Violence is not to be glorified in itself, nor will it serve to prove one's macho or manhood. The blessings of a just peace are certainly preferable to war, yet sometimes violence is the only way and people or nations must fight. Even so, violence should be used wisely. It is useless to strike angrily at someone physically and indeed verbally only to find that the other person can harm you far more than you can harm him or her. Also, one must be careful not to descend to the lower moral level of a threatening enemy. A patient must learn to respond to threats with neither undue violence nor undue restraint, but with practical wisdom and with a strong sense of right.

MISPLACED MERCY, MISPLACED VIOLENCE: KING SAUL

Biblical Narrative

As it is not helpful to be tough when one should be gentle, so it can be equally unhelpful to be gentle when one should be tough. The Talmud (Yoma 22b-23a) cites King Saul as the classic example of this error, despite his greatness of character and his many accomplishments.

God had commanded the Israelites, through Moses, to totally obliterate the Amalekite tribe. When Saul became the first king of Israel, this duty devolved upon him. Saul, indeed, attacked the Amalekites and won a smashing victory. However, when the prophet Samuel arrived at the army camp, he was shocked to find that the Israelites had spared not only the Amalekites' sheep and cattle but even Agag, their king. Samuel remonstrated bluntly with Saul on his failure to carry out God's clear command and then himself slew Agag. Saul could only try to excuse himself by claiming that he had merely followed the wishes of his people. Samuel then informed Saul that God would take his kingship from him and give it to someone more worthy.

On a later occasion, Saul grew angry when it was reported to him by Doeg, one of his agents, that a priest of the town of Nob had supplied food and a sword to David, who at that time was fleeing from Saul. The priest had not known that the relationship between Saul and David had so deteriorated, and he had acted in good faith. Saul, however, would not accept the priest's protestations of innocence, and he ordered his men to slay all the priests of Nob. When they refused in horror, Saul turned to Doeg, who slew eighty priests.

As the Talmud puts it, to King Saul's unwarranted mercies to Amalek are applied the verse in Ecclesiastes, "Do not be overly righteous" (7:16). To his treatment of the priests of Nob is applied the verse, "Be not overly wicked" (7:17). A righteous person must be kind and forgiving and modest but not inappropriately so.

Clinical Implications

Consider a man who feels pushed around by his boss at work. He is totally unable to stand up to the boss but winds up displacing his anger on his wife and children when he arrives home. Feelings of anger and rage do not simply disappear. If they are not addressed to the eliciting targets, they will be displaced on innocent victims. This does not mean that anger must become violent, only that the feeling of anger needs to be expressed appropriately.

PROTECTING THE INNOCENT: MOSES

Biblical Narrative

Moses was a deeply humble and compassionate man who had learned much of the meaning of peace and of goodness both from God's direct teaching and from his own life experience, yet he was not totally free of strong or even violent reactions. Let us view four incidents in his life. In two, his strong reaction was appropriate, but in two it was not.

1. Moses descended Mount Sinai after forty days of study with God. He was bringing to the Israelite people the Ten Commandments inscribed by God on two tablets of stone. Moses walked down the mountain and saw people worshiping the golden calf, "And he saw the calf and the dancing, and Moses reacted angrily and cast the tablets from his hand, breaking them at the base of the mountain" (Exodus 32:19). Moses' anger was in this case very suitable. The people had behaved badly, and they did not deserve the divinely made tablets. God later signaled approval of Moses' act by spending a second forty days with him on the mountain and by giving him a second set of tablets.

2. Exodus 2:11-15. Moses was raised as a prince in Pharaoh's palace, but the princess, his stepmother, had informed him of his Hebrew origin. When he grew old enough, Moses went forth to see the Hebrews oppressed in their slavery, and his heart went out to them. A certain Egyptian overseer was beating a slave. Looking around and seeing no other Egyptians, Moses killed the man and hid his body in the sand. Moses had been careless. He could accomplish nothing for the slaves by killing one taskmaster. Perhaps the taskmaster did not even deserve to be killed for beating the slave. More dangerous for Moses was that he had been careless of his own safety. Someone, perhaps one of the slaves, reported Moses' deed to Pharaoh, who sought to arrest Moses and to execute him. Moses was forced to flee Egypt. He returned many years later when God sent him to lead the Hebrew exodus from Egypt. Again, Moses' killing of the Egyptian was noble, fed by his compassion for the slaves. However, it was ill-considered in that it was too violent and, in fact, accomplished little, putting Moses in danger.

3. Many years passed. By now, Moses had long been the leader of the Israelites in the wilderness. The people came with a legitimate request for water. God told Moses to speak to a certain rock and it would bring forth water. However, feeling that the people's request was out of line and rebellious, Moses overreacted, addressing them harshly, "Hear ye rebels" (Numbers 20:10). In his anger, Moses then smote the rock with his staff instead of speaking to it as he was commanded. God punished him by decreeing that he would not be permitted to enter the land of Israel.

4. Moses had endured many months of dealing with Pharaoh's cruelties toward the Hebrews and with his constant reneging on promises to let them depart from Egypt. After the ninth plague—darkness—Pharaoh finally told Moses that "you will never see my face again for on the day you will see my face you shall surely die" (Exodus 10:28). Moses could deal with the frustrations and disappointments of his labors and even with the hardships and sufferings of his people, but until now there had always seemed some small hope that Pharaoh could still be dealt with peaceably and successfully. Now Pharaoh himself seemed to be rejecting with finality all of Moses' goodwill as well as his own human duty to the Hebrews. It seems to have pained Moses deeply to see a human being so persistent in his foolish wrongdoing and purposefully hurtling to his own self-destruction. Moses became angry—"And Moses departed in anger from before Pharaoh" (Exodus 11:8). The Scripture give no indication that Moses' anger was in any way wrong or unjust.

Clinical Implications

A person must know when to show anger. Many events occur in life that are frustrating and even unjust, yet we cannot show anger in all of these instances. Sometimes, we become prisoners of our own anger, which deepens our misfortune. Other times, we become trapped through trying to overcontrol our anger. Learning when, where, and how to show anger is an important clinical lesson.

ESCAPING CYNICISM: HEZEKIAH VERSUS RABSHAKEH

Biblical Narrative

Some people, unable to tolerate others' belief in goodness, have the effrontery to accuse those people of being as empty, forlorn, and cynical as they are. The story of King Hezekiah and the Assyrian Rabshakeh illustrates this pattern. It is told in 2 Kings 18-19 and again almost verbatim in Isaiah 36-37.

King Hezekiah of Judah was a man of great ability and of noble character, known especially as one who trusted in God (2 Kings 18:5). In Hezekiah's time Judah remained one of the few countries that had not yet been conquered by the growing might of Assyria and its cruel and aggressive armies. Finally, after much political and military exchange, the Assyrian King Sennacherib invaded Judah and set about conquering its cities. Soon little more than Jerusalem remained. Hezekiah strengthened the city defenses and tried to buy time by paying Sennacherib a heavy tribute of gold and silver. Still, the Assyrians came on, and a powerful army was soon encamped around Jerusalem.

Three high-level Assyrian leaders were sent to parley, and Hezekiah dispatched three of his advisers to meet them. The Assyrian Rabshakeh (this was a title, not a personal name) addressed not only Hezekiah's representatives but also the Judeans standing on the walls. He spoke in a loud clear voice and in the Hebrew language so that all could understand. Many scholars believe that Rabshakeh was a renegade Judean because of his apparent knowledge of both Judah's language and religion. His speech was deeply threatening and highly cynical. He first attacked directly the deep faith that was central to Hezekiah's personal thought and to his governing: "And Rabshakeh said to them . . . 'What trust is this in which you have trusted. . . . Now on whom do you trust that you have rebelled against me?'" (Isaiah 36:4-5). He argued first that Judah certainly could not rely for help on Egypt for Egypt is but a "broken reed" (Isaiah 36:6). Then he attacked the whole idea of faith in God and accused Hezekiah of forfeiting God's support by his iniquities. "But if you say no to me: We trust in the Lord our God; is it not He whose high places and whose altars Hezekiah has taken away" (36:7). Hezekiah had indeed removed the illegal private altars so that people would offer sacrifices only in the Jerusalem temple. In this, Hezekiah had followed the teachings of the Pentateuch and of the prophets of his own day, but Rabshakeh cynically twisted this around, presenting Hezekiah as ignoring true religion to build the prestige of his own capital city, thus making Hezekiah no different from any pagan king. Rabshakeh may have been seeking to arouse support among Judeans who opposed removal of the private altars. Hezekiah's deep and sincere piety was projected as an expression of cynical self-promotion. Judah was being ravaged because of Hezekiah's impiety, not despite his piety.

Rabshakeh went on. Resistance to Assyria would be useless, for her power was too great, and God favored her too—"Have I now then come without God upon this land to destroy it? God said to me, 'Go up against this land and destroy it'" (36:10). Finally Rabshakeh revealed his own total disdain for faith and indeed for God himself. (He mockingly used the word *äbtkhã,* trust or faith, seven times in his speech, in an attempt to denigrate Hezekiah's real sense of faith.) We have conquered many nations, and their gods could not help them, said Rabshakeh. "Who among all the gods of these lands saved their land from my hand that your God will save Jerusalem from my hand?" (36:20). This world is ruled by power and the Assyrians are more powerful than gods.

Hezekiah had done what he could to prepare Jerusalem's defenses for the war, and now that the moment of decision had come, he knew exactly what to do next. He put on sackcloth, and went to the temple to pray and sent word to Isaiah the prophet to ask for his help. To Hezekiah, the contest was not only over Jerusalem but also over the cynical boasting and threats of Rabshakeh—"It may be that the Lord your God will hear the words of Rabshakeh whom the king of Assyria his master has sent to taunt the living God" (37:4). Hezekiah's own prayer to God centered on his belief that the Assyrians had conquered many lands and burned their gods. They did not realize that those gods were false, nor did they realize that it was now the true God with whom they were warring (37:20). "Now therefore, Lord our God, save us from his hand, so that all the kingdoms of the earth will know that you alone are God." This was not an appeal to God's vanity. It was a hope that this was an opportunity for people to come to recognize God's rule over the world, which is the main purpose of human history.

God's answer came through Isaiah. All that had happened is part of God's plan for the world. The Assyrians boasted that their conquest and power proved their greatness. However, in truth, all that was happening, the whole war, was from God. "Have you not heard? Long ago I made it; from the earliest days I formed it. Now I have brought it to pass. Let it be so that fortified cities should turn into desolate ruins" (37:36). God struck Sennacherib's army with a plague and 185,000 men died in one night. Sennacherib abandoned the siege of Jerusalem and returned to Nineveh, his capital, where his own sons stabbed him to death (37:38).

Clinical Implications

It is often tempting to project a worldly cynicism to protect oneself from hurt or disappointment. "I didn't really expect anything," one might say, "and you are naive to have hope." This can extend to protecting oneself from rejection in love and failure in work.

From such a vantage point, hope seems naive, faith is to be dismissed, and love is illusory. Goodness is merely weakness, and right and truth are determined by might. The difficulty is that the cynical response sounds so much more sophisticated. Mistrust sounds so much more worldly and smart than trust, and negativity sounds so much more rooted in experience than optimism. Indeed, the sense of the tragic seems to reflect a deeper vision than a hopeful stance.

A biblical approach to therapy suggests that the opposite is true. Hope in the face of all the onslaughts of life may, in fact, represent a clearer and deeper vision than the tragic. The things that cannot be seen may be even more important than those that can be. This does not mean that patients should be encouraged to act foolishly or to put their lives at risk through meaningless and illusory attempts to illustrate power and freedom. True freedom can come only from putting oneself in God's hands and relinquishing a need to control everything in the environment. True freedom allows one to experience a sense of awe in the wonders of the world.

Chapter 6

Various Disorders

INTRODUCTION

"Unfortunately," writes critic Stanley Crouch in an article about jazz great Louis Armstrong (2000, Part 2, p. 16), "our aesthetic sense of tragedy and comedy, sorrow and happiness, derived from the Greeks, has convinced us that spiritual affliction is a more serious subject than spiritual exultation."

Many humorous activities that can produce joy, be uplifting, and promote personal growth can be garbled and distorted so that they give instead pain, anger, and frustration, which deplete and stifle the human spirit. They feed into human tragedy not into man's natural love of life. The Bible enjoins that people should "serve God with joy and awe" and "rejoice before Him with trembling" (Psalms 2:11). Let people focus not on the tragic view of life but on life's bounties and opportunities. In all human activities, it helps immensely to have a clear and positive perspective and to understand both one's responsibilities and potential. People can handle problems and not be crushed by them.

This section highlights the stories of five biblical characters whose lives were disrupted by their inability to deal with matters that should have been simple and joyous. Many are problems that involve ordinary day-to-day matters—eating, drinking, working, having sex, and acquiring possessions.

Common to all these stories is an inability to establish boundaries around the self and to regulate walls between the self and the outside world in healthy ways. Food, work, sex, and material possessions all have their proper place. They can be enjoyed in a fruitful and positive way and can enhance a person's life. Taken to excess, however, they can poison and make one a captive of an obsession or addiction.

The story of Adam and Eve approaches the problem of an eating disorder. The second story, Noah, discusses drunkenness and the disrespect that often results from it. The third story, again of Adam, offers a distinction between healthy work in service of a transcendent goal and workaholism. The fourth, Cain, deals with being unrealistically overwhelmed by a heavy burden. Finally, the story of manna distinguishes hoarding from enjoying.

OVERCOMING EATING DISORDERS: ADAM AND EVE VERSUS ERYSICHTHON

Biblical Narrative

Eating disorders include a wide range of problems from dangerous anorexia to being a few pounds overweight, and they have become highly noticeable in modern society. A report in 1999 claimed that since the introduction of television in several of the South Pacific Islands a few years earlier, the number of eating disorders there had increased fivefold. However, eating disorders are not an invention of modern civilization. Ancient literature also features stories of anorexia, overeating, and the like. The Bible offers its own approach to eating, and there is a striking difference between the story of Adam and Eve eating the forbidden fruit and the Greek myth of Erysichthon, who ate himself. Several motifs in the two stories are indeed amazingly similar, yet the stories offer totally different views on eating.

Erysichthon, as portrayed by Ovid in his *Metamorphoses,* wickedly chopped down an old huge tree that was sacred to Ceres, the goddess of grain. Ceres punished him by giving him an insatiable appetite. The more Erysichthon ate, the hungrier he became. He finally sold his own daughter for food. However, with Neptune's help, she changed her form and escaped her slavery. When Erysichthon learned that she had this ability, he continued to sell her over and over. Even this, however, did not supply him with enough food, and he finally devoured himself.

Similar to the Genesis story of the Garden of Eden, this story includes an attack on an important tree and a problem involving eating, but here the similarities end. Adam and Eve were not angry and hostile. They did not chop down a sacred tree, although they did yield to temptation and ate the forbidden fruit. Also, no deity tried to help or rehabilitate Erysichthon, as God did to Adam and Eve. Food was the medium of punishment for Erysichthon. Adam and Eve sinned by once eating forbidden food, but they were not punished with self-destruction through food. They could still eat well and enjoy food, although they had to work harder for it. "By the sweat of your brow, you shall eat bread" (Genesis 3:19), but they could indeed have good food. Production and the preparation of food became one way for people to express their creativity and to enjoy God's bounty.

Erysichthon was then unlike Adam and Eve. He was an angry, vicious man who destroyed everything around him: (1) the sacred tree, (2) a man who tried to stop him from attacking the tree, (3) his daughter, and (4) himself. Adam and Eve were not inherently wicked. Their act of eating the fruit was propelled perhaps by misguided sensuality or philosophy, but not by depraved hostility or cruelty.

Indeed, Erysichthon resembled more closely the serpent in the Garden of Eden, who sought to destroy Adam and Eve with no tangible benefit to himself beyond the false thrill of causing trouble for them. The serpent's end too was similar to Erysichthon's. He would crawl on his belly, which seems to indicate that after having induced the people to sin through eating he would himself never enjoy the full pleasures of the belly (i.e., joy in eating). For both Erysichthon and the serpent, eating is a punishment, for they can never enjoy it or be satisfied with it. "On your belly you shall go, and dust you shall eat all the days of your life" (Genesis 3:14).

The Greek myth offers no resolution to Erysichthon's eating problem except his self-destruction. The Bible's response is very different. God intervenes in the manner of an expert therapist, not only to save Adam and Eve, but also to relax the strain that had developed in their relationship. The Bible develops the approach that eating, like all activities of this earth, should be sanctified and made into a form of service to God. Physical pleasure can enhance human holiness. Thus the Bible ordains that some foods may be eaten while others are prohibited, and people must express gratitude to God for their food (e.g., Leviticus 11; Deuteronomy 8:10). Eating is a form of expressing and contributing to the joy of life and of marking special occasions such as Sabbaths and festivals. Both the nutrition and the pleasure of eating offer people a means of enjoying and sanctifying God's creation and their role in it.

Clinical Implications

The Bible's approach to food has great practical significance for treatment of eating disorders. Eating must not stem from aggression or loneliness nor should withholding of eating be used as an attempt to establish boundaries. In these cases the underlying attitude toward eating is destructive, and this negativity will be manifested in the eating disorders.

A healthy individual approaches food in the context of one's entire life. It can and should be enjoyed without descending to gluttony. Likewise, one may eat moderately and keep to a desired weight without vomiting what is eaten. One can have a healthy appetite without degenerating into insatiable hunger. One can eat moderately without starving to death. A good therapist will approach eating disorders by seeking to change underlying attitudes to food that are projections of a miserable and unfulfilled personality. For a healthy individual, eating becomes a means of social and spiritual communication.

DRUNKENNESS AND DISRESPECT: NOAH

Biblical Narrative

The story in Genesis 9 of Noah's drunkenness and the insult from Ham and Canaan, his son and grandson, presents a number of important themes: (1) a picture of Noah as the survivor of a world catastrophe, (2) the problems of substance abuse, and (3) father-son relations. We shall look at another aspect—how to relate to the human body and especially to nakedness. This story takes on increased significance in an age when the Internet has added new dimensions to the use of pornography.

Leaving the ark after the great flood had receded, Noah turned to farming, which he had always loved, and he planted a vineyard (Genesis 5:29 and 9:20). When the grapes ripened, he made wine, and he drank himself into a deep sleep. His son Ham came into the tent and saw his father sleeping drunk and naked "in the middle of his tent," which might mean not on a bed but on the floor. "And Ham the father of Canaan saw the nakedness of his father, and he told his two brothers outside" (Genesis 9:22). Instead of helping his father in his debased condition, Ham and his son Canaan mocked and degraded

Noah. They acted with a distinct lack of respect for a human being. Ham may well have been expressing his own low self-image by seeking to bring Noah down to his own level of misery. Nakedness is not frequent in the Hebrew Bible, and modesty of dress has been normative in Jewish tradition through the ages. The ancient Israelites did not show any known interest in depicting the naked body in portraits or statues. The human body, in biblical teaching, was created by God and, although man may do evil with his body, the body is inherently good and can accomplish many good things. Modesty guards the sanctity of the body and of human sexuality.

Ham, however, sought to capitalize on Noah's nakedness and vulnerability to demean him. Shem and Japheth, Noah's other sons, heard Ham's story and brought a cloak to cover Noah. They entered the room backward and covered him without seeing his nakedness. They showed the respect that Ham did not.

All this contrasts with classical Greek art, which gloried in nakedness, whether the sublime beauty of the statues by Phidias and Praxiteles or the exhibitionist paintings of vulgar figures and obscene acts on drinking vessels. Particularly in the latter, the human body and sexuality are treated not as sacred but as hostile, insensitive, and grotesquely physical. Sexual intercourse becomes a means to proclaim one's manhood by degrading and dominating others, not to achieve greater intimacy and commitment and certainly not to create. Sexuality was widely associated with orgiastic phallic cults and with drunkenness (e.g., Dionysus). These cults may have arisen to some extent due to an innate need to seek a nobler expression of sexuality. They did not succeed, however. Greek mythology recounts numerous stories of gods committing rape. The Greeks, in a sense, rendered fearful homage to drives that they would not control or sublimate. Sexuality in this form cannot be fulfilling, and the physical cannot connect maturely with the emotional or spiritual. By requiring modesty of dress and behavior, and indeed perhaps even by the practice of circumcision, the Hebrew Bible offers the means to sublimate and redirect physical drives into a mature pattern of life and to find fulfillment in a sexuality that focuses on intimacy and mutual respect.

In our story, Noah blessed the respect for a fellow human being that Shem and Japheth showed even to a person in a debased condition. He cursed the poor behavior shown by Ham and Canaan, who found in human lowliness and nakedness a reason to show disrespect to a fellow human being.

Clinical Implications

This story is important for modern society, which is oversexed but unsatisfied. Nakedness between two lovers should be an essential means of establishing intimate knowledge. It is a private act and deeply personal, and the very opposite of the public exhibitionism and exploitation of the human body. A therapist must help patients to accept their own bodies and care for them respectfully as temples of the soul. They must not mutilate or disfigure them in any way. On the other hand, they must not glorify their bodies at the expense of good character. Such worship of the physical becomes almost idolatrous.

Our society's obsession with sex is an outright denial of the deep sexual component of human relations. A therapist must help patients feel comfortable in their physical beings without becoming obsessed by seeming physical perfection and symmetry at the expense of the spiritual. The biblical approach to therapy would insist that the patient learn to harmonize body and soul. The two are indispensably unified. Trying to sever this unity leads to disaster.

WORK VERSUS WORKAHOLISM: ADAM

Biblical Narrative

Labor unions and workers' strikes are thought of as part of twentieth-century history. It may be surprising then to learn that a very ancient Mesopotamian epic, *Atrahasis,* tells the story of a strike. The Igigi gods had labored 3,600 years digging canals. Physically and emotionally spent, they finally smashed their tools, surrounded the palace of the Annunaki gods, and threatened violence if they did not obtain relief. The attempt to achieve some suitable balance between work and leisure appears often through history, and many Americans have trouble effecting this harmony between work and play. Such imbalance can lead to workaholism or to the neglect of responsibilities, to the extremes of the work ethic or of the life of total leisure, which are really two sides of the same coin.

The Hebrew Bible discusses the issue of work in its very earliest chapters. God placed the first people in the Garden of Eden to "work it and to guard it" (Genesis 2:15), though not to work all day every day on backbreaking labors as the Igigi did. God had already established the principle that people should work six days and cease to work on the seventh, just as he had created the world in six days and rested on the seventh (2:1-3). In those first days of history, people did indeed work. In that beautiful garden, the physical burden was not crushing and people had ample opportunity for study and for personal growth.

When, after eating the forbidden fruit, the people were sent out of the Garden of Eden, their work became harder. They could plant their crops and often harvest little more than thorns and thistles (3:18); yet, their work could also be creative and joyful. For they did not have to eat only what nature offered ("the herbs of the field," 3:18), but with creative effort they could produce bread and other wonderful and enjoyable things—"By the sweat of your brow you shall eat bread" (3:19). This statement offers humans an opportunity, not a curse. Work can continue to be a means of expressing God-given creativity and of producing enjoyable things, thereby becoming a means of blessing and not merely a crushing burden.

The Scripture outlines many ideas and laws on these topics of work and rest—the weekly Sabbath and the Sabbatical year and the many rules on how to manage one's employees. The essential point is that work is not merely a way to earn great sums of money. More important, both work and rest become ways to sanctify one's life and to come close to God. Although God does want us to work, we must learn that success comes from God, not directly as a result of our labor. When we understand and accept this, we are free to create and grow, and we learn to leave other burdens to God.

Clinical Implications

Modern human beings hold an ambivalent attitude to work. We seem obsessed with it, not out of an intrinsic love for the process of creativity but almost out of a compulsion to work for work's sake. However, we cannot wait to retire, to enter an equally polarized life of leisure for leisure's sake. Totally lost in this polarity is the biblical connection of work and rest both rising from a deeper purpose. The therapist must instill in the patient a desire to work for some significant purpose, which has the intrinsic meaning of allowing an expression of creativity.

One must also rest and refresh oneself from the rigors of work, but rest does not simply mean mindless leisure in which the inner self is lost. Rest must be part of the entire human enterprise as a pause, which is itself part of one's life's work.

Such a stance would do much to overcome the workaholic/play-aholic cycle in modern society, which compartmentalizes a soulless work and a mindless play. The therapist must inculcate in the patient a psychological sabbath—a pause to rejuvenate one's strength.

UNREALISTICALLY HEAVY BURDENS: CAIN

Biblical Narrative

The Hebrew Bible is a great book with many varied interpretations. Here is another view of Cain, which uncovers a wholly different slant on that important story. We all complain occasionally about being overworked, having too much to do, and being stressed. For some people, however, everything in life appears to be an unbearably heavy burden. They may acquire many things, but they do not seem able to enjoy them easily. Relationships for them are typically more burdensome than easy and loving. They may have a strong—even punitive—sense of responsibility, but often they overburden themselves with matters for which they have no moral or social obligation. This can result in not being properly able to fulfill duties that they truly should fulfill.

Cain, the first son of Adam and Eve, was a man of many strengths and abilities. However, as he grew up he became deeply enmeshed and dependent on the land he farmed so that it was difficult for him to give of himself or to relate lovingly, especially to his brother, Abel. Both Cain's actions and his conversations with God in Genesis 4 reveal much of his view of the world. First, he decided to bring an offering to God. This in itself was a fine gesture. However, Cain also saw the sacrifice as a heavy burden so that he did not do it wholeheartedly and did not give his best produce.

God was displeased with Cain's approach and spoke to him—but mildly, in very careful phrases,

Why are you angry? And why is your countenance fallen? If you do well, shall you not be uplifted; and if you do not do well, sin couches at the door, and unto you is its desire, but you may rule over it. (4:6-7)

It was not important for Cain to offer a particular sacrifice but simply to do well, God told him. However, Cain, as usual, had not done what he demanded of himself, and he became very distraught and hostile. God tried to make Cain understand that it was necessary for him only to do as well as he could, "If you do well, will (you) not be raised up?" Cain, however, could not really understand that; he thought that God was demanding too much of him, overburdened as he already was. He reacted with intense anger by killing Abel. Then, when God again tried to approach him, Cain expressed his distraught state by lashing out at God, "Am I my brother's keeper?" (4:9). Cain's words belied his thoughts—Why do you expect me to carry the burden of being my brother's keeper?

Cain's hostility toward Abel was, at least in part, the result of his mistaken feeling that he alone was saddled with the responsibility of being Abel's guardian. In hopes of breaking through Cain's destructive pattern, God finally told him that he could no longer till his land but must wander away from it. Cain responded in a phrase that expressed again the terrible burden under which he saw himself living. Similar to the Greek Atlas, Cain feels he bears the world on his shoulders—"Greater is my sin than I can bear" (4:13). The sin was not only great. It was "greater than *he could bear.*"

Cain then went on to voice another debilitating concern. People will hate him and reject him. Cain's set of personal problems was closely connected to his inherent feelings of rejection. God's reaction to his offering may have exacerbated those feelings, and now even his land, in a sense, rejected him. People too will hate him.

Behold, You have driven me today from the face of the land and from before you I shall be hidden, and I will be a vagabond and a wanderer in the land and whoever will find me will slay me. (4:14)

Cain was crying out to God from the mire of rejection in which he was wallowing. So God gave him a sign, not a sign of Cain's evil deed but one that showed God cares for him and will protect him and did not reject him even after his great crime. However, Cain must try to change.

It seems likely that he did change, inasmuch as he went on to a productive life—had a family and even built a city (4:17). His descendants were very creative and successful, inventing new technologies and forms of music (4:20-22). God tried to help Cain face his problems realistically. When Cain was unwilling or unable to handle this, God changed tactics, altering Cain's lifestyle while giving him a show of support by means of a sign.

Clinical Implications

Our society often confuses laborious, unpleasant tasks with serious work. Enjoying what one does seems to be a sign that it is not serious. Work must be onerous and performed under great pressure. The Bible offers a different view, suggesting that such an attitude may be rooted in passive aggression. We should instead learn to work in a way that suits our own personalities. If we see our giving as being an unrealistic burden, we may not be giving the right thing in the right way. If we are truly giving of ourselves, the sense of burden will lift, and underlying resentment will dissipate. We must learn that it can feel good to express ourselves by giving of ourselves. This is an important lesson in this highly depersonalized world.

HOARDING OR ENJOYING: MANNA

Biblical Narrative

People all too easily lapse into thinking that success is measurable in the accumulation of wealth and material objects. What matters more is that one should enjoy what one does have, using it wisely to pursue useful goals. Wealth can help one to live a more complete life, but one cannot place reliance or trust in money instead of in God.

The Israelites ended their long enslavement in Egypt and went to freedom in the wilderness of Sinai. Freedom was wonderful, but it carried with it many adjustments to new responsibilities. People began to worry about how they would eat, although they had many cattle and other food supplies with them. They even remembered somewhat overfondly how they "sat by the meat pots as we filled up with bread" (Exodus 16:3). Certainly this was an illusion, for slaves in Egypt did not eat well.

God now promised that, "I will rain down to you bread from the heavens, and the people will go out and gather each day's portion that day, so that I will try him whether he will go with my Law or not" (16:4). This food, or manna as it was called, would cover the ground around the camp, and each person would gather what the household needed for that day, one *omer* per person. Even if they tried to collect more or less than they needed, they would still find, upon returning to their tents, that they had one *omer* for each member of the household (16:18). Moses had an additional instruction—"Let no one leave over from it till morning" (16:19).

God was providing food for the Israelites in a miraculous manner, and he was also providing an important lesson about the meaning of work. God does want people to work and be productive; however, the relationship between work and income is more apparent than real. One's sustenance is provided by God not by one's own labor. God gives everyone what he wants them to have. People should use and enjoy God's bounty and should not hoard up for tomorrow. Certainly, in the long run they will not "take it with them." A man might save up wealth and end up leaving it to people he does not like, perhaps even his wife's next husband. Some Israelites did not listen to Moses and tried to save some manna overnight only to awaken the next morning and find "that it was rotten with worms and it stank" (16:20). The first lesson of the manna then was that hoarding is counterproductive to the real purpose of working and possessing.

Conversely, one day in the week, Friday, people were supposed to gather a double portion of manna. The added manna was needed because none would be provided on Saturday—the Sabbath. On the Sabbath, people would eat from the double amount gathered on the previous day. The people were to learn that they must not hoard and then they were to learn that sometimes planning is necessary. All this would depend on the realistic needs of the moment. In any case, the purpose of earning is not unending acquisition for its own sake. It is to fulfill God's will in this world.

Clinical Implications

The acquisition of material goods is important to enhance the enjoyment of life. Having enough food in the house is important. Likewise, having financial security can ease one's mind. The problem arises when the individual is done in by the process of acquisition. The aim of enjoyment becomes distorted into hoarding the material itself. No level of security is enough; the individuals need to put more aside, far more than they will ever need, and they will never enjoy it. The idea of "saving for a rainy day" is betrayed. The rainy day never comes but the present sunny days are obscured by the fear of rain clouds. The therapist must work with a patient such as this to achieve a deeper kind of security, somewhat independent of material possessions.

Chapter 7

Overcoming Family Problems

INTRODUCTION

A striking difference emerges in the patterns of biblical and Greek families. The biblical matriarchs were devoted both to their husbands and to the raising of their children as continuations of the covenant with God. They intervened strongly and successfully in family affairs and were profoundly important in maintaining both the high quality of the covenental relationship and the unity within the family. The Bible and the rabbinic writings regard women as equal and sometimes superior to their husbands in spirituality and in prophecy.

Through the various vicissitudes and disagreements of the lives of the founding families, the husbands and wives were able to support and enjoy each other while carrying out the duties that God had placed upon them. The children in these families grew up in a milieu where fulfillment was not found in narcissistic acquisition of goods nor by destroying their relatives. Instead, satisfaction was found in a steady development toward building a nation with a unique theocentric unity. This development was affirmed anew in each generation by the fathers blessing the children.

Of course, there were some sad failures in biblical families too. Abimelech, the son of Gideon and his concubine, murdered all but one of his seventy brothers in an attempt to become ruler. Perhaps his outsider status left him feeling unblessed by his father (Judges 9:5). In David's family, David's son Amnon raped his half sister Tamar. Amnon was then murdered by Absalom, another son. Absalom later led a revolt against David. Another son of David, Adonijah, tried to seize the throne from Solomon, the designated successor, and was put to death. The text explains that David did not sufficiently discipline him (1 Kings 1). David still managed to build a line of royal succession that ruled Judah for over four centuries until the Babylonian conquests. Some of the Davidic kings were outstanding personalities, including Solomon, Hezekiah, Josiah, and others.

The narrative of Oedipus illustrates an important principle in the Greek family. As the father recedes as a threat, previously repressed sibling rivalry and hatred becomes free to emerge. This is because the earlier banding together of the sons was not done out of any filial love or mutuality of purpose, but out of a devil's pact against the murderous father.

Consider, for example, the story of Castor and Pollux, half brothers who, by all accounts, seem to get along quite well with each other. Perhaps no paternal threat exists. Nevertheless, their friendship seems to be without purpose. They join in adventures that typically involve violent exploits such as rape or theft. This type of bonding through violence is exactly what Jacob criticizes in Simeon and Levi. Castor and Pollux do nothing to build families in which to raise future generations. The children they beget are generally born of rapes and casual relationships (Apollodorus iii, l. 2).

Five family narratives are presented in this section. The story of Rachel and Jacob explores how a husband and wife can learn to trust each other even if the relationship was formed in a deceitful manner. Achan's story shows the impossibility of successfully covering up a family problem rather than dealing with it. The story of David and Bathsheba returns to the problem of how to overcome a less than honorable beginning of a relationship. The fourth story, that of Rebecca, Isaac, and Eliezer, discusses the qualities that should be involved in a healthy approach to mate selection, since choosing a mate wisely goes a long way toward having a happy family. Finally, the story of Boaz and Ruth illustrates how mutuality of kindnesses can lead to a deep bond between partners.

FORGIVING DECEIT: RACHEL AND JACOB

Biblical Narrative

Mate selection, to be successful, need not be a clear-moving, unruffled process with no problems or imperfections. Facing great troubles in his own life, but at the same time working toward God's promise of a great future, Jacob found a woman of unusual compassion, whom he grew to love very deeply. The road to marriage and after, however, was beset with many difficulties. The story of Jacob finding his wife (actually his four wives) parallels his parents' story in several motifs. Jacob too journeyed from Canaan eastward and met his future wife by the well in Haran, yet the stories are different in important ways. Eliezer had traveled as a representative of a wealthy family, his camels laden with good things. Jacob left his father's home as a fugitive, fleeing his brother Esau, who had threatened to kill him because of the paternal blessing that he accused Jacob of stealing from him (Genesis 27:41). Jacob came to Haran alone and without worldly possessions. Poor as he may have been in worldly goods at that moment, Jacob's soul had been greatly buoyed by his wonderful dream (28:10f). He saw a ladder with its top reaching into the heavens and angels going up and down on it. Standing above the ladder, God promised Jacob that he would bless him in all his endeavors and that he would be the father to a great nation. Jacob would find great trials ahead, but this vision greatly uplifted him. After a long journey, he arrived at Haran and stood before the well. Jacob was a man of great intellect and deep feeling. Certainly, he knew the story of Eliezer's visit to Haran and to that very well. Now this same scene aroused in Jacob thoughts of his mother and also symbolized to him at many levels God's promises of his great spiritual and historical future.

The shepherds, with three flocks of sheep, were gathered waiting for more shepherds to come, for it took a number of men to move the large stone that covered the well. Jacob inquired about his Uncle Laban, Rebecca's brother, and was told that Laban's daughter, Rachel, was approaching with her sheep. While they were still talking, Rachel came near. After all his trials, the sight of Rachel by the well aroused in Jacob the longing for home, family, and, above all, his mother, Rebecca, to whom he was especially close (25:28).

> And it was when Jacob saw Rachel, the daughter of Laban his mother's brother, and the flocks of Laban his mother's brother, and he [Jacob] drew near and rolled the stone off the mouth of the well and watered the flocks of Laban his mother's brother. (29:10)

Three times the Scripture mentions the connection to Rebecca. Rachel must have stood in amazement, watching the stranger perform so prodigious a feat of strength as to move the stone by himself. Jacob, however, was using not only muscle power but deep spiritual inspiration. Rachel must have been amazed too as he gave water to her sheep and then came over and kissed her and broke into loud weeping. Jacob was a strong and thoughtful personality who could see Rachel's beauty both in her form and in her character, yet he recognized that the future held many uncertainties and that her beauty too would one day waste in the earth (to use the Talmudic expression). Regaining his self-control, Jacob then explained that he was her father's nephew and Rebecca's son (29:12).

Jacob stayed with Laban and later agreed to work for him for seven years after which he would marry Rachel. Rachel was a very beautiful girl; however, this was not the only factor in Jacob's mind. Indeed, Scripture first mentions her beauty only somewhat later (29:17). More important, Rachel was very nurturing. Jacob could see this in the way she handled her sheep (29:10). She had a special love for children too and her years of barrenness later before the birth of her sons Joseph and Benjamin were very trying to her. She also showed an ability to let Jacob care for her. Jacob was perhaps much like Rebecca in this ability to take the initiative in caring for others. When Jacob came to the well at Haran, it was he who watered the sheep, and later when Rachel despaired over her childlessness, it was Jacob to whom she turned for help (30:1). Rebecca, likewise infertile in the first years of her own marriage, had prayed to God for herself just as Isaac, her husband, prayed by himself (25:21).

After some years, when Jacob and his family returned to Canaan, Rachel died in giving birth to Benjamin, her second son, and was buried near Bethlehem, not in Hebron with the other patriarchs and matriarchs including Jacob. Many centuries later, her love for her children would again be felt in a deeply trying moment. The land of Judah had been conquered by the Babylonians, and its inhabitants were being marched into exile under the harshest conditions. The prophet Jeremiah describes the scene as the sorrowing captives were being led past Rachel's tomb.

> A voice is heard on high, lamentation, bitter weeping, Rachel crying for her children, she refuses to be comforted for her children for they are not [on their land]. So says the Lord, "Hold back your voice from weeping and your eyes from tears, for there is reward for your work," says the Lord, "and they shall re-

turn from the land of the enemy. And there is hope for your future," says the Lord, "and the children will return to their own border." (Jeremiah 31:15-17)

Rachel's compassion stood strong and steadfast and inspired her descendants many generations after her own day.

Her compassion toward her sister Leah was also great, although it caused tension for a time in her relationship with Jacob (see Alshich, 1970, on Genesis 29). Laban was determined to marry off Leah to Jacob too. Polygamy was not unusual then. However, Jacob was deeply in love with Rachel, so Laban did not approach Jacob directly with his plan. Instead, he simply substituted a heavily veiled Leah for Rachel at the marriage ceremony. Not until the next morning did Jacob discover the deception and the fact that Rachel had not warned him and perhaps had actively taken part in the plan. Leah loved Jacob as did Rachel, and it seems that Rachel felt so deep a compassion for her sister that she was even willing to risk her own future with Jacob. Jacob was at first very hurt, but apparently he soon recognized the sincerity of Rachel's kindness and was more than reconciled to her. He married Rachel too as soon as the week of celebration of his marriage to Leah was ended (Genesis 29:28, 30). Jacob and his wives went on to become the parents of the twelve sons who founded the twelve tribes of Israel.

Clinical Implications

A person needs both to pick the right partner and to be the right partner. Although physical attraction is certainly a factor, inner psychological beauty is more important. One must be able to trust one's partner's humanity deeply with both heart and head. This requires respect for the other's intelligence and kindness and makes it possible to try to understand actions that appear on the surface to be unfathomable. Trusting a partner allows one to withhold judgment until the results of an action become apparent. Like Jacob, a man must sometimes go along with his wife even if he does not fully comprehend her actions at the moment. Not everything that is sensed can be communicated verbally, and it is important to have enough faith in the qualities of one's partner and let situations work themselves out.

COVERING A FAMILY PROBLEM: ACHAN

Biblical Narrative

Joshua led the Israelites across the River Jordan to began the conquest of the land of Israel that God had promised them. Their first effort was indeed spectacular as they took Jericho aided by the miraculous collapse of its walls. Next, Joshua sent 3,000 men to conquer the smaller town of Ai. However, here the Israelites were put to flight with the loss of thirty-six men. It was clear to Joshua that this was more than a small military setback. It was a sign of divine displeasure. He and the elders tore their garments, put dirt on their heads, and lay prostrate before the holy ark all day. Why did God not help them? Why had so many died? Could the Israelites no longer rely on divine assistance in conquering Israel? Must they send out larger armies? Surely now all the Canaanites would feel encouraged to fight against them (Joshua 7:6-9). God answered Joshua,

> Israel has sinned and they have transgressed My covenant which I commanded them, and they have also taken of the consecrated things, and they have also stolen, and also dissembled, and they have also put into their vessels. (7:11)

Specifically, one man had secretly taken from the spoils of Jericho, which were to have been utterly destroyed. God would not help them in battle until this problem was dealt with. Joshua called all the people together, and by drawing lots revealed, with God's help, that the guilty man was Achan of the tribe of Judah. Strangely, when Joshua confronted Achan, he not only made no effort to cover up but even admitted to several previous offenses of a similar type. He quickly specified what he had taken from Jericho,

> And I saw among the spoils a good Babylonian cloak, and 200 shekels of silver and a wedge of gold weighing fifty shekels, and I coveted them and took them. And behold they are hidden under the ground in the middle of my tent, and the silver is beneath. (7:21)

Achan's answer suggests the possibility of a compulsion to steal. He apparently had done this more than once (7:20). He had taken a cloak that might have aroused suspicion had he worn it in public. He confessed so easily that he may have felt relieved to have his problem out in the open. His family may have had some knowledge of his criminal acts and had not dealt with it. Perhaps if Achan had found help earlier, his problem could have been healed. Now, however, Achan had commited a crime that had resulted in an Israelite defeat in battle and the loss of thirty-six men. He was put to death, and all his property was destroyed. In their next attack on Ai, the Israelites were entirely successful, conquering the town without the loss of a man.

Clinical Implications

This story has deep meaning for psychotherapy: Problems swept under the rug can come back to haunt, whether the problem is known to the patient or not. If the problem is known consciously, covering it will probably cost a great deal of psychic energy that could be better applied elsewhere. However, what if the family is unaware of the underlying problem? The problem may be associated with all sorts of subsidiary issues that drain the family's energy from positive coping. Also, the family can experience the vague sense that a problem exists without being able to identify it, which can be even more devastating. The best solution, of course, is for the family to identify the problem and attempt to resolve it, thus resulting in a psychic structure that has more energy to cope in a positive manner.

OVERCOMING A BAD START: DAVID AND BATHSHEBA

Biblical Narrative

Imagine a man coming to a therapist for advice with the following problem:

> Doctor, I saw my neighbor's wife and had her brought to my house where I had sexual relations with her. When I learned she was pregnant, I had her husband sent home on furlough from the war so that people would think the child was his. When that didn't work, I had him sent to the most dangerous part of the fighting where he was soon killed. I then married the woman,

but our child died shortly after birth. Can we make this marriage work?

A relationship begun with so many problems is unlikely to thrive. The biblical story of David and Bathsheba, told in 2 Samuel 11-12, is exactly this story. Their relationship not only turned out to be a fulfilling one, but their son became the wise King Solomon. This is an important story for studying the biblical view of male-female relationships, for the obstacles here were enormous. The greatness of David's character and faith turned an almost sure disaster into a moving story of human acceptance and growth. Here is the Bible's account.

King David went one spring evening to stroll on the roof of his Jerusalem palace. From there he spied a woman bathing in her home, and he was struck by her beauty. Learning that this was Bathsheba, daughter of Eliam and granddaughter of Ahitophel, his brilliant adviser, David sent his aides to bring her to the palace, where he lay with her. David was probably moved not only by Bathsheba's great beauty, but also by her distinguished family background and her intelligence. He recognized in her immediately a woman who was fit to be mother to the next king of Israel. Nevertheless, David's actions were exceedingly high-handed. Bathsheba sent word to David that she was pregnant. Seeking to avoid publicity, David recalled Uriah, her husband, who was with the army besieging Rabat Ammon, the Ammonite capital. David hoped that people would think the child was Uriah's, conceived during his visit. However, Uriah never went to his home, sleeping instead among the palace servants. David then sent Uriah back to the front with orders to the generals to place him in the sector of greatest danger. This was done, and Uriah was killed by an arrow from the city walls. David then took Bathsheba as his wife.

David felt that he had done no legal wrong. According to the practice of the time, Uriah had given his wife a bill of divorce before going to the war. This was so that if the man was missing in action, the wife could remarry rather than sit as a grass widow. So in a legal sense, Bathsheba was indeed unmarried. Nathan the prophet came to David to express God's great displeasure with what David had done (see Chapter 4). The child that Bathsheba was carrying would die, said Nathan. David fasted and prayed for his new son's life, but the child lived only a week.

Could the marriage survive such a rocky start? Rabbi David Kimchi (see *Mikraot Gedolot,* 1978), the Medieval Spanish commentator, suggests, based on 2 Samuel 12:24, that David wanted to have another child, but Bathsheba wanted to leave him. They had sinned grievously, she argued, and God had already punished them. If they would have another child, everyone would point to him as the son of the sinful union.

Few people could have handled all this, but David did so in a manner that provides a model of dealing with one's own bad behavior and also of marriage relations. David never lost the sure feeling that God still loved him, even after his sin and punishment. He expressed his deep and sincere repentance in the moving Psalms 51, "A psalm of David when Nathan the prophet came to him after he had gone in to Bathsheba." David recognized his sin and was deeply contrite. He did not deceive himself nor justify himself—"My sin is ever before me" (51:5). David had no illusions about himself. He understood his sin and what he needed to do. There was sin and there would be consequences, including the death of the child. "Wash me thoroughly from my iniquity" (51:2). David accepted cleansing even in the form of punishment, for no pain was as hurtful for him as feeling distant from God. His main aim was not to avoid the necessary consequences of his behavior, but to live up to the closeness that God feels to all mankind and which was so important to David. David accepted his guilt and his punishment hoping that it would cleanse his sin and thereby show himself and others that his guilt was erased. "Purge me with hyssop, and I shall be clean. Wash me, and I shall be whiter than snow" (51:7). David asked for forgiveness and healing based on God's own kindness and mercy. "Be gracious to me, God, according to Your kindness; like the multitude of Your mercies, blot out my sin" (51:1). Whether David was as great as the patriarchs or Moses is debatable, but it is difficult to imagine that anyone surpassed him in the quality of heart. "Create for me a pure heart, Lord, and an upright spirit renew within me" (51:10). David felt close to God and trusted him with all his heart. Only such a level of trust could have enabled David to face his sin and to seek renewal.

This quality of utmost faithfulness and loyalty was displayed by David in his friendship for Jonathan and for King Saul. It could overcome even incidents of apparent disloyalty and betrayal. Most important were not the formalities of repentance but the profound and sincere contrition. "Offerings to God are a broken spirit. A broken and contrite heart, You O God, will not despise" (51:17). David understood that all people are capable of sin, but they can also renew their hearts and open them to all good. People can neither completely ignore nor completely forget their sins even after a long time has passed. However, they should not become obsessed with them. They can learn and grow from their sins and transform them into positive experiences. Their hearts and spirits can be renewed and life can go on joyfully and productively. They may gain greater insight into themselves and into their relationships with God even through sin and punishment. If they can do this, then they are indeed renewed and uplifted.

David possessed a courage born in total trust of God, enabling him to win great contests of spirit that would have destroyed other men. David was not in the long term embittered, frightened, or depressed by his experience. He overcame Bathsheba's reluctance to go on by convincing her that God had indeed forgiven them, as Nathan had reported, "God has caused your sin to pass and you will not die" (2 Samuel 12:13), and by promising her that their next son would succeed to the throne of Israel. Their marriage did indeed revive, and Bathsheba eventually bore a healthy son, whom she named Solomon (peaceful or fulfillment). "And David comforted Bathsheba, his wife, and he came to her and slept with her, and she bore a son" (2 Samuel 12:24). God, speaking through Nathan, named the boy Jedediah (beloved of God). The names mark the restoration of peace and fulfillment and of God's love in the lives of David and Bathsheba.

Clinical Implications

This story illustrates a crucial truth for couples in therapy. A terrible event can occur in a marriage that seems to make it impossible to go on. The partners may feel powerless and thus be tempted to blame each other for their misfortune. The mutual recriminations may be worse than the initial misfortune itself. At the very point where partners need most to support each other, accusations and rejection can make each partner feel frightened and alone.

This need not be the case. A wise therapist can help a couple contain a misfortune and deal with its larger implications—without blaming each other. It is possible to accept a joint responsibility for a misfortune without seeking to shift blame. This approach can make a marriage even stronger than it was before. The misfortune can become a means of bonding instead of dissolution and conflict.

WISE MATE SELECTION: REBECCA, ISAAC, AND ELIEZER

Biblical Narrative

The Western world now accepts "dating" as the main method of mate selection. However, about half of American marriages end in divorce, and some number of those that do endure are not very fulfilling. The Catholic Church has introduced a course of prenuptial training for couples who are planning to marry, and rabbinic leaders have discussed instituting a similar process for Jewish couples. The Book of Genesis recounts several stories that present a healthy approach to mate selection. One such story is in Chapter 24.

Abraham was growing older and his son Isaac was not yet married, so Abraham called his servant Eliezer and entrusted him with finding a bride for Isaac. This was a task of great importance for upon it depended not only Isaac's personal happiness but the future of Abraham's divinely appointed mission to found a great nation that would bring God's blessing to the world (Genesis 12:2-3). Abraham gave Eliezer instructions: He was not to select a woman from among the Canaanites among whom Abraham dwelt in Canaan, for they were too accustomed to lewdness. Instead, Eliezer should go back to Haran, Abraham's own homeland, to seek a wife for Isaac. The Mesopotamians too were idol worshipers. However, this was merely an intellectual error, and they were basically of better character. What if Eliezer found a suitable woman, but she was unwilling to come to Canaan? This would be unacceptable for Isaac. The fulfillment of the mission of Abraham and Isaac and of God's promises to them was deeply bound with the land of Israel.

> The Lord God of heaven, who took me from my father's house and from the land of my birth and who spoke to me and who swore to me saying, "To your seed, I will give this land," He will send His angel before you, and you will take a wife for my son from there. (24:7)

Isaac must remain in the land. God would certainly help Eliezer, Abraham told him. Abraham then added, probably to reassure Eliezer, that if the woman would not be willing to come to Canaan, then Eliezer would have no further responsibility. Eliezer then took ten well-laden camels and journeyed to Haran. They arrived at the city toward evening and went to the well just at the time people were coming to draw water. The servant prayed to God to do kindness with Abraham.

> Let it be that the maiden to whom I will say, "Incline your pitcher and let me drink," and she will say, "Drink and also I will water your camels too," that one have you set for your servant, Isaac. And in this I shall know that you have done kindness with my master. (24:14)

Eliezer's request was uncomfortably similar to the practice of divination so common in the ancient Near East, i.e., of predicting the future by means of signs. However, Eliezer was clearly relying on God and on his own knowledge of human behavior and not on magic forces. His request was immediately filled for along came Rebecca, pretty and refined (24:15-25).

The servant saw that God was answering his prayers, and he ran to her and asked her for water. Rebecca could have told him to get his own water, but she assumed that he must be weary from a long journey or perhaps was sore or injured. "Drink, sir," she said, and she hurried to give him a drink (24:18). When she finished taking care of Eliezer, she said, "I will draw water for your camels too" (24:19). She hurried down to the well and brought pitcher after pitcher of water until all ten camels were satisfied. Eliezer stood in silent wonderment seeing the girl's compassion, quickness, and intelligence.

He gave her a golden ring and bracelets and asked who her family was, and if he could spend the night with them. She responded that she was the daughter of Bethuel and that they could easily handle Eliezer and his train. Learning that she was of the family of Abraham and seeing that she practiced Abraham's style of warm hospitality, Eliezer knew that God had helped him to accomplish his mission, and he bowed to the ground and worshiped. Rebecca returned with Eliezer to Canaan, where she married Isaac. Love, tenderness, and mutual support characterized their marriage.

Several elements in this story of mate selection are worth noting. First, it was necessary to find a mate who could support one's deeper aims in life; in this case, a woman who could join in the covenant with God, which was the central meaning of Isaac's life. Physical compatibility was important too. However, both Abraham and Eliezer felt that something more was needed. Both men prayed to and trusted God. Eliezer's test was in fact a prayer to God.

Clinical Implications

Mate selection based on the fulfillment of selfish needs will produce a husband and wife who will continue to work each for his or her own selfish interests. It will be difficult to establish any mutuality or harmony of interest in the marriage. A marriage, like any other relationship, is far more likely to succeed when it begins with and helps to develop the partners' sense of harmony with God, the world, and each other.

Patients need to develop the capacity to look into the deeper meaning of interactions. A deeper understanding can help resolve what appear at more superficial levels to be conflicts between self and others. A marriage is a covenantal unit, and when this is understood emotionally, acts that are aimed at benefiting the marriage or one's partner can also develop one's self as well. Finding a compatible partner who shares one's visions is essential to attaining this harmony.

KINDNESS FOR KINDNESS: BOAZ AND RUTH

Biblical Narrative

Ruth's exemplary kindness toward Naomi, her former mother-in-law, is described in the biblical Book of Ruth (see Chapter 8). Boaz, whom she would marry, was a man with considerable empathy and perception as well as strong moral character. A match between them seemed unlikely. She was a childless widow of Moabite birth who came with Naomi from Moab to Bethlehem after their menfolk had died. They lived in deep poverty, and Ruth was reduced to gathering the leavings of the harvesters from the fields to sustain the two of them. Boaz was a wealthy and prominent landowner and communal leader. Their eventual union was founded on their kindness and on their ability to recognize each other's good qualities.

When Ruth went out to gather the leavings, which the law allotted to the poor, she came first to the field of Boaz. There Boaz noticed her and inquired of his foreman what she was doing there. Bethlehem was not a large metropolis, and Naomi was a relative of Boaz so he certainly knew about the women's arrival. Nor was Boaz the sort of low fellow who would inquire idly about a woman. He may have noted Ruth's modesty in that she did not flirt with the workers (Ruth 2:9). The foreman answered that this was the "Moabite woman who returned with Naomi from the field of Moab" (Ruth 2:6). Perhaps Boaz saw that she felt uncomfortable in a new land whose ways and people were strange to her and that the workers referred to her merely as "a Moabite woman," i.e., a stranger and not one of us. A deeply compassionate man, Boaz sought to make Ruth feel welcome.

> And Boaz said to Ruth, "Do not go to collect grain in any other field and do not pass from here and so you stay close to my women. Keep your eyes on the field, which they will reap and follow after them. Have I not ordered the young men not to bother you. . . ." (2:8-9)

Boaz addressed directly her feeling of being an outsider. Ruth was pleased but also surprised, "Why have I found favor in your eyes to recognize me, *and I am a foreigner?*" (italics ours) (2:10). She expressed her feeling of being foreign and wondered why a person of Boaz's high rank would be so kind to her, when others were not.

Boaz's answer was both kind and direct. He had heard how supportive Ruth had been to Naomi "and you left your father and mother and the land of your birth, and you went to a people whom you did not know yesterday or the day before" (2:11). Her kindness and selflessness showed her good character, and she came to Bethlehem with the highest motives, not as a threatening low-class alien. "May God repay your deeds and may your reward be complete from God under whose wing you have come to be sheltered" (2:12). Boaz states that God has recognized Ruth's kindness and her devotion to Him as well, and He will bless Ruth greatly, i.e., Ruth is welcome among the Israelites both as a fine human being and as a Hebrew by religion despite her foreign origins.

Boaz was able to look at her character, not at the trappings. Such words of welcome and acceptance from so important a man as Boaz moved Ruth deeply. She could accept sincere kindness as well as give it to others. "May I find favor in your eyes, my lord, for you have comforted me, and you have spoken to the heart of your maidservant" (2:13).

A basic trust now existed between them. Boaz encouraged her to partake of the food and water that the workers brought out to the fields. Ruth continued to glean the leavings in Boaz's fields and supported Naomi and herself. Some months passed. Then occurred the famous incident in which Ruth came quietly by night to Boaz while he slept on the threshing floor as he customarily did after the threshing. She uncovered his feet as he slept, probably to indicate that she was willing to marry him. Boaz indeed thought very highly of Ruth but had been hesitant to seek to marry her, perhaps because there was a large age difference between them (3:10). Now that he saw she was willing, he could declare his interest too.

The die was now cast, but one impediment existed. Another man was, like Boaz, a kinsman of Ruth's first husband, and he had a prior claim to Ruth and to the piece of land that her husband had left her. Boaz approached the man that very day, as the latter entered the town gate. "Turn aside here and sit down, So-and-So" (4:1). No other person in the Hebrew Bible is called "So-and-So." It may well be Scripture's way of indicating how insignificant a person So-and-So was. At a historical moment so deep in meaning, the man could not step beyond his very narrow attitude toward people. He was too insignificant to be referred to by his name. Boaz told him about the field and So-and-So was interested, but when he heard that to acquire the field he would have to marry Ruth he hastily and emphatically backed off. "I cannot redeem it for myself lest I ruin my inheritance" (4:6). Apparently So-and-So thought that marriage to Ruth would ruin him because of her foreign background. Like the foreman, he could see only that Ruth was Moabite. He could not see her beautiful humanity and could not sense, as Boaz had, that she was welcomed by God to her new nation and that she was a person of the highest quality ("a woman of valor") (3:11). So-and-So quickly passed out of the picture. Boaz married Ruth and despite the differences in their ages and origins, they produced a distinguished family, including David and the kings of Judah (4:17-22).

Clinical Implications

In a happy couple, the partners belong not only to each other but to a larger purpose. This purpose provides a framework for them to express their love for each other. The more they pull together, the deeper their love becomes. In contrast, a therapist may be faced with two people who are strongly attracted to each other but who want very different experiences out of life. In trying to make their relationship work, they each suppress something of deep emotional and intellectual meaning. In a sense, each is giving up too much of himself or herself to have a happy marriage. The couple is trying to make it on their own without the foundation of a larger common purpose. In such a situation the two partners, despite their mutual attraction, eventually resent each other and see each other, correctly or incorrectly, as the cause of their respective feelings of nonfulfillment.

Chapter 8

Parental Blessings, Permission, and Support

INTRODUCTION

The importance of parental blessings, permission, and support cannot be overestimated. A highly successful physician may experience a breakdown at midlife because she never felt she received parental support in her medical endeavor. A young talented teacher may sabotage his career through absenteeism because he never felt he received his father's blessing to surpass him.

Successful parenting involves blessing children's endeavors, giving them permission to succeed, and supporting them in this process. A failure to provide this can lead to disaster for the children unless they are able to find a parental substitute. "Cast me not off, neither forsake me O God of my salvation. For though my father and my mother have forsaken me, the Lord will take me up" (Psalms 27:9-10).

This section contains five biblical stories, each illustrating a psychological issue. The story of Isaac, Jacob, and Esau focuses on the need of parents to be careful in what they assign to each child. Although they may care about all of their children, they must be careful to give each child the correct support. The second story, Joseph, extends this message, arguing that different children may receive different blessings and support. The third story, of Hannah and Samuel, focuses on the need of the parent to consider what the child needs first, even if it entails sending the child away from home. The fourth story, Naomi and Ruth, portrays two people evolving their relationship with the realization of their respective developmental needs. If the parent encourages the child in his development, the parent will gain from it in the long run as well. Finally, the story of Lot and his daughters focuses on the father's need to see his daughter as a person in her own right, and not simply as a possession to be manipulated.

BEING CAREFUL WITH A BLESSING: ISAAC AND HIS SONS

Biblical Narrative

Stories of blessings appear constantly through the Bible and particularly in the Book of Genesis. God blesses the newly formed world and its creatures (Genesis 1:22), the Sabbath day (2:3), and especially man, "Be fruitful and multiply and fill the earth and conquer it . . ." (1:28). There are later blessings from God to Noah, Abraham, and others; Abraham's family begins the record of parents blessing their children.

A blessing is not a magic formula aimed at producing good luck, nor is it an idle statement of good wishes. The givers instead offer the receivers a show of love, support, and confidence, carefully planned to acknowledge their unique strengths and needs. The receivers gain recognition from the parent and a measure of self-understanding, which work to produce in them a sense of direction, purpose, continuity, and strength. In Genesis, the blessing connects people with their sacred obligations and with the need to fulfill their own missions in their own form of creativity.

We shall study the blessings that Isaac gave to his two sons, Jacob and Esau. Keep in mind the great contrast to the Greek hero Oedipus who, deep in bitterness, cursed his sons to kill each other. Oedipus' wish was fulfilled when his two sons killed each other and his daughter Antigone hanged herself, all heavily burdened by their father's ill wishes.

Isaac's blessings, although initially met by Esau with resentment and anger, resulted ultimately in the two sons finding greater personal fulfillment and also a measure of peace with each other. Isaac's blessing was carefully thought out and deeply truthful—after Rebecca's intervention.

Isaac was aging and failing of sight. Feeling that his end was near, he sought to bless his sons. As wise as Isaac was and as carefully as he had prepared his blessings, all would have gone wrong had it not been for Rebecca's intervention (in the best therapeutic style). Isaac had tried his best to see the good in Esau and had closed his eyes to Esau's wildness. He hoped that by giving Esau the blessing of material well-being, he would be providing him with what he needed most. Isaac did his best to prepare Esau to receive the blessing, sending him to perform at least one act of kindness for his father. Esau was a hunter (Genesis 25:27 and 27:3), and he had some affinity toward food (25:30, 34). Isaac asked Esau to provide him with fresh venison before the blessing, hoping that Esau would understand that his physical drives must be turned to the service of God.

Jacob, as the more spiritual of the sons, would receive the spiritual blessing only. Rebecca, however, realized that Jacob's spirituality could not endure if separated from material well-being, so she arranged her great mummery (see Chapter 3), by which Jacob received a blessing for material success as well. Isaac's blessing, originally intended for Esau, was now received by Jacob:

> See the smell of my son is as the smell of the field which God has blessed. And may God give thee of the dew of the heaven and of the fatness of the earth and abundance of grain and wine. Peoples will serve you and nations will bow down to you so that your mother's sons will bow down to you. Who so curses you will be cursed and who so blesses you will be blessed. (27:28-29)

Isaac had wished for Esau what he now gave actually to Jacob—political ascendancy and economic productivity, as well as spiritual strength.

Esau, returning with the venison and learning that Jacob had received the blessing by means of Rebecca's mummery, asked for a blessing for himself too. Isaac blessed him with economic prosperity, but Esau could attain political power only when Jacob would stumble. Apparently, Isaac had never intended to pass Abraham's unique world mission on to Esau, for he gave it neither in his blessing originally intended for Esau nor in the next blessing, which he actually gave him. This full unique spiritual legacy of Abraham could be borne only by Jacob, and thus Isaac blessed him a second time with the blessing he had planned for him all along, "And God the All-Sufficing bless you and make you fruitful and multiply you that you may be a company of peoples. And He will give you the blessing of Abraham to you and to your seed . . ." (28:3f).

Clinical Implications

This story illustrates the complexity of familial relationships and the impossibility of treating all children in the same manner. It is normal for Isaac to care about Esau. His mistake, however, is in allowing this care to overwhelm his judgment in terms of the future and well-being of the family. Esau receiving the covenant would not only be bad for Isaac and Jacob but for Esau as well. Isaac's wife, Rebecca, is wise enough to realize this, yet she cannot confront Isaac directly because he might be hurt and would find it difficult to accept her judgment.

A therapeutic intervention must involve creating in the parent an acceptance of the principle of different strokes for different folks. This may sound trite, but it is very tempting for parents to want their children to be like themselves, without regard to their abilities. It is important for parents to accept the biblical truth that a child is created in God's image, not in the parents' image. A wise therapist may foster this understanding in the patient in some form.

This situation emerges often in families. The father may want his eldest son to follow him in his profession, yet the younger son is more suited for this. The mother may realize the situation. Trying to force the eldest son into a path for which he is not suited will do damage to everyone involved. Trying to deny another son an opportunity for which he is well-suited can be equally hurtful.

SPREADING THE BLESSING AROUND: JOSEPH AND HIS BROTHERS

Biblical Narrative

Isaac had been the recipient of Abraham's special mission, and Jacob had been the principal recipient of Isaac's. Jacob's own situation, however, was more complex. He had been blessed by God with the command to "spread west and east, north and south" (Genesis 28:14) and to found a nation that would carry God's message to all mankind. Through a life that often brought him great pain and hardship, Jacob devoted himself to raising his twelve sons and preparing them to build the twelve tribes of the Israelite nation. They were strong personalities, at times in conflict with the world around them, with one another, and even with themselves. However, Jacob was successful in raising them to a strong sense of their spiritual mission and also to maintaining harmony despite serious strains.

When he felt his own end approaching, he called his sons together to give them his last blessing. It was important to impress upon the sons that each could function in his own distinct personality and had both the responsibility and the potential for great fulfillment. Jacob sought to help each define himself and to assume his role with hope and devotion. He needed to address unresolved grievances and guilt and also assure the sons of his own confidence in them. This required a combination of bluntness, tact, and paternal approval.

Two examples: Reuben, the eldest, had been plagued with guilt over his interference in Jacob's relationship with Jacob's concubine, Bilha, and over the failure of Reuben's own effort to stop the brothers from selling Joseph into slavery. Jacob reassured Reuben that he still had a special feeling for him as his firstborn, despite Reuben's own errors and despite the trick played on Jacob when Laban gave him Leah, who later bore Reuben, as his bride in place of Rachel whom Jacob loved. Reuben was prone to hasty reactions that were not clearly thought out and he would not be a good leader, but he was a valued part of the nation of Israel.

Simeon and Levi too had brought pain to Jacob both by their violent attack on the town of Shechem and later by their role in the sale of Joseph. Jacob warned them about their anger to which he could not reconcile himself, yet their tribes too would have their place in the new nation. The descendants of Levi would be priests in the temple and the tribe of Simeon, says the Talmud, supplied many scholars and teachers.

In this manner, Jacob blessed each of his twelve sons, addressing each as a unique personality with his own strengths and weaknesses and trying to give each support, recognition, and freedom in making his own contribution to the people of Israel. Jacob noted too the importance of the process of blessing, "Your father's blessings are mighty beyond the blessings of my progenitors to the farthest boundary of the everlasting hills" (Genesis 49:26). The children of Israel could now proceed on their great mission bearing not only the spirituality and wisdom that they learned from the patriarchs but also their parental approval and support.

Jacob's action broadens the idea of parental blessing. Unlike Isaac, Jacob attempts to give each son what is suited for him. Joseph is not Reuben, and Reuben is not Benjamin, yet each can inherit something unique and valuable. The fact that Joseph can spread blessings among all children indicates the potential power of differentiated parental blessings.

Clinical Implications

This story is especially relevant to the blended families endemic in our modern age. Jacob had multiple wives as many men today do, and the children of each wife play out the conflict of their mothers. A wise and discerning father can overcome this with appropriate attention and differentiation.

The role of a therapist is to help the parent see the uniqueness of each child. Parents should help their children develop their particular talents. Letting each child know he or she is loved in his own way goes a long way toward overcoming sibling jealousy and conflict.

SUPPORTING ONE'S SON: HANNAH AND SAMUEL

Biblical Narrative

Parental support helps provide a child with a sense of continuity and connection and also with a feeling of confidence in his or her road in life. This support helps children both to develop healthy roots and later to strengthen the wings they need to gain healthy independence. The biblical story of Hannah illustrates a strong if unusual mother-son relationship. Hannah, wife of Elkanah, a Levite of some distinction, was deeply saddened by her failure to bear children even after many years of marriage. Elkanah was loving and supportive, but Hannah still longed for children.

Once when the family went on pilgrimage to the tabernacle in Shiloh, Hannah departed alone from the festival meal and went to pray near the door of the tabernacle. Hannah wept and prayed to God for a child and vowed that if God would give her a wise and healthy son, she would dedicate him to serving in the tabernacle.

She prayed silently and fervently. Eli, the High Priest, seeing that she came from the meal, rebuked her as being drunk, but Hannah explained that it was her longing and not wine that affected her. Eli replied that God would grant her request.

Whether Eli was transmitting a prophetic message or giving her a blessing of his own, Hannah was satisfied and she returned to the feast in good cheer. Sure enough, soon afterward Hannah conceived and gave birth to a son whom she called Samuel, meaning "I have borrowed him from God."

Hannah kept Samuel at home for several years and when she judged him ready, she brought him to Eli at Shiloh in fulfillment of her vow. "For this child I did pray, and the Lord granted me my request, which I asked of Him. And I also have lent him to God; for all his days he is lent to God" (I Samuel 1:27-28). She believed that Samuel and, in a larger sense, all things are a loan from God and not owned by people, a belief that was likely strengthened by the many years of waiting. This was perhaps also Hannah's way of informing Eli that she was not abandoning or rejecting her child. Rather, this child was a special answer from God to her longing, and he was as though under special care of God. (As Rashi [1961] puts it—Hannah told Eli that he should not punish the lad. God has borrowed him for I have lent him to God, and he must restore him to me.)

Hannah then recited to God a hymn of her own composition in which she exulted in the strength and kindness of God and thanked him for the joy he had brought her. She would later bear other children, but she remained devoted to Samuel as well.

Every year as he grew, she made him a small robe that he wore during his work in the tabernacle. It signified her love for her son and her recognition of his special accomplishment and his personal growth in serving with Eli. Samuel continued to wear such a robe all his life so that it became almost an identifying trademark. He was buried in a robe and, according to the Midrash, he wears it in the next world as well (1 Samuel 28:14 with Rashi).

Apparently Hannah understood her son well. He was exceedingly bright and aware, and bringing him to serve as Eli's disciple and helper at a tender age greatly enhanced his spiritual and intellectual development. She loved him deeply and must have missed him a great deal, but she also loved him realistically and unselfishly, and she knew that it was better for him to be with Eli. Samuel was a brilliant thinker who was gifted with prophecy at an early age, and he later became the judge and prophet of the Israelites and one of the greatest personalities of the Hebrew Bible, compared even with Moses and Aaron (Psalms 99). Hannah realized too that a child of such unusual ability needed to be encouraged, nurtured, and taught not only by his parents in his early attachments but also by people of greater accomplishment when the time came for him to go on to the later stages of his life. Nevertheless, one opinion in the Midrash (Yalkut Shimoni on 1 Samuel 1:78) suggests that Hannah's prayers and hopes for Samuel were excessive and even contributed to his early death at age fifty-two.

Clinical Implications

This story touches on a poignant dilemma that parents of an especially gifted child may face. As much as parents may love the child and wish to keep the child near, they may realize that the child needs training that can be only developed elsewhere. Not to understand this can block the child's development. It can happen with children of various ages either out of selfish possessiveness or simple obliviousness.

On the other hand, it is also wrong for a parent to push a child to live out the parents' frustrations. Therapy offices are filled with patients whose parents had pushed them in childhood to compete in the classroom or on the athletic field in ways that did violence to the child's emotional vulnerabilities. The message is twofold: support one's child in constructive development but do not push the child ahead to satisfy the parent's own purposes. What Hannah did was exemplary because she supported Samuel's development not for her own sake, but for the sake of Samuel's development and his service to a cause greater than himself or his mother.

A vivid example was portrayed in the Oscar-winning film *Shine* (1996). David Helfgott, a brilliant, young pianist from New Zealand, was blocked by his father from accepting a scholarship to America to study music. Rather, the father, out of his own selfishness, kept the son at home. When young David finally accepted a scholarship in London, he was disinherited by his father and ultimately experienced a psychotic break. It may be very difficult for a parent, especially a single parent, to allow his or her child to grow because of the separation this may entail, but the parent must do this in order to encourage the child to develop.

RECIPROCITY BETWEEN GENERATIONS: NAOMI AND RUTH

Biblical Narrative

Although the Hebrew Bible is filled with stories of women of great character and significant accomplishment, almost no information exists in the biblical text specific to mother-daughter relationships. The story of Naomi and Ruth is one exception, and it actually describes a relationship between mother-in-law and daughter-in-law. This story is remarkably contemporary in a number of ways. First, it treats what is commonly assumed to be the most problematic of all relationships. Second, it deals with acclimating to a new environment far from one's birthplace. Third, it deals with reactions to loss. Fourth, it touches on the problem of being a single parent, especially with regard to letting children grow up and lead their own lives. Finally, it stresses the rewards that come from treating the other as an end in himself or herself rather than as a means to an end.

The story begins when Naomi, her husband, and their two sons leave Judah to reside in Moab. This in itself is not insignificant given the Israelites' ambivalent view of the Moabites. On the one hand, they are not to be attacked and God has given them their lands as an inheritance (Deuteronomy 2:9). On the other hand, Moabite men are never to be allowed to join the Israelite religious community. This is because they hired Balaam, the Mesopotamian prophet, to curse the Israelites (Deuteronomy 23:4-7). In Moab Naomi suffers her first loss—her husband dies. After the death of her husband, Naomi's two sons marry women of Moab, Orpah and Ruth.

Naomi then suffered a second grievous loss—the death of her two sons. She set out to return to Judah accompanied by her two daughters-in-law. Naomi blessed her daughters-in-law and told them to go back to Moab, to their own people. They both wept and insisted that they would return with their mother-in-law to Judah. Naomi again urged them to go, stating that she is too old to have more sons for them to marry (Ruth 1:11-12). Unlike Clytemnestra and Electra, Naomi did not try to bind her daughters-in-law to her but unselfishly urged them to go on their way to find husbands. This in itself is remarkable. She had asked the people of Bethlehem to call her Marah (bitter) rather than Naomi (sweet). However, now Naomi seemed to overcome her bitterness and what must have been her isolation as a widow to recognize the right of her daughters-in-law to their own lives, even if it meant Naomi would be abandoned in the process. She was a strong and healthy enough woman to realize that her daughters-in-law are not simply objects to serve her.

Orpah kissed her mother-in-law and departed, but Ruth would have none of it. In a moving speech, Ruth expressed her devotion to Naomi as a person in her own right rather than as only a producer of a son. Ruth refused to abandon Naomi, bonding instead to Naomi's land, people, and God.

And Ruth said,

> Entreat me not to leave thee, or to return from following after thee: for whither thou goest, I will go; and where thou lodgest, I will lodge: thy people shall be my people, and thy God my God. Where thou diest, will I die and there will I be buried: the Lord do so to me, and more also, if ought but death part thee and me. (Ruth 1:16-17)

Strikingly, the rabbis concluded that the women of Moab would be exempt from the ban against conversion to the Israelite nation "Moabite but not Moabitess" (*Babylonian Talmud*, Yebamot 76b based on Deuteronomy 23:4-7). The Moabites were descended, argued the rabbis, from the union between Lot and his two daughters. Lot had sunk into the depravity of Sodom while his two daughters had continued to behave in a decent and moral way (Genesis 19:8).

How different this story is from that of Oedipus whose father Laius is warned by an oracle not to let him reach man's estate lest Laius be killed by him. Naomi was not afraid to let Ruth grow. Ruth was not driven to abandon Naomi, and Naomi accepted Ruth among her people. This beautiful reciprocity continues throughout the story. Naomi continually encouraged and helped Ruth to fulfill her own needs, and Ruth was certain to include Naomi in any good fortune she may experience. Ruth met Boaz, a kinsman of Naomi's late husband, who was greatly moved by Ruth's treatment of Naomi: "It has fully been told me, all that you have done to your mother-in-law since the death of your husband" (Ruth 2:11). Naomi continued to look out for Ruth's welfare unselfishly. Rather than diminish Ruth's self-esteem or block her development, Naomi instructed Ruth in what she should do to win Boaz (3:1-4).

Ruth followed Naomi's advice, and ultimately married Boaz. She did not fail to include Naomi in her happiness. Naomi became the nurse to their son and is even described by the neighbors as the child's mother:

> And he shall be unto thee a restorer of life and a nourisher of thine old age; for thy daughter-in-law, who loveth thee, who is better to thee than seven sons, hath borne him. And Naomi took the child, and laid it in her bosom, and became nurse unto it. And the women her neighbors gave it a name, saying, "There is a son born to Naomi." And they called his name Obed; he is the father of Jesse, the father of David. (4:15-17)

The Moabite woman Ruth is a fit ancestress of the Davidic dynasty.

Clinical Implications

What are the therapeutic lessons of this story? This story continues the theme of encouraging one's child to develop and to separate. This time, the story involves not a daughter but a daughter-in-law and not a child but a grown woman who has been widowed. Naomi is herself widowed and must find it comforting to have the company of Ruth, yet she understands Ruth's need to live her own life. She pushes her to remarry, taking the risk that Ruth will go her own way, but Ruth returns the love and respect Naomi has shown her by including Naomi in her life after she remarries.

Not everything can be known in advance, and sometimes a parent must make a sacrifice to help a child (whatever the age) develop. One must have faith that the act is right in itself and hope that it will bring the parent joy as well. A failure to do this can create a great deal of family bitterness and can leave the child unfulfilled. An example of this was portrayed in the Spanish film *Like Water for Chocolate* (1993) in which a widowed mother blocked her daughter's romance with a suitor because she wanted to bind the daughter to her as a servant. No good can come from blocking a child's development. This, of course, does not mean throwing the child to the wolves. Rather, it means letting the children develop in ways that they must. A therapist can help a parent loosen the reins on a child who needs to find his or her way, and then have faith that the parent and the mature child will achieve a rapprochement. Loosening the reins does not necessarily mean letting go completely. It means finding an equilibrium between letting go and holding on too tightly—a delicate balancing act that a good therapist can help facilitate.

CONTROLLING ONE'S DAUGHTER: LOT

Biblical Narrative

Although neither vicious nor sadistic, Lot, the nephew of Abraham, was a man of weak ego who often showed an unwonted carelessness in dealing with people. This, combined with a need for control, as demonstrated in his relationship with his two daughters, led him into some tragically bizarre behaviors.

Lot had accompanied Abraham and Sarah on their journeys from Haran through Canaan, and later down to Egypt and back again to Canaan, and he learned something of the virtues of kindness and hospitality, which were so greatly emphasized in Abraham's household. Lot also grew very wealthy, amassing vast flocks of sheep and herds of cattle so that he finally decided to part from Abraham and go out on his own. He moved his household to the more fertile grazing lands of the city of Sodom, despite that city's reputation for greed and inhumanity. Perhaps Lot felt more comfortable as the best among wicked people than as the least of Abraham's more high-minded household. Settling into his new home, Lot prospered and was even named judge. Then events took a sharp turn. The wickedness of Sodom and its four sister cities had become so blatant that God decided to destroy them. The same angels that he had sent to announce to Abraham the forthcoming birth of Isaac were to go to Sodom and rescue Lot and his family from the impending destruction of the city. Lot's handling of the subsequent events showed his weakness of character.

The angels, in human appearance, arrived at Sodom. The Sodomites never showed hospitality to travelers and only Lot invited the strangers, urging them to lodge in his house. The travelers refused and Lot, insulted, grew angry with them. His anger did not result from any lack of courtesy on the part of the travelers. Nonetheless, Lot took their polite refusal of his offer as a personal insult, an ego threat. Finally, they did agree to come with him.

That evening, a large mob gathered before Lot's house, demanding that Lot surrender his guests to be gang raped. Lot stepped out of the house, closing the door behind him. He sought to calm the mob, even offering to hand over his own two daughters to them rather than violate the rules of hospitality to his guests. Even if Lot's offer were a bluff, and there is every reason to believe that it was not, it was unbelievably foolish. The Midrash remarks that Lot was saving the two girls for himself.

In any case, the mob was interested only in the guests, not the daughters, and they surged forward to break into the house. At this point, the angels intervened, striking the mob sightless and informing Lot that he had better collect his family and leave the city because God planned to destroy Sodom with fire and brimstone that very night.

While God rained fiery destruction on the cities, Lot and his daughters escaped, eventually making their way to a cave, where the Sodomites had stored barrels of wine. Lot's daughters believed that the whole world had been destroyed by fire, as it had been by flood in Noah's time, and that they were the only survivors. Continuation of the human race therefore depended on the three of them. Fearing that their father might not go along with their plan, the daughters got him drunk on successive nights and slept with him hoping to produce children. They indeed became pregnant, and in due course gave birth to sons who became the ancestors of the nations of Moab and Ammon.

Lot was hardly innocent. Offering his daughters to the mob was a demonstration of his control over them. Sleeping with his daughters was again a way of showing his disdain and control over them. It was probably his immature ego that had originally prompted him to leave Abraham, to whom he had felt inferior, and to move to Sodom where he could feel far superior to his wicked neighbors.

Many generations later, the nations of Moab and Ammon used their own daughters to lure the Israelites to join in their idolatry just as Lot had degraded his own daughters by offering them to the mob and later sleeping with them himself.

Clinical Implications

This story illustrates the obligation of a parent to see the child as an independent being who must be respected in his or her own way. Lot treats his daughters as possessions to be used rather than as offspring to be treasured. He, like Medea, is ready to sacrifice them for his own needs, and as a result creates dangers for his own people.

So it is with any parent who refuses to see a child as a person in his or her own right. A father frustrated in his athletic ability may become overinvolved in his daughter's tennis abilities and may push her in this direction beyond her emotional capability. A mother unfulfilled in her career may push a son of average ability into a career for which he is not suited. Both cases are likely to bring disastrous results, making the children miserable and ultimately estranging them from the parents.

The therapist must encourage the parent to love the child not as his or her own possession but as God's. The parent may take joy from the children's achievements but must still respect them as independent beings. This realization would do much to prevent the widespread child abuse in American society, which substitutes possessiveness for genuine love.

Chapter 9

Good and Bad Development

INTRODUCTION

Any developmental theory worth its salt must explain how a given person develops from an infant, or even before, to adolescence, adulthood, and old age. Human development is a complicated process involving a number of important life events. Not everyone navigates these life events successfully or at the same speed. Some people develop steadily over their lives; others are late bloomers. Still others, even some with bright beginnings, do not fulfill their early promise. Questions of how to integrate concern for self and for others abound in this context. Also important is the balancing of intellect, emotion, and physical prowess. Cultures differ in their views of the developmental process. Indeed the Greek riddle with which the Sphinx confronts Oedipus: "What walks on four legs in the morning, on two legs in the afternoon, and on three legs in the evening?" represents a cyclical curvilinear view of aging. If one looks at physical strength, perhaps this view is partly correct, but what if one looks at cognitive or emotional development? Is it possible for people to grow stronger as they get older?

The five biblical stories in this section all deal with healthy versus distorted psychological development. Balaam's story portrays the evil resulting from an intellectualism devoid of a moral sense. The Tower of Babel story warns of the dangers of a misguided utopianism. Solomon's story teaches how to acquire wisdom. The fourth story portrays Jeroboam, a man undone by ambition. The final story, Amnon, teaches us the dangers of using other people.

AMORAL INTELLECTUALISM: BALAAM

Biblical Narrative

The Bible demonstrates great admiration for knowledge and intellect. However, these traits can be destructive when not combined with good character. Numbers 22-24 tells the story of Balaam, a Mesopotamian wise man and seer, whose intellect was exalted but whose character was petty and greedy and who could be vindictive when he felt his ego threatened.

The Israelites, nearing the end of the forty years in the Sinai Desert, had just conquered the kingdoms of Kings Sihon and Og, east of the Jordan River, and they were encamped near the border of neighboring Moab. King Balak of Moab, sorely frightened by their presence and their recent victories, sent for help to Balaam—"Come curse this people for me." Mesopotamia was a land with institutes of higher learning and great scholars who probed the limits of knowledge available in that time. We still know some of their writings on anatomy, law, poetry, and dreams. Other important areas of study included astrology and divination (predicting the future by the reading of sacrificial entrails of or omens in nature such as the flights of birds). Scholars devoted lifetimes of study to these topics and wrote detailed treatises on them. Balaam, says the Scripture, was a widely acclaimed wise man who was able to speak with God and pronounce prophecies. King Balak now called upon Balaam to "come curse this people for it is stronger than I . . . for I know that whom you bless is blessed and whom you curse is cursed" (Numbers 22:6).

Tempted by Balak's promises of great wealth, Balaam was most anxious to accompany the king's messengers to Moab. However, he knew he had to consult God first. Much to Balaam's disappointment, God ordered him not to go to curse the Israelites for they are a blessed people (22:12). Balak then sent new messengers promising even greater rewards. Again Balaam asked the messengers to remain overnight, although warned that even if Balak were to give him a house full of silver and gold, Balaam could not go unless God permitted it. Balaam's imagery reveals his drive for wealth and recognition. God decided to teach Balaam a lesson in humility. Despite his great knowledge of magic, Balaam would soon be shown to be no more than a pawn in God's hands.

God appeared to Balaam that night and told him to go to Balak but to say only what he would tell him to say. Balaam was so happy to receive the permission to go that he woke up early in the morning and even saddled his own donkey for the journey. The donkey now became the means by which God would teach Balaam his lesson. As they traveled, the donkey saw an angel with a drawn sword blocking the road ahead. Three times it turned off the road, banging Balaam's foot. Balaam could not see the angel and reacted by cursing and beating the animal. How foolish Balaam looked. The powerful sorcerer was on his way at a king's behest to destroy a great nation with his curses, but he could not control even a single little donkey. Balaam was furious, fulminating at his humiliation, when the angel finally revealed himself to Balaam (22:31). The angel pointed out to the prophet that the donkey had seen better than he, the great wise man, had. Balaam should go on to Balak, but he must say only what God would tell him to say.

Balaam came to Moab but, to Balak's chagrin, God had Balaam deliver a great paean of praise and blessing for Israel instead of the planned curses. Balaam was sent away by Balak in utter disgrace.

Balaam was a towering intellectual and scholar with a special knowledge of divination and prophecy. He lacked, however, good character and integrity. It is not enough to be an intellectual. It is far more important to have the good character to make that intellect a source of blessing to oneself and others rather than a source of misery. Balaam's efforts at cursing the Israelites had failed most ignobly. He sought to redeem himself in Balak's eyes by offering him a piece of cynically cruel advice. Let the women of Moab and Midian seduce Israelite men and lead them thereby to worship their gods. God would be angry at the Israelites and destroy them (Numbers 31:16). The two nations followed Balaam's advice, and God did indeed grow angry at the Israelites, sending upon them a plague that left 24,000 dead. The total would have climbed much higher if Phinehas had not intervened as related in Numbers 25 (see Chapter 5). Eventually, the Israelites caught up with Balaam, his magic completely failed him in the face of their spirituality, and they slew him with the sword (31:8).

Clinical Implications

This story has strong implications for therapy with overintellectual patients. Intellect itself can be used to block the development of self-awareness as easily as it can help one to know oneself. This insight squares with the traditional psychoanalytic view of intellectualization as a defense against awareness of one's emotional side.

In the contemporary United States with its emphasis on attending college, people can easily be educated beyond their intelligences. True intelligence is not simply pure intellectualizing but is rooted in emotional understanding and compassion. It is warm and involved, not cold and detached. To the extent that intellect is involved with emotion, it becomes a warm intelligence that can illuminate one's self-knowledge and heighten awareness. A therapist must always direct intellect toward illuminating rather than obscuring.

TOTALITARIAN UTOPIANISM:
THE TOWER OF BABEL

Biblical Narrative

One might well be surprised upon walking into a good library and seeing the great number of books on utopias, or ideal societies. From ancient times to the present, people have dreamed these fictional ideals—Plato's *Republic,* Thomas More's *Utopia,* Jonathan Swift's *Gulliver's Travels,* Aldous Huxley's *Brave New World,* and many more. U.S. history features many attempts to build real life utopias, such as New Harmony, Indiana, in the mid-nineteenth century. All of these utopias, fictional and real, have been deeply flawed.

The Book of Genesis describes what must have been man's first attempt to build an ideal society in the story of the Tower of Babel (Genesis 11). Human population multiplied after the great flood of Noah's time, and the people eventually traveled westward, finally deciding to build a new home in the valley of Shinar (Mesopotamia). There they built a new city. So far so good, for God wanted mankind to work toward a good life. However, the people's motives were misdirected. "Let us build a city and a tower with its head into the sky and let us make a monument for ourselves lest we be scattered over the face of all the earth" (11:4). The utopia had formulated for itself a mission that had no real meaning. The goal of this society was not to enable man to come to closer to God, to grow spiritually and emotionally. No mention was made of helping the disadvantaged, of educating the young, of developing new ideas in science or art. The purpose of the tower society was security based on self-aggrandizement, "Let us make a monument . . ." Ancient man indeed built huge pyramids and ziggurats whose purpose was to glorify the kings and societies that built them. They did succeed, at least in the sense that we can still see today the remains of those great structures and remember some of the names of the builders.

The people of Shinar stated a second purpose: "lest we be scattered over the face of the earth." That is—the society must form certain controls to prevent people from leaving or changing. People must be rigidly controlled, which is characteristic of totalitarian societies all through history. Subdue progress; stifle disagreement. The tower society was arrogant too—"Let us build a city and a tower with its top in the heavens" (11:4). The goal of the society was again not producing people who were whole in body and soul. Building a tower all the way to the heavens would keep the masses occupied and would demonstrate the greatness, even the godlike character of the leaders of the society. Harmony and unity are wonderful goals that are in some measure attainable. However, not every aggregation of people holds these aims. A characteristic of totalitarian societies, including many of the great utopias of literature, is that they foster laws and practices that rigidify and preserve the society, while the population becomes secondary. The citizens are often little more than slaves. The seeming harmony in the society is false and deceptive. It is merely conformity. Indeed, some societies, Plato's Republic for example, even eliminate newborn babies who are judged unfit, and refuse medical treatment to people who may not be able to keep up their jobs.

This was not the biblical God's intent in creating the earth and the human race. Humans were designed to love, create, think, and grow—to fulfill God's purpose for them. The tower society had no goals beyond its own desires. Such a society and its leaders must inevitably seek to perpetuate their own selfishness and their hunger for power. God looked upon what the people were doing in Shinar and saw that they were pursuing their own goals rather than his, "and now nothing will be withheld from them, whatever they purpose to do" (11:6). The people began to find cooperation difficult. The unity that such a society needed collapsed before the demands and egos of individuals and factions. God may have miraculously befuddled their languages, but most commentators say an increase in quarreling occurred among these people who basically had no healthy purpose for their society. The people of Shinar eventually split into many smaller and uncooperative groups, and the tower remained unfinished.

Clinical Implications

So it is with many people. They focus on their achievements, building altars to themselves rather than to God. Such people become obsessive and narrow careerists rather than placing their careers in God's hands. Work becomes for such people an end in itself rather than a means of bettering the human condition. People who fall into this trap often appear wooden, humorless, and rigid. They seem obsessed with achievement for its own sake. They may be perfectionist and intolerant of flaws. Their ideals may remain so distant and cold as to exclude human warmth and liveliness.

When working with a patient of this type, it is important to stress that the aim of achievement is human betterment and that success is not an end in itself. Whatever dreams the patient has must be human dreams. It is ill-conceived to sacrifice real human beings in the name of some abstract vision of humankind.

ACQUIRING WISDOM: SOLOMON

Biblical Narrative

It is probably always better to be wise than foolish, and particular times can arise when one needs greater wisdom than ever before—when facing an important decision or striving toward existential knowledge, for example. The Greek philosophical literature describes Socrates' search for wisdom. The god Apollo, speaking through the oracle of Delphi, had pronounced Socrates to be the wisest of all men. Socrates did not know what that meant, so he accepted in the sense of a command from Apollo the obligation to learn what the god's statement did mean. Inquiring of many people—poets, tradesmen, politicians, and so on, Socrates learned that he knew something none of the others knew: no man is truly wise, and true wisdom belongs to the gods alone.

This is similar to the biblical dictum "The beginning of wisdom is reverence for God" (Psalms 111:10). However, the Bible adds an important new level to the human drive for wisdom. Solomon was still young and lacking confidence and awed by the tasks facing him when he succeeded his father David as king of Israel (1 Kings 3:7-8).

> I am a young lad and I do not know how to go and come. And Your servant is in the midst of your people whom You have chosen, a great people whose multitude cannot be numbered or counted.

When God told Solomon to ask for what he wanted most, the young king asked for "a heart to hear and to judge Your people, to understand good from evil" (3:9). Inexperienced as he was, Solomon was already wise enough to know that he could rule well only with wisdom and with faith in God.

Two brilliant men, the Greek philosopher and the king of Israel, have points in common in these accounts. Both sought and attained great wisdom. Socrates is described as the father of Western philosophy, and Solomon was admired by all the wisest people of his time (1 Kings 8:3).

> And God gave Solomon wisdom and very great understanding and a heart as broad as the sand on the sea shore. And Solomon's wisdom was more than the wisdom of all the peoples of the East and the wisdom of Egypt. And he was wiser than Ethan the Ezrachite, and Heman and Calcol and Darda the sons of Machol, and his name was among all the surrounding nations. And he spoke 300 parables and 1,005 poems, and he spoke of trees from the cedar of Lebanon to the hyssop which grows out of the wall, and he spoke on beasts and birds and on creeping things and fish. And there came from all the peoples to hear the Wisdom of Solomon from all the kings of the earth who heard of his wisdom. (1 Kings 5:9-14)

Tradition attributes to Solomon the authorship of Ecclesiastes, Proverbs, and the Song of Songs, three brilliant and intricate works.

However, the two approaches to wisdom show significant differences. Socrates never dealt directly with Apollo. Apollo hinted at the mission of seeking wisdom, but he actually gave Socrates no help and did not teach him. The idea of a personal relationship with a loving and omniscient God was nearly unknown in the Hellenic world.

Solomon, in contrast, felt close enough to God to ask directly for wisdom as a gift. Indeed, Solomon's entire sense of direction and his prophetic dream began with his love of God—"And Solomon loved God" (3:3). God promised great wisdom to Solomon and assured him of material support as well—"wealth and honor which no man ever had like you among kings . . ." (3:13). Solomon can be very wise not only in recognizing his own limitations and God's greatness and wisdom but also in many areas of knowledge. Indeed, God had commanded all people to study and acquire knowledge and to pass this on to their children in the most thorough manner—"And you shall teach your sons diligently" (Deuteronomy 6:7). This is a great responsibility, but God offers loving help. God began the chain of transmission by personally giving the commandments to the Israelites at Sinai and many more laws and ideas as well during the forty years in the wilderness. Even earlier, God taught Adam in the Garden of Eden all about nature and science (Genesis 2:19-20). Certainly a wise person ought to be humble. However, wisdom involves much besides humility, and God gives of his own wisdom and creativity to humanity and helps and supports them in their searching and development.

Clinical Implications

An individual may, like Socrates, be intelligent enough to realize the limitations of human wisdom. Intellect can take one only so far—and then one seems to have reached a brick wall. As did Socrates, the patient may despair, feeling that true wisdom belongs only to the gods and that the entire human enterprise of acquiring knowledge is futile and even tragic.

Alternatively, one may react as Solomon did, who also realized that his intellect could take him only so far, but that God would help him understand. Such an individual will listen to the wisdom of his or her heart, understanding that wisdom is not of the intellect alone but of his or her entire being. Intellect need not manifest itself in rebellion toward one's emotional life, but should be in harmony with it. God will help us on our path in life, not the snake in the Garden of Eden.

UNDONE BY AMBITION: JEROBOAM

Biblical Narrative

Biblical thought is not opposed to ambition per se. Indeed, it is healthy for people to want to improve themselves and their lot. Wisdom, wealth, and physical well-being are all part of God's bounty to humanity and all worth working for. However, ambition can expend itself pursuing wrong goals and can be mixed with unhealthy motivations such as arrogance, greed, or lust for power. 1 Kings 11:26f tells of the career of Jeroboam, whose great drive and talent were thrown off track by his own arrogance.

Jeroboam was marked by the great King Solomon as a young man of special ability, and Solomon named him to a high government post. All people need some bit of self-confidence, but Jeroboam had showed a good deal of arrogance. He seems to have thought of himself as being as great as King David. God recognized Jeroboam's talent and brilliance but worried about his pride.

Many troubles came on Israel in Solomon's last years, and God sent Ahijah the prophet to inform Jeroboam that the kingdom would be split in two after Solomon's death. Two tribes would follow Solomon's son in the kingdom of Judah, but ten would name Jeroboam as their ruler in a new kingdom of Israel.

Ahijah made clear to Jeroboam that God still loved David and would leave the two tribes and the city of Jerusalem with David's progeny "for the sake of my servant David" (11:32). Ahijah went on to mention David's name five more times to confirm God's continuing love and support for the rule of David's descendants in Judah. God knew Jeroboam's pretensions well and wanted to make his role clear to him. He could

> rule over all which your heart desires, and you will be king over
> Israel. . . . And it will be if you obey all which I command you
> and you will walk in My ways, and you will do the right in My
> eyes to guard My statutes and My commandments as did David

My servant, then I will be with you and I will build you a firm house. (11:37-38)

God emphasized that Jeroboam had an important role to play. At the same time, he would not supplant David. However, this was exactly what Jeroboam wanted. He would be David as well as Jeroboam.

In the course of time, Solomon died, and his son Rehoboam greatly disappointed the people of Israel, ten of whose tribes seceded and formed a new kingdom with Jeroboam as their king. Here, Jeroboam showed that despite his brilliance, his character did not equal David's. When a seeming threat to his rule arose, he failed to follow God's wishes and laws and to trust God's promises to him.

Jeroboam began to fear that his new subjects' loyalties to David's family might be renewed when they went to worship at the temple in Jerusalem. And Jeroboam too—should he go to Jerusalem and seem to be second to Rehoboam? Should he stay in his new capital Shechem and not go to worship in Jerusalem? His response was to proclaim to his new subjects that God was to be found everywhere, not only in Jerusalem—a very clever argument. He set up new religious centers in Bethel and Dan, presided over by priests who were not of the family of Aaron, and featuring statues of golden calves, which served as symbols of his rule. The new centers still probably worshiped the biblical God and not idols. However, this was very different from the form of worship that the Bible enjoined.

Jeroboam's new nonbiblical religion was initiated solely to support his own ambition for power. It is striking that he showed such moral weakness in his attitude toward the Jerusalem temple, inasmuch as he had once criticized Solomon, states the Talmud, for blocking some gates that made access to the temple easier for pilgrims. This fact highlighted the corruption of Jeroboam's ambitions and the failure of his attempt to be King David. He could have been a very great leader of an Israelite kingdom. Instead, he lived to see Ahijah thoroughly disappointed with him. Two years after his own death, Nadab, Jeroboam's successor, and the entire family were murdered by his general, Baasha.

Clinical Implications

This story can help a patient balance the various forces in life—a desire to succeed as an individual within the context of appreciating the larger collective enterprise. Patients must be supported in their striving to be all they can be, and psychological blocks that impede this progress must be removed. At the same time, patients must be helped to set appropriate goals rather than striving for something that is not good for them.

This distinction is a delicate one, which must be transmitted to patients delicately. They must be encouraged neither to underreach nor to overreach, but to seek what suits their character and abilities. Ambition in the service of fulfilling one's potential must be encouraged, but this must be distinguished from mindless self-aggrandizement and perpetual discontent.

USING OTHERS: AMNON

Biblical Narrative

King David's liaison with and marriage to Bathsheba and the death of their newborn child must have shaken the stability of the royal household of Israel. Soon after, Amnon, son of David, developed a fixation for the beautiful Tamar. She may have been a half sister to Amnon, and a full sister to Absalom, David's son by another wife. In any case, Amnon's behavior was criminal. Amnon became so preoccupied with his desire for Tamar that he fell ill. This was not love in any positive sense. He did not cherish or admire Tamar for her good character or even her beauty. Marriage, romance, or passion was not suggested. He single-mindedly plotted to rape her.

Amnon's friend and cousin, Jonadab, noticed that Amnon was wasting away and, learning why, he suggested that Amnon pretend to be seriously ill and invite Tamar to bake him some pancakes, a specialty of hers. It is possible that Jonadab did not realize Amnon's full intentions and sought merely to calm him, but more probably he was a jealous, unfeeling man who enjoyed making trouble. Amnon liked the plan for it would give him his chance to encounter Tamar. King David had visited the ailing Amnon and now supported his request to have Tamar come to make the pancakes.

As Tamar was preparing the cakes, Amnon suddenly ordered everyone else to leave the room. He seized Tamar and said, "Come lie with me, my sister" (2 Samuel 13:11). Not even a hint of love or romance, not even the momentary excitement of a graceful seduction, Amnon became violent. To him, Tamar was merely an object, not a human being. She pleaded and remonstrated and probably fought back but to no avail. Amnon would not be moved. He seized her roughly and raped her.

> Then Amnon hated her with a great hatred, for the hatred he now held for her was greater than the love he had held before. And he said to her, "Get up and leave." And he called his servants to drive her out and lock the door behind her. (13:15-17)

Tamar was devastated, and the news of the rape shook the family. Absalom, Tamar's brother, burned for revenge. Two years later, Absalom had Amnon murdered.

The thought pattern of a man such as Amnon is complex. First, Amnon saw people only as objects to be used. He did not respect Tamar as a human being. She meant nothing at all to him. Amnon seemed also to need to dominate others and to use violence. Tamar apparently tried to resist him, but he forced her violently, which fit his need to see other people as inferior, indeed nonhuman, and to crush them. Amnon may have also hated his father, King David, deeply resenting David's multiple wives and particularly his recent addition of Bathsheba. Amnon probably was very disturbed that Bathsheba's son, Solomon, was named to succeed David on the throne. Probably the eldest son, Amnon had likely thought of himself as heir apparent. Now he sought his revenge against David by raping and humiliating his daughter, and in the process disrupting the entire extended family. He even duped David into asking Tamar to cook for her supposedly ailing brother.

Thus Amnon was able to show his power and gain some attention by hurting Tamar, David, and the popular and handsome Absalom as well. There was no tangible gain for himself. One thinks of the great maxim, so original in the Hebrew Bible—"Love thy neighbor as thyself" (Leviticus 19:18). Amnon's attitude toward people was crude and hostile, and not at all biblical, with no concern for people, God, morality, or holiness.

Clinical Implications

Using people ultimately cheats the user as well as the used. To see another as simply a tool or as a means to an end deprives the user of the wonderful mystery of coming to know another human being. The clinician can instill in a patient the sense of adventure in human relations—one does not know the outcome of a relationship in advance.

Likewise, one must give up the need to control another. Paradoxically, by attempting to control the other's responses one destroys the other—turns him or her into something wooden and deprived of life. Therefore, one destroys what one is trying to possess. Only through accepting the other as intrinsically valuable can one achieve fulfillment in human relations.

Chapter 10

Recovery from Misfortune, Weariness, Loss, and Disability

INTRODUCTION

All human beings experience misfortune in their lives. The key is to acknowledge it without being overwhelmed and paralyzed. Likewise, individuals can become weary and mistake their way, often losing the glow of life. The poet Dante and the medieval figure Charles of Orleans both wrote about being lost in the middle of life. Individuals may also face loss, which grieves them greatly, yet can be overcome after the trauma has lifted. Finally, all human beings have areas of limitation and weakness. What is particularly difficult in therapy is when patients' weaknesses hamper their abilities to function in other ways as well. For example, a nearsighted man who needs thick glasses may find himself limited by extreme shyness as well. Consider the literary figure of Cyrano de Bergerac who, because of his protruding nose, felt incapable of being loved by the woman of his heart, Roxanne, despite his intellectual brilliance. Indeed he used his brilliance to help the empty-headed but handsome Christian to woo Roxanne, perhaps attempting to gain her love vicariously. People may compensate for a handicap by exaggerating other facets of their personalities. For example, a very short man attempted to make up for his disability through military and political conquest. We have a name for this: the "Napoleon Complex."

The biblical concept of repentance provides a means by which humans are able to treat personal and emotional problems rather than letting them fester and grow until they destroy. Repentance is so natural to the Bible that it is surprising to learn that Greek thought seems not to have developed a mature concept of repentance. Thus, the only way for a Greek to correct a personal flaw or sin, in many cases, was by means as extreme as suicide. Fate could not be altered. Gods such as Zeus were not forgiving and if they did forgive, it would carry little effect. The Midrash recognized how innovative the Jewish idea of repentance was. It held that Reuben, the son of the patriarch Jacob, was the first to do full-scale repentance (Genesis Rabbah 84:19 and 82:11) and he indeed is labeled as the "first-born for repentance." Adam and Cain may have repented of their sin but not as fully and only on God's suggestion, not of their own initiative.

All people make mistakes and commit wrongs or sins, which can harm every aspect of their relationship with God, with one's fellow, or with oneself. God recognizes that man is imperfect. However, God in his love and compassion for man gives him the possibility to correct his ways by means of repentance. Repentance does not mean self-deprecation or abject surrender or absorption in the overwhelming power and majesty of deity. It means instead that man refits himself for the service of his Creator after having left it. Repentance requires a feeling of guilt over one's imperfections and a renewed recognition of God as the one who rewards and punishes.

If circumstances or feelings hinder people from repenting, then God will help them along. However, much of the initiative is with people. The success of repentance is not merely in being forgiven and saved by God. Repentance is an end in itself, not a means toward some other end. It changes the equation of the relationship between God and people.

The main point of repentance is that it results in improving the people who repent, not that it merely induces a magical potion or catharsis for their faults. Repentance is also not merely a matter of correcting a wrong. It is a generic concept that concentrates on human growth as its aim more than on merely correcting a man's behavioral ledger. The intense activity of the High Holy Day season concentrates on the two inseparable ideas of recognizing God's sovereignty and of repentance, in the sense of assessing and straightening out one's relationship with God.

Beyond all this, repentance has a cosmic significance in bringing man close to God on the most exalted level. As the Talmud puts it, "Great is repentance for it reaches up to the Throne of Glory" (Yoma 86a). Judaism contains no notion of original sin. If the Jew seeks to come closer to God after having sinned, it is not mainly for purification, but because God loves when his creatures seek to approach him through repentance and prayer. Often individuals can even change themselves so that wrongs that they committed become a positive part of their experience, helping to make them better people (Ibn Paquda, 1963, Chapter 7).

Both the Hebrew Bible and the rabbinic literature contain many examples of the importance and efficacy of repentance. King David is one of the most notable. Unlike the Hellenic world, in biblical religion a person's life can be significantly altered by repentance and prayer. God watches over us, loves us, hears our prayers, and knows our needs. He will respond to our repentance by recognizing our spiritual development and also by changing our worldly lot.

This chapter discusses six biblical stories. The first, Jeremiah, provides a model for dealing with disasters. The second story, the Curser, portrays the unhappy tale of a person who is unable to overcome early rejection and alienation. The third selection is taken from Ecclesiastes and deals with the problems of aging. Sarah's story deals with the effects of trauma even after it has lifted. The story of Moses and Aaron discusses the biblical approach of overcoming a disability. The final story, the Fugitive, is about giving a person who slew another out of carelessness the chance to be rehabilitated (that is, to recover from his crime).

DEALING WITH DISASTER: JEREMIAH

Biblical Narrative

The Jewish people in their remarkable history have suffered repeated major cataclysms—destruction of their homeland, expulsions from England, France, Spain, and many other places, almost ceaseless religious persecution, social and economic restriction, and the Holocaust of the early 1940s. Each time, however, the Jews have revived and rebuilt, compiling an amazing record of accomplishment in numerous areas of human thought and activity. They have long outlived all the great empires from the ancient Egyptians to the Soviet Union. How does a people manage to restore itself after a seemingly overwhelming national disaster? The Jews established a method in reacting to the destruction of Jerusalem by Nebuchadnezzar and the Babylonians in 587 B.C.E. The land was devastated, Jerusalem and its temple razed, and most of the population slaughtered or carried into captivity. How would the Jewish people manage? The Hebrew Bible provided an answer in Lamentations, a book consisting of five poems, whose authorship tradition attributes to the prophet Jeremiah. In relating his own experience of dealing with cataclysm, Jeremiah set the paradigm for future cataclysms as well.

The five poems describe stages in the poet's effort to deal with God. Facing the terrible destruction, he first bemoans the fact that the friends and allies of the kingdom of Judah have proven false to her. They have not tried to help, have shown no empathy whatsoever, and have indeed rejoiced to think that perhaps the Jews and their faith were no better than anyone else. The Judeans were now suffering terrible brutality and starvation at the hands of pitiless conquerors.

They would have to confront their own misbehaviors too, although this was not the most important point. It was more important to feel and know their suffering and to understand it without denial. Why did God seem so cruel and merciless?

After a time, the prophet was ready to get hold of himself and to take on responsibilities: "I am the man who has seen affliction by the rod of his anger" (Lamentations 3:1). These terrible sufferings have come from God. Only by accepting and acknowledging his affliction can the man begin to feel the responsibility, "We have transgressed and rebelled. Thou hast not pardoned" (3:42), and only in accepting responsibility can the poet begin to feel hope, "Remember mine afflictions and mine anguish, the wormwood and the gall. My soul hath them still in remembrance and is bowed within me. This I recall to mind, therefore I have hope" (3:19-21). It seemed that God had covered himself with a cloud so that no prayer could reach him, but the poet cries out anyway, challenging him and demanding his mercy until he does take notice, "Thou hast covered us with anger and pursued us; Thou hast slain unsparingly. Thou hast covered thyself with a cloud so that no prayer can pass through" (3:43-44).

The poet again reviews the sufferings of his people, now showing how it was their own sins that aroused God's anger against them. Having arrived at this point, he can see hope, "Your iniquity is expiated, O daughter of Zion, He will not exile you again. He remembers your iniquity, daughter of Edom, He will uncover your sins" (4:22).

One must be realistic about suffering, neither denying it nor totally giving in to it as did the characters of the Greek tragic drama. People must accept that suffering comes from God. Only then can they understand that hope too comes from God (4:22). Without accepting responsibility, people cannot accept hope. God may seem to hide his face from people, but he does not abandon them. The prophet has explored the meaning of despair, but he must also understand and accept the meaning of rejuvenation. Suffering can be corrective and can lead to improvement. It is not the same as rejection.

The Talmud provides a profoundly important epilogue to Lamentations. Centuries later, after the Romans had destroyed the second temple, Rabbi Akiba and several other sages passed by the temple mount and saw a fox playing on the ruined site of the Holy of Holies. The sages wept, remembering the verse, "Over this our heart was faint; for these our eyes were dimmed; for Mt. Zion which lies desolate. Foxes walk in it" (5:17). Rabbi Akiba, however, began to laugh. When the others asked how he could laugh at such a scene, he answered that if the prophecies of destruction were so completely fulfilled, then God's promises of redemption were also sure to be fulfilled. History will not end in Greek-style suicide, but will bring God's redemption to his people.

Clinical Implications

This story has profound implications for the treatment of an individual who is suffering. It has become too easy in modern society to ignore or rebuke a person showing any signs of sadness. People even blame the sufferer for causing the suffering rather than acknowledging the reality of it and the need for the person to have time to heal. However, suffering does not simply mean feeling sorry for oneself and giving into despair, but instead represents an attempt to place one's pain in a larger context.

Although a person is suffering now, the suffering need not last forever. It is essential to maintain one's integrity and sense of a higher purpose through periods of misfortune. This is easier said than done and can be facilitated in therapy by recognizing the suffering while stressing the larger meaning and hope in life.

FEELING REJECTED: THE CURSER

Biblical Narrative

Feelings of rejection and alienation trouble most people, to some degree, through their lives. At times, the feelings may arise from real situations. In other cases, the feelings are endemic to a self-concept that has never developed in a healthy or realistic way, and also to a lack of knowledge and awareness of a purpose or meaning for one's existence. Such feelings of rejection and lack of confidence can be crippling to a person's endeavors in every area. The case histories of serial killers and recent shootings of high school students by their classmates typically show the perpetrators to harbor an extreme sense of alienation and of lack of acceptance from others. They respond with very antisocial and destructive behaviors.

The Bible in its characteristically brief style tells the story of such a man in a few verses. His name is never stated, and the later rabbinic literature refers to him only by his act—the *mekallel* (the curser or blasphemer). The very fact that his name is not given sets the focus on one of his main problems—a distorted sense of self. The blasphemer was born in Egypt to an Israelite woman, who was seduced or raped by an Egyptian overseer. The woman was of the Israelite tribe of Dan, but the Danites, years later, would not accept the young man as one of their own. Legally, they were correct. The young man, nevertheless, suffered from a sense of rejection, however mistaken, by the tribe, by the nation, and even from God. As time passed, his anger against God grew, and he picked quarrels with people "in the camp" to which he felt no sense of belonging. "And the son of an Israelite woman, whose father was an Egyptian, went out among the Children of Israel; and the son of the Israelite woman and an Israelite man strove in the camp" (Leviticus 24:10-11).

That the blasphemer felt rejected or alienated is understandable, given the circumstances of his birth and also his inability to gain full acceptance in his mother's tribe. It is understandable, but it was not beneficial. He could not grasp that he might have a duty to accept certain personal hardships or limitations for the public good as well as his own, nor did he seem interested in seeking possible solutions other than his quarreling and complaining, which were altogether misguided. He could still have lived a full and productive life in every aspect as a scholar, merchant, or craftsman, but he chose not to. Instead he quarreled and ridiculed as his frustration grew until finally "the son of the Israelite woman blasphemed the Divine Name and cursed" (24:11). His blasphemy of God's name was not merely an outburst of temper. It was a derogation and violation of the basic dignity and holiness with which God has invested the human being. In lashing out at God, the blasphemer showed his anger and spite at everything that God had created and, perhaps more important, his lack of interest in doing anything constructive. He was content to wallow in his own anger and misery.

Moses did not act hastily but instead consulted God. Perhaps Moses did not truly know what the proper punishment was, or perhaps he felt that his judgment would be unreliable since he was at fault for not preventing the crime in the first place (*Babylonian Talmud*, 1975, Sanh. 78b). God's answer was clear, and the blasphemer was put to death.

Clinical Implications

This story provides a motif for a therapist dealing with a patient from a troubled background. The therapeutic stance must be to show understanding of the hurt and rejection the patient has undergone without affirming the destructive tendencies, which can lead to even worse consequences. The therapist must offer the patient venues to express the hurt, but also to draw a positive outcome from it rather than to wallow in the pain and to act destructively to others and ultimately to himself or herself. For example, a man who experienced abuse as a child might be encouraged to pursue a career in mental health, where he can attempt to build the self-esteem of children who have suffered abuse. In so doing, the patient can affirm his own self-esteem—that he is worth something unconditionally no matter how badly he has been treated.

AGING: ECCLESIASTES

Biblical Narrative

"After I have withered, shall I become supple?" wondered the matriarch Sarah after hearing God's assurance that despite her ninety years of age she would bear her first child (Genesis 18:12). Certainly, aging can bring its pains and fears. Ecclesiastes 12:1f is most eloquent:

> Remember your Creator in the days of your youth before the evil days come and the years arrive of which you will say, "I have no joy in them." Before the sun and the light darken and the moon and the stars (i.e., When death comes), and the clouds return after the rain (i.e., the suppleness of the body withers) . . . (12:1-2)

The key to a successful adjustment to each stage of life, including old age, is this—"Remember your Creator in the days of your youth" (12:1), and be aware that the body will probably not be as strong or as swift as in younger years. However, even if you have not remembered your Creator in your youth, then turn to him in your mature years. Even until the moment of death, one can still improve.

The human body typically weakens as it ages. However, the Bible emphasizes that an old person can do wonderful things. "In the morning, sow your seed, and in the evening rest not your hand because you do not know which one will go well, whether this one or that one, or if both will be good" (11:6). Youth is wonderful only if it is well spent and only if it helps to prepare one for what comes afterward.

> Rejoice young man in your youth, and let your heart be glad in the days of your youth and go in the ways of your heart and after the sight before your eyes, but know that on all these, God will bring you into judgment. (11:9)

One should not lament the passing of youth as the romantic poets do. Instead, "remove vexation from your heart and draw evil off from your flesh, for youth and dark hair are vain" (11:10). The joys usually associated with youth are more seeming than real. A life devoted to good deeds and the development of faith and wisdom will help a person face the challenges of every stage of life, including old age.

Scripture commands respect for the aged. "Before gray hairs you shall rise up, and you shall honor the wise in counsel *(zaken),* and you shall fear your God" (Leviticus 19:32). Honor is indeed due to people for their years and their "gray heads." However, what is important is the wisdom that a lifetime of experience and study can bring to the aged. Even a younger person who has gathered great wisdom must be respected. The old person must show respect for his or her own age and wisdom by behaving in a manner that honors these accomplishments. Of course, one should respect all decent people, but to show respect to elders may be particularly important because they are sensitive to their own aging and so have more need of a show of respect. The elder should respect God and not be so arrogant or foolish so as to seek honor from others.

Westerners fear the coming of old age with its weakening of powers and the growing fear of being a useless burden. Old age also seems to be closing in on the end of life. How far all this seems to him from the warm blood and the sweet promise of youth. This view, so popular in Western thought, is nourished in ancient Greek myth, especially in the stories of Oedipus and Tithonus. Old age is presented as a time of deterioration and decline. A person is in full vigor during youth, but in old age can only plod along on "three legs" as the sphinx said in her famous riddle to Oedipus. That is, in old age one must walk with a cane.

Another myth tells of how Eos, goddess of the dawn, fell in love with Tithonus, a handsome mortal. She prayed that he be given immortality. The gods indeed gave him that gift but along with it played a cruel trick. Tithonus would live forever, but he would not keep his youth. He soon grew too old to be of interest to Eos, who left him in search of younger lovers.

Clinical Implications

The Bible recognizes the challenges of aging. However, it does not see old age as less useful or important than youth. Both are important stages in the human's progress. In every stage, one can grow in goodness and wisdom. "For if a person should live many years, let him rejoice in all of them, and remember the days of darkness for they will be many" (Ecclesiastes 11:8). People should live as best they can in every period of their lives. They should rejoice in them all without neglecting their responsibilities and opportunities and without forgetting God or their own humanity.

The implications for therapy with aging patients are great. An older woman, for example, may feel diminished in her physical condition. Her eyesight and hearing may not be as keen, she walks with a cane, and her memory is slower. The patient may bitterly complain that she is no longer the person she was and that she is worth nothing. The therapist needs to instill in the patient an appreciation of her strengths and abilities that have remained undiminished or have even increased, particularly her ability to transmit to a new generation what she remembers from a lifetime of experience. Central to this sense of a life span continuity is a chance for the patient to resolve her life story. This can be facilitated through a technique of guided reminiscences, allowing the patient to examine her progress through her life. She is in essence the same person she was as a child, a unique creature of God.

THE EXPERIENCE OF ALMOST-LOSS: SARAH

Biblical Narrative

Receiving very important and unexpected news, whether good or bad, can rouse powerful emotions so quickly and uncontrollably that a person's equilibrium, physical as well as emotional, can be deeply upset and serious trauma can result. The Scripture juxtaposes the binding of Isaac with the death of Isaac's mother, the matriarch Sarah. Although the text is cryptic, several midrashic passages argue that the shock of the unexpected news of the almost-death of her son was the direct and immediate cause of Sarah's death.

God had commanded Abraham to bring Isaac, his son, as a burnt offering. Abraham's trust in God was sufficient for him to carry out God's order, and he was at the point of actually slaughtering Isaac when God told him to hold back his hand. This was only a test to strengthen Abraham's devotion and faith. God had never actually wanted Isaac to be sacrificed, and child sacrifice was abhorrent to the Hebrew Bible—in contrast to its widespread use among other ancient peoples.

What was Sarah's role in this poignant drama? The initial command to sacrifice Isaac had come to Abraham alone, and Sarah knew nothing about it. She could have had little inkling of the powerful emotions working through Abraham's mind. It was only after the almost-sacrifice had taken place that Sarah learned that her son had been placed on the sacrificial altar and then taken off alive at God's command.

The Midrash offers conflicting pictures of the sequence of events. One suggests that the first report to reach Sarah led her to believe that her husband had actually sacrificed her son. A woman of profound faith, Sarah accepted God's will and was able to bear her sorrow. However, when she heard, shortly afterward, that God had indeed stopped the sacrifice and that her son was well, she was overwhelmed and "her soul departed."

In a second midrashic view, Sarah died upon hearing a first inaccurate report that Isaac had, in fact, been slaughtered on the altar. In this version, it was the first shock that caused Sarah's death.

Abraham faced God's command to sacrifice Isaac with turbulent emotions. His trust in God was very great, yet Abraham felt uncertain. Was it possible that he had misunderstood everything? Could God really want him to sacrifice Isaac? Abraham faced a second difficult decision as well. What should he tell Sarah? Sooner or later she would need to know. Apparently, Abraham decided not to tell her anything until later, but when Abraham returned from Mount Moriah, he found Sarah dead from the shock caused by the unexpected and perhaps misleading reports. A midrash interprets the verse, "And Abraham rose up from his dead." Sarah was *his* dead, i.e., Abraham felt responsible for helping to cause Sarah's death.

Perhaps if the news had reached her in a manner less sudden, less piecemeal, perhaps if the reports had been clear leaving no space for false impression or false hopes, Sarah could have summoned the strength to deal with both harsh and gentle news. Then she could have lived to rejoice with Abraham and Isaac in the highly uplifting experience of the *akedah.*

Clinical Implications

Every clinician dealing with suicidal patients knows the most dangerous time is when the depression begins to lift. Often the acute trauma puts the psychological system in shock. The shock can serve as a prophylactic protection allowing the individuals to develop a psychological response to their predicaments. However, the shock may begin to dissipate before the new psychological coping mechanism is fully in place. This becomes a volatile and dangerous period, sometimes leading to acute suicidal behavior. Suicidal patients must be watched most clearly at the very point when they seem to be improving. Even aside from suicide, patients may show relapses in their conditions at the very point that the original trauma passes. The patients' defenses are finally down and the therapist must guard patients closely.

DEALING WITH DISABILITY: MOSES AND AARON

Biblical Narrative

Few skills were more prized among the ancient Greeks and Romans than oratory. Demosthenes rose to fame in Athens as an orator despite some shady activities in politics and a poor military record. A famous story tells that he overcame a speech infirmity by practicing speaking with stones in his mouth. Cicero's speeches earned him wide repute in the last days of the Roman Republic. Fronto recommended the study of rhetoric over philosophy in a letter to his student, the Emperor Marcus Aurelius. Aristotle wrote a full-length treatise on the art of public speaking, and during Athens' Golden Age, Sophists were well-paid to teach their clients how to present arguments before a court of law or a political assembly. As Socrates put it, "they teach how to make the weaker argument defeat the stronger."

Remarkably, in the Hebrew Bible, oratory has no place. In fact, Moses, the great Hebrew lawgiver, had a speech defect. So also, says the Midrash, did the prophet Amos (Leviticus Rabbah 2). How could a man with such a handicap converse directly with God, confront the mighty Pharaoh, and teach the Torah to an entire nation? Moses expressed his concerns about his handicap during his first meeting with God, at the burning bush (Exodus 3). This meeting had the purpose of sending Moses on his mission of leading the Israelites out of Egyptian bondage and of teaching them the law during their journeys in the wilderness. However, God knew that Moses needed to deal with his own handicap if he was to be an effective leader, and God tried to support and direct Moses toward helping himself.

Let us look at the nature of Moses' defect, (which Rashi and other commentators interpret as stuttering), and then at the dialogue at the burning bush. Was the handicap of physical or emotional causes? This is unclear, although it could well have been both. The Midrash (Exodus Rabbah 1:26) offers a parable: As an infant, Moses had been rescued by the Egyptian princess when Pharaoh had decreed that all Hebrew newborn boys be cast into the Nile. The princess raised Moses at the royal court as her son. The Midrash tells that Moses, as a bright little baby, was a favorite at court. Pharaoh too liked to hold Moses in his lap, and Moses liked to take Pharaoh's crown and place it on his own head. This troubled the soothsayers, who predicted that Moses would grow up to usurp Pharaoh's crown. One counselor proposed a test. Place two trays before Moses—one with gold on it and the other with brightly burning coals. If Moses tried to grab the coals, it would mean that he merely was drawn to bright sparkling objects. If he reached for the gold, it would be a sure sign of danger. Moses was ready to grab the gold, but an angel redirected his hand toward the coals. Moses touched the burning coals, then in pain put his finger to his tongue, singeing it. Thus injured, Moses had difficulty pronouncing words correctly. Midrashic parables generally contain several levels of meaning. This story can mean that Moses grew up feeling like an outsider at Pharaoh's court. This contributed to the development of a speech impediment, which remained with him into adulthood and even as he stood before the burning bush.

Moses was not anxious to accept the mission on which God was sending him, and he offered five separate protests:

1. God said, "Go and I shall send you to Pharaoh, and bring forth my people from Egypt." Moses objected that he was not worthy to stand before kings nor was he able to handle the problems of the Israelites and bring them out of Egypt. God responded that he would make sure everything went well, and he would culminate the exodus with the great revelation on Mount Sinai (Exodus 3:10-12).

2. Moses tried again: The people will ask for some proof that God had indeed sent him. God explained to Moses how to make clear to the Hebrews that God had sent him and assured Moses that they would accept him (3:13f).

3. Moses again worried that perhaps the Israelites would not at all believe his story. God then showed Moses certain signs (i.e., the snake and the dose of leprosy) to indicate that he should not be so skeptical about the Israelites believing him. At face value, these were easy tricks that the Egyptian wise men could also perform. However, in Israelite thought, the snake and the dose

of leprosy are motifs associated with punishment for slander, and God was demonstrating to Moses and to the people that God would defend them, even from Moses himself if need be (4:1f).

4. Moses then raised his fears about his stuttering. He felt he was not a man of words. He was "heavy of mouth and heavy of tongue." God reassured him, "Who has given speech to man or who will make him mute or deaf or sighted or blind; is it not I the Lord?" (4:11). God knew Moses well. God did not need a dynamic polished orator to lead his people and to teach his law. God wanted a man of Moses' high character and intelligence, whose outstanding characteristic was not showmanship but humility. No man is perfect, but Moses was a wonderful man. His speech problem was not significant. "And now go, and I shall be with your mouth, and I shall teach you what you shall speak" (4:12).

5. Moses' humility was genuine, but his reticence about his speech defect showed also a lack of faith and confidence that needed to be remedied. Even with assurances of God's help, Moses' speech defect troubled him and weakened him. He did not accept God's reassurances and instead tried to back away from the dialogue— "Please Lord, please send whom You wish to send" (4:13). Commentaries suggest that maybe Moses did not want to seem to be usurping the leadership of his older brother Aaron. This reticence may have been noble but, whatever its reason, it was inappropriate.

God had set him on an important mission, and Moses had protested in one way after another, finally seeming simply to withdraw and try to close the discussion. When Moses seemed to back off unilaterally, God grew angry. In a sense, Moses had mistrusted both God and Aaron. He did not accept God's assurances of help, and he feared that Aaron might resent having to accept his younger brother as leader. Indeed, Moses had earlier assumed that the Israelites were such nonbelievers that they would not follow him.

Still, God knew Moses well and did not give up on him. He assured Moses that Aaron would be glad to see him and would approach him first. Moses' speech problem would do no harm, for God "will be with your mouth and with his (Aaron's) mouth." Moses will be the leader and Aaron will speak for him (4:14f).

One view in the Midrash suggests that when Moses received the law on Mount Sinai, he entered a new stage in life and his speech defect disappeared. In another way, however, the problem remained for Moses. Years later in the wilderness the people needed water. God told Moses to speak to a rock and streams of water would gush forth. Instead, Moses spoke in anger to the people over their manner of asking for the water, and he struck the rock with his staff rather than speaking to it as God had commanded. The old fear was apparently still not entirely overcome and Moses never did totally master the ability to excel in matters of speech, nor perhaps did he ever combine his sincere and wonderful humility with any great amount of self-confidence. His achievement in matters of the spirit is unsurpassed, but he had little feeling for politics.

The lesson of the dialogue at the bush is significant. The man who would lead the Hebrew people out of bondage and on to the great theophany at Mount Sinai was not a pushy hero but a kind, humble man. For God, wisdom and good character are important; eloquence and persuasiveness are not. This lesson is the opposite of that emerging from the story of Demosthenes mentioned previously. To lead the Hebrew people, one needs more than a mouth. He must use his eyes and ears too (4:11), and he must feel a sincere empathy for his people. Indeed, God chooses Moses specifically to show that the exodus would depend not on oratory and politicking, but on the work of God.

Clinical Implications

Moses' self-doubts, repeated several times, are expressions of the humility that will make his mission successful. Even his speech problem is beneficial, for how significant it will be that a stuttering, unpretentious man can defeat the mighty Pharaoh and his powerful empire. Moses should not become leader of the Hebrews merely by the power of oratory. Some people have great powers of persuasion but no other merit. Others are not convincing, and great truths coming from them are ignored. Moses was a man of great truths. People would know he was successful because of God's will rather than because of his own oratory. Moses and his people can succeed beautifully despite handicaps and despite not being perfect heroes, and maybe indeed because of these imperfections.

All human beings have areas of limitation and weakness. What is particularly difficult in therapy is when patients' weaknesses hamper their abilities to function in other ways as well. In treating this problem, a therapist can benefit from the biblical story of Moses, who lived a wonderful life, yet perhaps never fully overcame the emotional consequences of his early stuttering and was troubled by them even in later life when he apparently no longer stuttered.

KNOWING THAT LIFE HAS MEANING:
THE FUGITIVE

Biblical Narrative

People can feel so unimportant that they think their moral and spiritual acts and thoughts have no real meaning, that it is useless to be diligent and dedicated in their personal conduct. The Bible's account of "the cities of refuge" has among other aims that of presenting graphically to both the individual and society the importance of a human life. (We follow here the commentary of Samson Raphael Hirsch.)

Both individuals and societies regularly face the need to make certain moral decisions, and these decisions should be handled with full attention and diligence. Neglect or weakness can produce damaging effects. Numbers 35 and Deuteronomy 21 speak of the laws of the city of refuge. If a man slew another in an act of carelessness, i.e., neither deliberately nor wholly by accident, he must make his way with all haste to one of the six designated cities of refuge. There he would receive a fair trial. If it is decided that the killing resulted from negligence, then the killer must reside in the city of refuge until the death of the high priest. At that time, he is set free. The banishment to a city of refuge seems to aim at both the preservation of society and the rehabilitation of the killer. Perhaps most important, it cries out against diminishing the value of human life.

God designated the six cities of refuge even before the Israelites crossed the Jordan and began their conquest of Canaan. Commentators note that this commandment may have given special satisfaction to Moses, first because it was something he could do for the promised land, which he was not permitted to enter. Second, he himself had once been a fugitive (Exodus 2:15f) who sought and found a refuge.

But if he had pushed him suddenly without anger or hurled upon him any implement without aiming. Or with any stone wherewith a man may die, seeing him not, he cast it upon him so that he died, and he was not his enemy neither sought his harm. . . . Then the congregation shall judge . . . And restore him to the city of refuge. (Numbers 35:22-25)

Lack of concern for individual life destroys a society and "pollutes the earth" (Numbers 35:33). A human society that does not care for every drop of human blood is not holy and denies the whole purpose of its existence; it is, in fact, polluted.

And you shall take no ransom for him that is fled to his city of refuge. . . . So you shall not pollute the land wherein ye are; for blood pollutes the land. . . . And you shall not defile the land which you inhabit in the midst of which I dwell; for I the Lord am present in the midst of the Children of Israel. (35:32-34)

The killer must atone for his crime and prepare himself, justify himself to be restored fully into a society that aims at very high spiritual and moral standards and which is very aware of God's presence.

A moral society must rest on the recognition of the values of fellow beings created in the image of God. In a society of force, depravity, greed, and even negligence, love and sanctity suffer. Not that people must or can be perfect, but the guiding principle of the state must be acceptance of the value of human beings and of what they can strive to do. The most precious commodity of a state is its people. Banishing the unpremeditated killer to a city of refuge recalls the banishment of Cain after slaying Abel. The killer's exclusion from general life should teach him the meaning of having excluded his victim from the preciousness of human life. The aim of banishment is not primarily punishment but expiation—that a person should recognize and regret his wrongdoing, deal with his guilt, and go on living.

The term of his exile ends with the death of the high priest. This seems to point to a relationship between negligent homicide and the duties of the priest. In fact, the cities of refuge were inhabited by Levites. The Levites and priests taught the people and served in the temple. They did not make laws or judge cases; they were the moral teachers of Israelite society. Their task was to spread the principle of the importance and sanctity of human behavior and of every drop of human blood and to work against human thoughtlessness and negligence. The life of the high priest is lived in a sort of sympathetic suffering with the condemned so that the priest's death in a sense concludes the atonement. The priest had to some extent failed in his task of impressing society with the importance of moral diligence and care.

Clinical Implications

Patients who have wronged another must be made to acknowledge their acts and must be given the chance to atone. The atonement is essential to the therapeutic process and accomplishes several aims. First, it allows some compensation to the victim. Second, and no less important, it provides a mechanism for the patient to restore self-esteem. The biblical insight for the therapist is profound. The best way for a patient who has wronged another to feel better is to make amends to the person and atone for the action. In fact, such atonement may be the only way to restore the patient's self-image. Giving the wrongdoers a chance to meaningfully atone for their actions is one of the most important avenues to effective rehabilitation.

Chapter 11

Suicide Prevention

INTRODUCTION

The ultimate psychological problem is suicide, and the corresponding ultimate challenge for a therapist is suicide prevention. We have discussed this issue at length in the prologue to this book. Let us restate the central theme: Freedom is fundamental in the literature and thought of both the ancient Greeks and Hebrews, but the way in which the two cultures understand and deal with freedom is very different. To the Greeks, freedom is a struggle against the control of others and an effort to establish some sense of control over one's own life. The highest form of control over one's self is the freedom to decide whether to live or to die, i.e., suicide. Biblical thought, in contrast, sees freedom as essential, and the issue of control is resolved in a direct manner. Freedom can be achieved only in the acceptance of the realities of man's relationship with God. This sets the stage for a striking psychological contrast. For Greeks and Romans, suicide represents a very high form of creativity. Hebrew thought, in contrast, sees life itself is the essence of creativity and suicide destroys this opportunity.

Human development presents a series of life events that must be coped with wisely in order to grow. Adolescents must begin to separate from their parents and make friends. Young adults must successfully find mates. Middle adults must make successful career decisions. Older adults must plan wisely for retirement.

Although the presenting problems may be different from one life stage to another, the underlying issues may be the same. Psychologist Erik Erikson (1951 [1963], 1980, 1982) sees development proceeding epigenetically—the seeds of later stages planted in the earlier stages. Suicidal behavior at each life stage involves unsuccessful resolution of individuation-attachment conflicts. Suicides abound in Greek tragedy (some sixteen in the surviving plays of Sophocles and Euripides). The Hebrew Bible contains only six. Furthermore, the Hebrew Bible presents a number of narratives that specifically prevent the suicide of the central figure. We turn to five of these stories now (Kaplan and Schwartz, 1993; Kaplan, 1998).

The first deals with Elijah and his recovery from weariness with the help of food and water. The second tells of Moses' feeling of isolation and how this is overcome through the establishment of a Sanhedrin. The third speaks of Job who had to find reason to go on living despite lack of support from his wife or his friends. The fourth story discusses David's overcoming his sense of abandonment. Finally, the story of Jonah is offered as the quintessential suicide-prevention story in the Hebrew Bible, showing how God as a divine therapist protected Jonah in his suicidal conflict. In all of these stories, the central character recovers the will to live and overcomes suicidal tendencies.

RECOVERING FROM WEARINESS: ELIJAH

Biblical Narrative

Sometimes people become so bound up in their work that they lose their sense of direction and their ability to make decisions and to carry them out. This can happen even to the ablest of people serving the noblest aims. In such cases, individuals' work will suffer, their inner selves may fail them, and they will become sadly debilitated. This is what seems to have happened in the biblical account of the great prophet Elijah. When Elijah seemed to lose hope in the meaning of his life and work, God intervened to help by giving recognition to his past work and encouraging him toward new tasks, which were more realistic and useful for his new situation.

Elijah was one of the most fiery and energetic figures of the Hebrew Bible. However, in the moment after a great public and personal triumph, he fell into a deep weariness, and God needed to intervene and help him modify his goals so as to restore Elijah's strength and set him back on his life's work.

Under the rule of King Ahab and Queen Jezebel, the people of Israel had turned away from their own God and had lapsed into the worship of idols. Indeed, followers of God were persecuted and his prophets were forced to flee or to hide. God sent a drought on the land, but Ahab and Jezebel were not moved to repent of their ways. At this point, Elijah came forward to propose a contest. In sight of the multitude of Israelites gathered on Mount Carmel, the 850 priests of Baal and Astarte would slaughter a bull as an offering to their gods. Elijah, the lone prophet of his God, would prepare another bull on a second altar. The God that would answer with fire from heaven to consume his offering would be the true God.

Elijah was no compromiser. "How long," he said to the people, "will you hop between two ideas. If the Lord is God follow Him and if Baal, go after Him" (1 Kings 18:21). The drama unfolded as the prophets of Baal danced themselves into a frenzy as was their wont, calling upon their god and even gashing themselves with knives and spears till their blood flowed. They leaped and danced for hours but Baal, of course, did not respond. Finally, late in the day, Elijah took his turn. He offered a brief prayer, and God answered with fire, consuming the offering and the altar and its surrounding trench filled with water as well. Properly impressed, the people shouted, "The Lord is God. The Lord is God," and they slew all the priests of Baal (18:39-40). Even Ahab seemed sympathetic, but Jezebel was unmoved. She sent word to Elijah that she planned to murder him if he remained in Israel. So the day after his great moral victory, Elijah was fleeing for his life.

He went to Beersheba in the friendly kingdom of Judah and journeyed alone a day's walk into the desert. There, in despair at the dashing of his hopes, he asked God to take his life. "My life is long enough. Until when will I undergo this confusion" (19:4) (following translation by Rashi from Targum Jonathan). He fell asleep under a bush. God now began to intervene to restore Elijah to a better frame of mind. He would not allow Elijah to run away blindly. An angel came and woke Elijah to give him food. Elijah ate and drank and journeyed many days to Mount Sinai, to the cave where Moses had studied the Torah with God himself, where God had expressed his intense love for the people of Israel in a most beautiful manner. God sought to help Elijah to feel the difference between the love of that moment and Elijah's present anguish, hoping to arouse Elijah's love too, to help him regain contact with his inner self and with the need of the prophet and people for one another.

Elijah was worn out not by many years of hard work and danger but by the feeling that the task was too great for him and he had failed.

He was the only prophet of God left, and he felt alone and weak. God himself now intervened to revive Elijah's spirit. God addressed him, "What are you doing here, Elijah?" Elijah answered,

> I have been zealous for the Lord, the God of Hosts, for the Children of Israel have forsaken Your covenant. They have torn down Your altars. Your prophets they have slain with the sword, and I alone have remained and they have sought to take my life. (1 Kings 19:10)

Elijah again emphasized his feeling of being alone and unable to bear the burden of his people's decline. His zeal had destroyed the priesthood of Baal but had also led to his being driven away. God had understood that Elijah had spoken of "Your covenant," "Your altars," and "Your prophets," and he had emphasized his zeal for God but did not mention the people of Israel to whom God had sent him.

God then displayed mighty winds, earthquake, and fire, but God was in none of these. After the fire came a small still voice, and Elijah knew that God was in the voice, and he understood God's message. Elijah should have besought God to help the people of Israel instead of merely trying to overwhelm them by himself. Even now Elijah was expressing his own difficulties with the Israelites, not concentrating on helping them. Because of both the serious problems with the people and Elijah's own zealous approach, the task had become more than he could handle. He repeated to God word for word the same answer he gave before, " I have been zealous for the Lord . . ." (19:14).

Elijah was still a great prophet, and God still loved him, but the burden of his mission had indeed become too heavy for him. God then assigned him Elisha as a disciple and eventual successor. In a sense, Elijah had not been wrong in his zeal, for God now told him that times of great violence would indeed come upon Israel because of its waywardness.

God first sustained Elijah with food and then revived his spirit in a frank but friendly confrontation in which Elijah expressed his doubts about himself and his people. God responded by recognizing his despair and by showing Elijah the beauty and importance of the small quiet voice even while recognizing the validity of Elijah's problem. He then sent Elijah on to other tasks more suited to his current strengths and with the support of Elisha. He would continue to do valuable work for his Creator and his people.

Clinical Implications

This story illustrates quite well the importance of social support in mental health. A great argument currently rages about a person's right to die. Proponents begin their argument with physical illness but quickly go on to psychological discomfort. Missing in this emphasis on patient rights is any responsibility on the part of the mental health professional to try to encourage the person and broaden the patient's focus on reality. Even acknowledging a patient's right to suicide (which the Bible does not), does not imply that this is in the patient's best interests.

The role of the therapist with people who are "burnt out" is to help relight the spark to continue on their path. This often requires a simple physical act of nurturance. Elijah is provided with food and drink, which gives him the strength to continue on to Horeb. Significantly, the Greek hero Ajax is left neglected by his fellows, with no food or drink. He descends into depression and takes his own life.

The therapist must provide safety and rest to the weary patient. However, therapy must not end there. Ultimately the individual must have reason to want to live. Purposelessness often turns into depression, which can manifest itself as weariness or boredom. The therapist must deal with the weariness first and then deal with the deeper issue of depression. Strikingly, the preoccupation in modern society with death with dignity has coincided with a retreat from involvement in life with meaning.

FEELING OVERWHELMED: MOSES

Biblical Narrative

Even the most dedicated people can think that their work has been useless and that the challenges facing them are unmanageable and overwhelming. This once happened to Moses, a great wise man and prophet and a dedicated and selfless leader. Some Israelites in the wilderness came to Moses and demanded food beyond the miraculous daily portion of manna. "We remember the fish which we would eat in Egypt for free; the cucumbers and the melons and the leeks and the onions and the garlic. And now our souls are dry; there is nothing but the manna before our eyes" (Numbers 11:5-6).

"God became very angry, and in the eyes of Moses it was evil" (11:10). Moses understood how badly the people were behaving. Their criticisms of the manna expressed their rejection of God. People who had experienced such heights of spirit as the Sinaitic revelation and the crossing of the Red Sea could now complain about not having onions. Moses was deeply chagrined at the people's attitude and trembled over the punishment that was sure to come on them. He turned to God, saying that he had been parent and nurse to this people. Where would he find meat to feed such multitudes?

"I cannot alone carry this people, for it is too heavy for me" (11:14). Moses expressed his sense of the inadequacy of his own leadership. A man of great humility, Moses had never thought of himself in the way later generations would—as a great moral and spiritual leader. At this moment, he did not see that perhaps it was exactly because of his compassion and sincere humility that God had chosen him to lead the children of Israel.

The people did not come directly to Moses. Perhaps they thought that a man who had stood alone with God on Mount Sinai for forty days and nights without food or drink ("I ate no bread and drank no water," Deuteronomy 9:9, 18) could not be troubled with worldly people who yearned for meat. "And Moses heard the people crying among their families each at the door of his tent" (Numbers 11:10). The people would not come to talk to him, and perhaps Moses felt that he did not fully empathize with their needs. Moses ended by imploring God, "If thus You do to me, please kill me; if I have found favor in your eyes and let me not see this evil that will come upon them" (Numbers 11:15).

Perhaps Moses was, in a sense, offering to sacrifice himself for the people so that the punishment for his presumed failure would fall on him, not on the people. On a previous occasion, when Moses had seemed overwhelmed by his labors, Jethro stepped in and helped to organize a judiciary system, and to take some of the burden off Moses (Exodus 18:13f). In this new incident, God instructed Moses as to what needed to be done. Moses was to assemble a council of seventy respected men, who would function as a sort of parliament to help him bear the responsibilities of leadership. The people would no longer feel that their leaders were too distant to be approached about mundane matters.

Clinical Implications

Sometimes a person is unable to deal with problems that are very real and tangible. It is necessary to help this person set up an apparatus, perhaps in the form of a human support system, that can help make the necessary decisions and changes and prevent the person from falling into extreme behaviors that will prove ineffective and harmful.

A well-intentioned person can feel unable to cope with all of life's responsibilities. For example, a woman may come into therapy complaining that she is exhausted, there are not enough hours in the day to complete all the tasks that need to be done, and that she feels wholly inadequate to the challenges facing her. She may even speak of suicide, not because she really wants to die but because she seems unable to get help. Sisyphus in the Greek myth pushes a boulder up a steep hill only to see it plummet back down. The famous refusenik, Natan Sharansky, in his book *Fear No Evil* (1988), came upon a striking resolution to Sisyphus' dilemma. He was able to withstand the terrors of the gulag by holding his feeling of closeness to both God and his wife Avital. Together, he and Avital would roll a rock up the hill. He says movingly, "There is, of course, one solution—in the complete mingling of two faiths into one—together we will roll the rock up the mountain, together we stand under it, like Avital and me" (pp. 374-375).

People too must learn that they are not isolated. A sense of trust and community can help even in the heaviest endeavor. People in this situation may feel totally alone even when they are not, but they do not know how to ask for help or to utilize it when it is available. The highly individualistic U.S. culture perhaps accentuates this problem. The therapist's goal is to instill in patients the sense that they are not alone, that there is help, and that they are not showing weakness through interdependence. If one is lost, it is okay to drive into a gas station and ask directions. It does not make one's journey less one's own.

FRIENDS IN NEED: JOB

Biblical Narrative

People react to unhappy events in various ways. The story of Job has become a paradigm in world literature for human suffering. A wealthy man with a large family, Job lost his wealth and, soon after, his children. Then he was smitten with a terrible illness. Covered with suppurating sores, he sat on an ash heap with nothing but a potsherd to scrape his festering, miserable skin.

What could a man do in such a situation? Job not only suffered grievously but did not understand why this suffering had come upon him. He had done nothing evil to warrant these miseries. His wife's response was similar to the attitudes that relatives too often show to a family member who seems very ill. Either the relatives feel the patient cannot bear continued suffering or, because they do not wish to deal with the sufferings, the relatives may actually encourage euthanasia (so-called) or even direct suicide, whether unaided or doctor-assisted, as in Kevorkian's many cases. The patient comes to feel that he or she is no more than a burden to "loved ones" and may accept euthanasia or suicide as a means of generally lightening what is perceived as the burden placed on them.

Job's wife was much in the mold of these relatives. Feeling her own dreadful loss and not sensing at all her husband's need to understand what was happening to him, she took what seemed to her the way of least resistance and urged him to "curse God and die" (Job 2:9). Her suggestion neither made much sense nor was it at all positive. Was cursing God supposed to cause death? Probably not. Job's wife was merely expressing her deep hurt and anger, and her feeling that life was useless and that it would be best to end it.

The Hebrew Bible, of course, strongly opposes suicide and greatly prefers life to death. Job rejected his wife's view and began his long and determined course of questioning that finally brought him to a new closeness to God and to a higher understanding, both intellectual and emotional, of the purposes of human life. He refused to give in either to his wife's unthinking rejection of God's gift of life or to his friend's suggestions that Job must have sinned and was therefore being punished by God. Job, indeed, lived through his many sufferings, despite the pressure from his wife and his friends. He learned many new lessons about God's world and about himself and found new meaning and joys in his life.

Clinical Implications

Sometimes when a man, for example, is going through the most acute misfortune, many other friends may fail him. They may tend to dissociate themselves from him or even blame him for his misfortune—as if they can thereby save themselves from his misfortune. In such a situation, the clinician must help the patient develop an inner strength to withstand not only his misfortune, but also the abandonment on the part of many of his friends. Depending on a deeper faith in oneself and developing a discernment as to which friends to turn are important clinical lessons to be learned here.

ABANDONMENT: DAVID

Biblical Narrative

Some human dilemmas are existential, i.e., individuals can reach points in their lives when accomplishments, possessions, and even human relationships have little meaning for them. This can take the form of adolescent depression or midlife crisis. The problem can be touched off by feelings that they have accomplished less than they should have or that they have not attained a certain level of recognition.

The problem of despair often goes far deeper. King David was a man of intense poetic sensitivity and deep love, who on occasion wrestled with a powerful sense of existential abandonment. This is expressed poignantly in Psalm 22.

> My Lord, My Lord, why have You abandoned me?
> Far from my help are the words of my cry.
> My God, I call by day and you do not answer,
> By night, there is no rest for me
> But You are holy
> Dwelling on the praises of Israel. (22:1-3)

David expresses a feeling of being terribly alone and abandoned by God. Where is God? David goes on to say that his ancestors trusted in God and called upon him, and they were removed from danger. However, for David himself,

> But I am a worm and no man,
> Scorned of men despised by the nation
> All who see me scorn me.
> They will reject me with their lips
> They will shake their heads. (22:6-7)

Then, at the time when a person is weak and feels scorned and rejected by men and even by God, he can still turn to God.

> Cast upon God.
> He will protect him (the person).
> He will save him
> Because He cherishes him,
> Because you bring me forth from the womb,
> Giving me trust on my mother's breast.
> Upon you I have been cast from birth
> From the womb You are my God.
> Be not far from me for trouble is near,
> For there is none to help. (22:9-11)

David turns to his trust in God, who has been with him from before birth. Even his trust and reliance as an infant with his parents is possible only because of God. All through life this deeply ingrained trust empowers David to remember, even in the most difficult moments, that he is never truly abandoned, for God is always with him.

Surrounded or threatened by every evil, David will still turn to God to help him (22:16-22). David's thoughts were now freed to turn with assurance to the glory of the time when all men will accept God's rule over the world (22:23).

Clinical Implications

In a therapy situation, awakening a sense of closeness to God will give strength to some people who feel abandoned, but can this story be of use to one who is not a religionist? The fact is that the vast majority of Americans do believe in a deity. Those who do not may lack the emotional support of the sense of personal relationship, but the story of David can still offer the paradigm of working one's way through a crisis of abandonment by holding to one's ideals. It illustrates also the immense importance of handling even the most dire threats with a positive and confident attitude, even if the patient cannot understand why at the start.

Patients may come to the therapist with an overwhelming sense of abandonment. They have suffered grievous losses of loved ones (or ideals) and feel totally alone and devastated. Why should they go on living? What is the point? A therapist at this point must cut to the patient's basic life story and extract his or her basic life meaning. Despite all the temporary setbacks and narcissistic wounds, one's life is still worth living—one's life is indivisible and does not lose its intrinsic meaning because of one misfortune or another. Rather, patients must be helped to feel that their lives have unconditional value—that they are worth something whether they succeed at this or that. This is a very difficult lesson to communicate, but a very important one.

PROTECTED REGRESSION: JONAH VERSUS NARCISSUS

Biblical Narrative

Perhaps the quintessential suicide prevention story in the Hebrew Bible is the story of Jonah. We have used this story with great success in suicide prevention with both religious and secular patients. The metaphors are powerful and quite representative of biblical stories. It can be vividly contrasted with the Greek story of Narcissus. In the version of both Ovid's *Metamorphoses* (1955) and Conon's *Narrationes* (1798), Narcissus moved from disengagement to enmeshment before dying in despair.

In the first part of the narrative, Narcissus seems to be self-absorbed, treating his lovers as mere extensions or mirrors of himself (Ovid, 3:359-378). This trend becomes accentuated in his relationship with Echo who becomes a perfect mirror for Narcissus, reflecting back everything Narcissus says (3:379-382). Narcissus is insufficiently connected with his environment; yet he is not suicidal at this time. The events in the story proceed. A rejected suitor prays that Narcissus himself will experience unrequited love (3:405-406). Nemesis answers this prayer causing Narcissus, for the first time, to fall hopelessly in love. He now idealizes the face in the brook, not realizing that it is his own reflection (3:414f). Narcissus is now insufficiently differentiated from his environment; yet, he is still not suicidal. Ultimately, however, Narcissus recognizes the face in the brook is his (3:463-473). The reflection becomes simultaneously an ideal and a mirror. He is not self-invested, but self-empty, driven to grasp his self, which has now been projected onto the outside world. Such a psychotic juxtaposition rips Narcissus apart. As Ovid expressed it, "How I wish I could separate myself from my body." This represents an extreme statement of confusion in the boundaries between the self and the outside world and is suicidogenic. The story ends with Narcissus' death, either through plunging a dagger into his chest (Conon, *Narrationes,* 24) or through pining away (Ovid, 3:497-502).

The suicidogenic element in the myth of Narcissus is the inability of Narcissus to successfully integrate his individuation and attachment behaviors. First he is individuated at the expense of attachment; then he is attached at the expense of individuation. Finally, he is overwhelmed by the irreconcilable confusion between his individuation and attachment issues and resolves the conflict through self-murder. Narcissus represents the extreme example of the inability to integrate one's personal self and one's social self. One can only be obtained at the expense of the other. Some of this, of course, is present throughout Greek tragedy. The myth of Narcissus simply presents this dilemma in its most simple lethal form.

The biblical story of Jonah (discussed in Chapter 2) is dramatically different, creating a structure whereby Jonah is able to integrate individuation and attachment. The story begins with Jonah placed in a terrible dilemma. God calls on Jonah to go warn the people of Nineveh of their wickedness. However, Jonah does not want to go and runs away to Tarshish (Jonah 1:1-3). He does not confront God and he does not submit.

He runs away in a confused attempt to avoid his mission. When God sends a storm, Jonah tells the sailors to throw him overboard (1:4-16). The story could thus end in suicide, *but it does not*—God intervenes as a protective parent, swallowing Jonah in the protective stomach of a great fish until he overcomes his confusion. Then the fish vomits him out on dry land (2:2-10).

This same pattern occurs later in the story as well. God again asks Jonah to go to Nineveh. This time Jonah goes and gives the people God's message. They repent and are saved (3:1-10). Jonah becomes angry and expresses the wish to die and leaves the city to sit on its outskirts (4:1-5). Again, God intervenes, sheltering Jonah with a gourd from the burning sun (4:6). After a worm destroys the protective gourd, Jonah once again expresses suicidal thoughts (4:7-8). God once again intervenes, this time engaging Jonah in a mature dialogue in a successful attempt to end his confusion as to individuation and attachment (4:9-11).

Clinical Implications

The suicide preventive element in the story of Jonah is God's covenantal intervention providing a protective shield to allow Jonah to regress and harmoniously reconcile his individuation-attachment dilemma. God is teaching Jonah that these two alternatives are not contradictory, that the personal self and the social self need not be in contradiction to each other. His rejections of egoistic and altruistic resolutions need not lead to suicidal oscillation or to anomic suicide.

God protects Jonah with a covenantal wall to allow him time to work out his boundary confusion at his own pace. Jonah may need to regress to an earlier stage to do so, and he will need protection. In the biblical world, God provided this shield with a fish and a gourd (with Jonah), trustworthiness (with Job), and with food and drink (Elijah). In the modern world, parental understanding, therapeutic protectiveness, and hospitals may provide some shielding function. Covenantal walls may be suicide preventive, shielding the anomically confused individuals from environmental pressures until they can straighten out their individuation-attachment dilemmas.

Epilogue: Freud, Oedipus, and the Hebrew Bible

We have presented fifty-eight biblical stories for use in therapy over a host of practical situations. We want to conclude this book by examining in depth the question of why Sigmund Freud employed Greek rather than Hebrew foundation legends, specifically the story of Oedipus, as a basis for psychoanalysis. The Oedipus complex represents the third stage in Freud's view of psychosexual development and is critical to explaining how the individual identifies with his or her same-sex parent and how the superego is formed. Indeed an adage of psychoanalytic theory is that "the superego is heir to the Oedipus complex."

Over the past forty years, a question has been raised by Eric Wellisch (1954) and others as to what the implications would be of substituting a narrative from the Hebrew Bible for this Greek story. As the title of his book *Isaac and Oedipus* implies, Wellisch proposes a biblical approach to psychotherapy wherein the *akedah* (Abraham's binding of Isaac and his ultimate nonsacrifice) is offered as an alternative to the legend of Oedipus. For Wellisch, the biblical story offers a resolution of the father-son relationship not available to the Greek civilization. A covenant of love replaces the cold peace between father and son emerging out of the incomplete resolution of the Oedipus complex. Much the same argument has been made by Kalman Kaplan and his associates (Kaplan, Schwartz, and Markus-Kaplan, 1984; Kaplan and Schwartz, 1993) and has been suggested by Yosef Yerushalmi (1991) in his recent book *Freud's Moses.* More recently James Grotstein (1994) raised this same question in his essay "Why Oedipus and not Christ?"

The question immediately leaps out at us as to why this alternative approach did not occur to Freud himself, who after all was a Jew, even if in his own terms he was a "Godless Jew." In other words, why was Freud drawn to the Greek legend of Oedipus rather than biblical alternative as the basis of psychoanalytic theory? Why are the master stories of psychoanalysis in general borrowed from Greek mythology rather than from the Scripture? Freud's choice seems odd even on programmatic grounds because the latter tradition was better known to the general public than the former and could thus more effectively further the cause of psychoanalysis. Yerushalmi's work suggests that Freud was at least slightly familiar with the Hebrew tradition, and Freud's obsessive attempts to keep psychoanalysis from being seen as a "Jewish National Affair" will not do either. Freud's fascination with the Greek Oedipus must have deeper roots.

The real question is: Why did Freud believe the legend of Oedipus to have universal applicability to the human condition rather than a narrative emerging from the Hebrew Bible? Freud undoubtedly observed the Oedipal configuration in his patients, but this too provides an incomplete explanation of why Freud was so interested in the Oedipus complex.

The Olympian story of creation provides us with a key to understanding Freud's focus on the Oedipus complex. Nature exists before the gods. Sky (the male) marries Earth (the female) and produces first the hundred-handed monsters, and then the cyclopes (Apollodorus, 1:1-2). The family pathology then immediately commences, as the father takes the children away from the mother and throws them into Tartarus (Apollodorus, 1:3). Such action, of course, breeds reaction and Earth takes her revenge.

> Grieved at the loss of the children who were thrown into Tartarus, Earth persuaded the Titans to attack their father and gave Cronus a steel sickle. They all set upon him, except for Ocean, and Cronus cut off his father's genitals and threw them into the sea. . . . From the drops of the spurting flood were born the Furies: Alecto, Tisiphone, and Megaera. Having thus eliminated their Father the Titans brought back their brother who had been hurled to Tartarus and gave the rule to Cronus. (Apollodorus, 1:4)

Thus, the Oedipal conflict is born and, indeed, ingrained through the Furies into the fabric of the natural world as an unchanging law of nature. When Earth and Sky foretold that Cronus would lose the rule to his own son, he devoured his offspring as they were born (Apollodorus 1:5). The infant Zeus is saved through a ruse, as Cronus was misled by being given a stone wrapped in swaddling clothes instead.

When Zeus reaches adulthood he makes war on Cronus and the Titans (Apollodorus 2:1), fulfilling the prophecy of Earth and Sky.

The family pattern emerging from these stories is evident. Husband and wife are estranged from each other. The husband is disengaged and hurtful. The wife is enmeshing and vengeful. Family triangulation occurs, pitting mother and son against father. Generational boundaries are blurred and transgressed. Moreover, the pattern seems a natural consequence of creation, destined to repeat itself cyclically throughout the generations. Indeed the riddle with which the Sphinx confronts Oedipus is itself a statement of this cyclical curvilinear view of aging. Oedipus is damned by answering "man," and "rewarded" with his mother in marriage, the ultimate incestuous blurring of transgenerational sexual boundaries.

The centrality of the Oedipal conflict to the Greek conception of creation is clear. It is indeed a natural law, and quite understandable that Freud focuses on it as a universal motif, given his strictly deterministic outlook. Indeed the Olympian creation story gives a much clearer statement of the Oedipal conflict than the legend of Oedipus itself. The creation story shows the conflict to be an integral and necessary part of the entire Greek worldview. Again, the question is why Freud is drawn to the Greek story of creation rather than its biblical counterpart, which is, of course, much better known and markedly different.

In the Hebrew story, God exists prior to nature and in fact creates the heaven and the earth. "In the beginning God created the heaven and the earth" (Genesis 1:1). God then proceeds to create order out of chaos. First, light is divided from darkness (Genesis 1:4). God then divides water from the land (Genesis 1:9). At this point, God begins to prepare this world for the entrance of man. He has the earth bring forth vegetation (Genesis 1:11). He then places living creatures in the sea and fowls in the air (Genesis 1:20). Next God places living creatures on the earth: cattle, creeping things, and other beasts (Genesis 1:24).

The world is now ready for man in God's plan. God creates man, his ultimate handiwork, in his own image and gives man dominion over all of nature that God has created.

> And God created man in His own image in the image of God created He them. And God blessed them and God said unto them: "Be fruitful, and multiply and replenish the earth, and

subdue it; and have dominion over the fish of the sea, and over the fowl of the air, and over every living thing that creepeth upon the earth. And God said: "Behold, I have given you every herb yielding seed, which is upon the face of all the earth, and every tree, in which is the fruit of a tree yielding seed to you it shall be for food." (Genesis 1:27-29)

Some lines further, man is specifically described as being formed from the dust of the ground and the breath of God (Genesis 2:7). Woman in turn is described as being taken from the rib of man (Genesis 2:22). And the man said: "This is now bone of my bone, and flesh of my flesh. She shall be called Woman because she was taken out of man" (Genesis 2:23). Certainly there is no sign of an Oedipal conflict here nor any antagonism between man and woman such as exists in the Greek story of creation. So why was Freud not influenced by this Hebrew view of creation rather than its Greek counterpart?

An answer to this question has been provided by the work of Lev Shestov, a largely ignored Russian-Jewish philosopher in his work *Athens and Jerusalem*. European man, writes Shestov, even religious European man, has been basically Greek rather than Hebrew. He has shied away from the biblical proclamation that God created the heaven and the earth, instead subordinating him to the very nature and material laws he has created. To put it differently, the creator of the world has himself become subordinate to Necessity, which he created and which, without at all seeking or discovering, has become the sovereign of the universe (Shestov, 1966).

The Greek and Hebrew creation stories embody two radically different worldviews. The former is deterministic; the latter is intrinsically open to the possibility of change and transformation. The two views are perhaps best reflected in the role of God(s) in the respective traditions. Bruno Snell, in *The Discovery of the Mind* (1982, 1935), makes the distinction between the God of the Bible and a Greek deity clear and powerful. To the biblical God, nothing is impossible: He can cancel the natural order of things, alter it in any number of ways, or, indeed, create something out of nothing, just the way he created nature. A Greek god is confined to acts of precipitating coincidences, occurrences that are of low *a priori* probability, but that nonetheless rest completely within the confines of natural law. The upshot is embedded in the two creation stories we recounted: Nature precedes the gods in the Greek version, but God precedes nature in the Hebrew account. The differences in the respective orderings are not just chronological, but logical and psychological as well.

The radical conception that God created nature and is thus able to change what seem to be immutable natural laws is incompatible with that much more deterministic view that nature creates the gods and, in fact, governs them. Freud correctly understood that the latter, deterministic alternative was immutably tied to an Oedipal conflict. "Earth and Sky foretold that Cronus would lose his rule to his own son" (Apollodorus l. 5). Freud had no ultimate faith in the transformative powers of the God of Abraham, of Isaac, and of Jacob and thus was not able to use biblical master stories as a basis for psychoanalysis. In Yerushalmi's terms, "Like Sisyphus pushing his rock, Oedipus and Laius must contend forever. At one point in the cycle the father must be slain by the son, at another, that of the return of the repressed, the father returns, the return is only illusion, for the cycle will begin again" (Yerushalmi, 1991, p. 95). That ever-repeating cycle represents Freud's tragic understanding of the psychological processes intrinsic to a deterministic universe.

May contemporary psychology recover an understanding of the biblical message of freedom necessary to overcome the deterministic and tragic view in the classical Greek world and in the Oedipal configuration. Then truly, the words of the prophet Malachi will ring out: "And He shall turn the hearts of the fathers to the children, and the hearts of the children to their fathers . . ." (Malachi 4:6).

We hope the stories presented in this book represent a step in this direction.

Bibliography

Aeschylus (1938). The Seven Against Thebes. In W. J. Oates and E. O'Neill Jr. (Eds.), *The Complete Greek Drama,* Volume 1. New York: Random House, pp. 89-122.

Alschich, M. (1970). *Torat Moshe.* Israel: Shiluh.

Apollodorus (1976). *The Library.* M. Simpson (Tr.). Amherst: University of Massachusetts Press.

Avot D'R Nathan (1887). S. Schecter (Ed.). Vienna: n.p.

Babylonian Talmud (1975). Jerusalem.

Boman, T. (1960). *Hebrew Thought Compared with Greek.* Philadelphia: Westminster Press.

Cicero (1914). *De Finibus Bonorum et Malorum.* H. Rackham (Tr.). New York: Macmillan.

Cicero (1945). *Tusculan Disputations.* J. E. King (Tr.). Cambridge, MA: Harvard University Press, Loeb Classical Library.

Cohen, Meir Simcha (1978). *Meshech Chochma.* Jerusalem.

Conon (1798). *Narrationes Quinquaginta et Parthenii Narrationes Amatoriae.* Gottingae: J. C. Dietrich.

Crouch, S. (2000). *The New York Times,* March 12, Part 2, p. 16.

Erikson, E. H. (1951 [1963]). *Childhood and Society.* New York: W. W. Norton.

Erikson, E. H. (1980). *Identity and the Life Cycle.* New York: W. W. Norton.

Erikson, E. H. (1982). *The Life Cycle Completed.* New York: W. W. Norton.

Euripides (1938). The Phoenissae. In W. J. Oates and E. O'Neill Jr. (Eds.). *The Complete Greek Drama,* Volume 2. New York: Random House, pp. 171-220.

Freud, S. (1912-1913). "Totem and Taboo." *Standard Edition of the Complete Psychological Works of Sigmund Freud,* Volume 13, J. Strachey (Tr. and Ed.). London: The Hogarth Press.

Freud, S. (1914). "The Moses of Michaelangelo," *Standard Edition of the Complete Psychological Works of Sigmund Freud,* Volume 13, J. Strachey (Tr. and Ed.). London: The Hogarth Press.

Freud, S. (1939). "Moses and Monotheism," *Standard Edition of the Complete Psychological Works of Sigmund Freud,* Volume 23, J. Strachey (Tr. and Ed.). London: The Hogarth Press.

Gay, P. (1987). *A Godless Jew: Freud, Atheism, and the Making of Psychoanalysis.* New Haven: Yale University Press.

Gayley, C. (1893). *Classical Myths.* Boston: Athen Press.

Golden, W. W. (1990). Maimonides' prayer for physicians. *Transactions of the Medical Society of West Virginia,* 33, 414-415.

Grotstein, J. (1994). Why Oedipus and not Christ? Presented at the 102nd Annual Meetings of the American Psychiatric Association. Los Angeles, California, August.

Hesiod (1914). The Shield of Heracles. In H. G. Evelyn White (Tr.). *Hesiod: The Homeric Hymns and Homerica.* Cambridge, MA: Harvard University Press, pp. 221-253.

Hesiod (1914). *The Theogony.* In H. G. Evelyn White (Tr.). *Hesiod: The Homeric Hymns and Homerica.* Cambridge, MA: Harvard University Press, pp. 78-154.

Hippocratic Writings (1984). In R. M. Hutchins (Ed.). *Great Books of the Western World,* Volume 10. F. Adams (Tr.). Chicago, IL: The University of Chicago Press.

Hirsch, Samson Raphael (1976). *Pentateuch.* Isaac Levy (Tr.). Gateshead, United Kingdom: Judaica Press.

The Holy Scriptures (1917). 2 vols. Philadelphia: Jewish Publication Society of America.

Homer. *The Iliad.* (1951). R. Lattimore (Tr.). University of Chicago Press.

Homer (1967). *The Odyssey.* R. Lattimore (Tr.). New York: Harper and Row.

Ibn Paquda, Bahya (1963). *Duties of the Heart.* Moses Hyamson (Tr.). Jerusalem: Kiryah Neemanah.

Kaplan, K. J. (1998). *TILT: Teaching Individuals to Live Together.* Philadelphia, PA: Brunner/Mazel.

Kaplan, K. J. and Schwartz, M. B. (1993). *A Psychology of Hope: An Antidote to the Suicidal Pathology of Western Civilization.* Westport, CT: Praeger.

Kaplan, K. J., Schwartz, M. B., and Markus-Kaplan, M. (1984). *The Family: Biblical and Psychological Foundations.* New York: Human Sciences Press.

Laertius Diogenes (1972). *Lives of Eminent Philosophers,* 2 Volumes. R. D. Hicks (Tr.). Cambridge, MA: Harvard University Press, Loeb Classical Library.

Leibowitz, Nechama (1981). *Studies,* Fourth Edition. Aryeh Newman (Tr.). Jerusalem: Alpha Press.

Luzatto, Moshe Chayim (1966). *The Path of the Just.* Shraga Silverstein (Tr.). New York: Feldheim.

Midrash Rabbah (1975). Jerusalem.

Midrash Tanhuma. Shlomo Buber (Ed.). Israel.

Midrash Yalkut Shimoni (1944). Author unknown. New York: Title Publications.

Mikraot Gedolot (1978). New York.

Muntner, S. (1977). Medicine in ancient Israel. In *Medicine in the Bible and the Talmud* (pp. 3-20). F. Rosner (Ed.). Hoboken, NJ: KTAV.

Numbers Rabbah (1978). Jerusalem.

Ovid (1955). *The Metamorphoses.* M. Innes (Tr.). London: Penguin Classics.

The Oxford Classical Dictionary, Second Edition (1970). N. G. I. Hammond and H. H. Scullard (Eds.). Oxford: Clarendon Press.

Plato (1954). *The Last Days of Socrates* (including *Euthyphro, The Apology, Crito,* and *Phaedo*). M. Tredennick (Tr.). Middlesex, United Kingdom: Penguin Classics.

Plotinus (1918). *Complete Works*. K. S. Guthrie (Tr.). London: George Bell and Son.

Preuss, J. (1978). *Biblical and Talmudic Medicine*. F. Rosner (Ed. and Tr.). Northvale, NJ: Jason Aronson, Inc.

Rashi on Genesis (1961). Jerusalem.

Rosenberg, A. J. (1996). *Samuel I*. New York: Judaica Press.

Rosner, F. (1977). *Medicine in the Bible and the Talmud*. Hoboken, NJ: KTAV.

Seneca, L. A. the Younger (1971). *Seneca*. R. Gunmere (Tr.). Cambridge, MA: Harvard University Press.

Shafranske, E. and Maloney, H. N. (1990). Clinincal psychologists' religious and spiritual orientations and their practice of psychotherapy. In *Psychotherapy: Theory, Research, Practice, Training*, 27, 72-78.

Sharansky, N. (1988). *Fear No Evil*. New York: Random House.

Shestov, L. (1966). *Athens and Jerusalem*. New York: Simon and Schuster.

Simon, B. (1978). *Mind and Madness in Ancient Greece: The Classical Roots of Modern Psychiatry*. Ithaca: Cornell University Press.

Snell, B. (1982/1935). *The Discovery of the Mind*. New York: Dover.

Sophocles (1938). Oedipus at Colonus. In W. J. Oates and E. O'Neill Jr. (Eds.). *The Complete Greek Drama*, Volume 1. New York: Random House, pp. 613-670.

Sorotzkin, Zalman (1961). Oznaim LaTorah. Jerusalem.

Tanhuma Buber. Israel.

Urbach, E. E. (1979). *The Sages: Their Concepts and Beliefs*, Second Edition. I. Abrahms (Tr.). Jerusalem: The Magnes Press, The Hebrew University of Jerusalem.

Wellisch, E. (1954). *Isaac and Oedipus: Studies in Biblical Psychology of the Sacrifice of Isaac*. London: Routledge and Kegan Paul.

Yerushalmi, Y. (1991). *Freud's Moses. Judaism: Terminable and Interminable*. New Haven, CT: Yale University Press.

Index

SPECIAL 25%-OFF DISCOUNT!
Order a copy of this book with this form or online at:
http://www.haworthpress.com/store/product.asp?sku=4985

BIBLICAL STORIES FOR PSYCHOTHERAPY AND COUNSELING
A Sourcebook

_____in hardbound at $29.96 (regularly $39.95) (ISBN: 0-7890-2212-5)

_____in softbound at $18.71 (regularly $24.95) (ISBN:0-7890-2213-3)

Or order online and use special offer code HEC25 in the shopping cart.

COST OF BOOKS_____

OUTSIDE US/CANADA/
MEXICO: ADD 20%_____

POSTAGE & HANDLING_____
(US: $5.00 for first book & $2.00
for each additional book)
(Outside US: $6.00 for first book
& $2.00 for each additional book)

SUBTOTAL_____

IN CANADA: ADD 7% GST_____

STATE TAX_____
(NY, OH, MN, CA, IN, & SD residents,
add appropriate local sales tax)

FINAL TOTAL_____
(If paying in Canadian funds,
convert using the current
exchange rate, UNESCO
coupons welcome)

☐ **BILL ME LATER:** ($5 service charge will be added)
(Bill-me option is good on US/Canada/Mexico orders only;
not good to jobbers, wholesalers, or subscription agencies.)

☐ Check here if billing address is different from
shipping address and attach purchase order and
billing address information.

Signature_____

☐ **PAYMENT ENCLOSED: $**_____

☐ **PLEASE CHARGE TO MY CREDIT CARD.**

☐ Visa ☐ MasterCard ☐ AmEx ☐ Discover
☐ Diner's Club ☐ Eurocard ☐ JCB

Account #_____

Exp. Date_____

Signature_____

Prices in US dollars and subject to change without notice.

NAME_____

INSTITUTION_____

ADDRESS_____

CITY_____

STATE/ZIP_____

COUNTRY_____ COUNTY (NY residents only)_____

TEL_____ FAX_____

E-MAIL_____

May we use your e-mail address for confirmations and other types of information? ☐ Yes ☐ No
We appreciate receiving your e-mail address and fax number. Haworth would like to e-mail or fax special
discount offers to you, as a preferred customer. **We will never share, rent, or exchange your e-mail address
or fax number.** We regard such actions as an invasion of your privacy.

Order From Your Local Bookstore or Directly From
The Haworth Press, Inc.
10 Alice Street, Binghamton, New York 13904-1580 • USA
TELEPHONE: 1-800-HAWORTH (1-800-429-6784) / Outside US/Canada: (607) 722-5857
FAX: 1-800-895-0582 / Outside US/Canada: (607) 771-0012
E-mailto: orders@haworthpress.com
PLEASE PHOTOCOPY THIS FORM FOR YOUR PERSONAL USE.
http://www.HaworthPress.com   BOF03